Fangs of Malice

STUDIES IN

THEATRE HISTORY & CULTURE

Edited by Thomas Postlewait

Fangs of Malice

Hypocrisy, Sincerity, & Acting

MATTHEW H. WIKANDER

UNIVERSITY OF IOWA PRESS Iowa City

VUM.
W64f
2002

University of Iowa Press, Iowa City 52242
Copyright © 2002 by the University of Iowa Press
All rights reserved
Printed in the United States of America
Design by Richard Hendel
http://www.uiowa.edu/~uipress

The publication of this book was generously supported by
the University of Iowa Foundation.

Printed on acid-free paper

Library of Congress Cataloging-in-Publication Data
Wikander, Matthew H.
Fangs of malice: hypocrisy, sincerity, and acting / by
Matthew H. Wikander.
p.   cm. — (Studies in theatre history and culture)
Includes bibliographical references and index.
ISBN 0-87745-809-X (cloth)
1. Acting — Psychological aspects.   2. Theater and society.
3. Actors — Social life and customs.   I. Title.   II. Series.
PN2058.W54   2002
792'.028'019— dc21   2001055640

02   03   04   05   06   C   5   4   3   2   1

FOR CHRISTINE

Contents

Acknowledgments

Thanks are especially due to the librarians of the libraries where I have been made welcome: the University of Michigan Graduate Library, the University of Toledo Libraries, the Williams College Library, and the Cambridge University Library. The Newberry Library made an extended visit possible with a Short Term Fellowship in the summer of 1996. The University of Toledo has supported this project through the sabbatical leave program, the summer research fellowships program, and the Small Grants Program of the Office of Research. I am especially indebted to the Humanities Institute of the University of Toledo, which has offered me the opportunity to develop this work all along the way: I first tried out some of the ideas as Distinguished Humanities Lecturer in 1992 and was able to present some of the last phases of the project as Distinguished Doermann Lecturer in 2001. To my colleagues in the Humanities Institute Anniversary Seminar I am especially grateful: Friedrike Emonds, Peter Linebaugh, Sara Lundquist, Susan Purviance, and Dan Watermeier. Richard Axton made my stay at Cambridge particularly memorable by generously permitting me the use of his office and by entrusting his students to my supervision in the spring of 1995. I have presented portions of this work at meetings of the Shakespeare Association of America and the American Society for Theatre Research, and I am grateful to Donald Morse of Oakland University for inviting me to Rochester and to the symposium at Williams College which he organized in honor of Don Gifford. Laurence Senelick at Tufts University and Jeffrey Ravel at Oberlin College also gave me opportunities to discuss my work with faculty and students. Michael Manheim goaded me into writing about Eugene O'Neill for *The Cambridge Companion to O'Neill,* and a revised version of the essay published in that volume appears here with the permission of the Cambridge University Press. Portions of Act One and Act Two have previously been published by *Comparative Drama* and appear here in revised form with the permission of the editors. David Bevington, Michael Goldman, and Martin Meisel have all been most generous in their encouragement and support. My students have always kept my ideas from sitting still, and I especially want to recognize four whose participation in *Henry IV* seminars over the years has helped to shape my thought: Celia Maddox, Page Elrod, Christopher Herr, and Joseph Sullivan. My fellow members of the North Coast Theatre Acting Ensemble always surprise me with their Protean inventiveness: David Clark, David Dysard, Chris Herr, Madge Levinson, Nora Warejko, and Irina Zaurov. Tom Postlewait's contribution to the final shape of this book is immeasurable; Barbara Hodgdon's thorough and generous critique of the manuscript came at just the right time in many ways. The errors and infelicities that remain are all my own. John Styan's inspiration and example have always shaped my engagement with drama. I dedicate this book to Christine Child, playwright, director, and spouse.

Prologue

THE ACTOR AS HYPOCRITE

"Are you a comedian?" Olivia asks the disguised Viola in William Shakespeare's *Twelfth Night*. "No, my profound heart," she replies; "and yet, by the very fangs of malice I swear I am not that I play" (1.5.178–80).[1] Swearing, as Juliet reminds Romeo, requires a constant term to swear by: "O, swear not by the moon, th'inconstant moon," she pleads in the balcony scene (2.2.109). The fangs of malice, then, must be constant at least in Viola's mind. Viola also invokes "my profound heart": in fact, both her profound heart and the fangs of malice attest to the truth of her confession: "I am not that I play." Viola is determined (perhaps overdetermined) that Olivia not mistake her for a professional actor (a comedian), but the malice she invokes — gossip, scandal, slander — is in some special ways a constant companion to members of that profession. Viola is in a bind here, because she wants to make it clear that while she is acting, playing the role of Cesario, Orsino's page, she is not untrustworthy, like a comedian. She wants to assure Olivia of her private, personal integrity and wants especially to distance herself from the charge of hypocrisy. That is, both Viola's desire to repudiate Olivia's suspicion that she is an actor and her fear that the "fangs of malice" will always attach themselves to this repudiation stem from a futile attempt to separate the notion of acting from the idea of hypocrisy. It is futile because, unable to declare the full truth about herself, Viola is engaged in the very kind of entrapment — "Fortune forbid my outside hath not charmed her!" (2.2.18) — that she associates with malicious gossip about comedians and not with herself.

The idea that acting is hypocrisy was a constant in moral pamphleteering in the seventeenth and eighteenth centuries in England and France. The malicious charge that an actor must necessarily be a hypocrite, false at the level of the profound heart, finds expression in innumerable tracts railing against the theater. These diatribes express, less ambivalently but with no less moral passion, Viola's anxiety that her acting can be mistaken for the social sin of hypocrisy. "If we seriously consider the very forme of acting Playes," William Prynne argues in his mighty volume *Histriomastix,* "we must needes acknowledge it to be nought but grosse hypocrisie." Quoting "sundry Authors and Grammarians," Prynne forges the etymological link to *"stile Stage-players, hypocrites; Hypocrites, Stage-players, as being one and the same in substance; there being nothing more familiar with them, then to describe an hypocrite by a Stage-player; and a Stage-player by an hypocrite."*[2] Prynne sticks to "Latine Authors"; had he turned to the Greeks, he would have discovered a closer connection. On the ancient Greek stage, as Gerald Else has pointed out, the professional actor — the actor who was not the tragedian, the actor who was only an actor — was dubbed the answerer or *hypokrites.*[3] The etymology proves the point: an actor is a hypocrite, nothing more, nothing less.

In a lively false etymology, John Northbrooke, one of the first of the English antitheatrical polemicists, moves in another direction, linking *Histriones,* actors, to *Histrices,* porcupines: "Histrix is a little beast with speckled prickles on his back, which he will cast off and hurt menne with them, which is, as Plinie sayth, a porkepine."[4] Stay clear of actors; they only look harmless, Northbrooke suggests. But what exactly are the "speckled prickles," the quills in the metaphor as it attaches to actors? The porcupine shoots its quills into the unwary person who pets or strokes it or tries to pick it up: so too do actors "hurt menne" who trust them, who believe their protestations of good faith, who place credence in their tears.

"What wouldst thou think of me if I should weep?" Prince Hal asks Poins, confessing that his "heart bleeds inwardly" at the thought of his father's illness. "I would think thee a most princely hypocrite," Poins rejoins, and the prince ruefully agrees: "It would be every man's thought, and thou art a blessed fellow to think as every man thinks" (*2 Henry IV* 2.2.49–53). The prince is in a sense doomed to act the part of indifference to his father's sickness lest his true feelings be interpreted as feigned. Where Viola swears by the constant calumny that tracks the actor, the prince must submit to its inevitability. Regardless of his true feelings, "every man" will consider his tears false.

The grieving Hamlet repudiates this kind of seeming. "Seems, Madam? Nay, it is. I know not 'seems,'" Hamlet snaps, when his mother wonders why he seems to be taking his father's death so hard. Hamlet goes further than Hal to set himself apart from the hypocrisy, double-talk, and double-dealing that characterize Denmark. He counters a principle of misleading and ambiguous seeming with a principle of being, of true denotation, of "that within which passes show" (1.2.76, 85). Invoking her profound heart, Viola struggles to survive amidst the playing and dissembling that surround her and determine her actions; Prince Hal reluctantly submits to the suspicions of every blessed fellow, but Hamlet goes on the attack. As preacher, moralist, and satirist, he takes arms against the sea of seeming.

As Hamlet attempts to differentiate what he is from what can be acted, the "actions that a man might play" (1.2.84), he shares with Prynne, Northbrooke, and other early modern opponents of theater a deep suspicion about the value of theatrical mimesis. But, because he is a character in a play and not an antitheatrical divine, there is a paradox at work. Audiences have always recognized Hamlet to be a grieving son because of his customary black cloak and because of his behavior, complete with sighs, tears, and downcast eyes. In fact, these are the only means available to the actor, whether we call him Richard Burbage or Mel Gibson, to communicate Hamlet's grief. Hamlet's rejection of playable actions is a challenge to actor and audience: the actor must show that he can play "that within," and not merely the outward appearances of grief, and audiences must not rest content with conclusions they have arrived at by conventional means. But how can "that which passes show" be played in a theater? Hamlet's contention that nothing he does, nothing that we can see him do, can "denote me truly" is a radical challenge to the medium in which he appears.

In Hamlet's first speech, to put it another way, an audience can hear the voice of the character reproaching the actor: Burbage or Gibson can never reach me, can never convey my mystery, my uniqueness. "The rest is silence" are Hamlet's last words. Perhaps the voice that audiences hear ventriloquizing through Hamlet is the playwright's: in Hamlet I have written a character so rich, so real, so truly mysterious as to be unplayable.[5] Rather than merely challenging an actor to transcend conventional ways of portraying grief and the audience to overcome conventional ways of seeing it, the playwright repudiates either's ability to penetrate the veil of seeming and truly know what is.

Hamlet's frustration with the hypocrisy of those around him finds expression as he stigmatizes them all as players. Ophelia is a painted wanton who jigs, ambles, and lisps; his uncle a villain who smiles and smiles; his mother, seeming virtuous, must be instructed to play at virtue and so habituate herself to abstinence. "Ere I could make a prologue to my brains, / They had begun the play," he tells Horatio of Rosencrantz and Guildenstern, whom he has entrapped in a script of his own making. For Hamlet, hypocrite and player are one and the same in substance.

The mighty opposite that the play poses to this ready identification is the ideal of sincerity, truth to one's self. The word comes into the English language in the late sixteenth century in specific reference to the quality of Christ, but it rapidly spreads into secular contexts, where it is immediately prized and privileged. Lionel Trilling saw Hamlet as a play "suffused by the theme of sincerity." In his first lecture on *Sincerity and Authenticity*, Trilling quoted Polonius:

This above all, to thine own self be true
And it follows, as the night the day,
Thou canst not then be false to any man.

Trilling found it impossible to read this statement ironically, in a way that would "consort with our low opinion of the speaker"; instead it is a "moment of self-transcendence, of grace and truth," for Polonius. "He has conceived of sincerity as an essential condition of virtue and has discovered how it is to be attained."[6] Like the secret voice that speaks through Hamlet's first great speech, Trilling's response to Polonius defies theatrical representation by seeing Polonius's speech as self-transcendent. Exempted from our low opinion, out of character, Polonius in this one speech repudiates all of the live seeming that the actor invests in making the role of Polonius whole and convincing — whole and convincing as the performance of a hypocrite, that is.

The idea that a true self, an own self, a sincere self, is unplayable is at the root of one of the great paradoxes of Hamlet, and it affords Trilling a starting place for his critique of the Freudian and post-Freudian quest for authenticity. It is also profoundly antitheatrical, for the self-transcendent Polonius imagined by Trilling cannot exist on the stage. As Jonas Barish has pointed out in his important book *The Antitheatrical Prejudice*, hatred of theater runs high in Western philosophy: its exponents are not only "hard-shelled, mole-eyed fanatics," Barish points out, but also "giants like Plato, Saint Augustine, Rousseau and Nietzsche." All these great thinkers, and a host of lesser figures in the

Western canon, have argued that actors, polished in their expertise at
seeming other than they are, pose a threat to society. Outbreaks of antitheatrical fervor, Barish notices, coincide with times when the theater
is prosperous, "when it counts for something in the emotional and
intellectual life of the community." Malicious gossip attaches most vigorously to actors when their profession is conspicuously successful.
The prejudice against theater and the concomitant attacks upon actors
that Barish traces are not solely negative, merely slanderous. Following
Plato, antitheatrical writers in the seventeenth and eighteenth centuries
celebrated simplicity and integrity: "Simplicity means purity, stability,
and health," in Barish's words: "Complexity spells impurity, instability,
distemper." These writers erected a binary opposition, which finds its
fullest early modern expression in Jean-Jacques Rousseau, that linked
both the institution of theater and the conditions of actors' lives with
poor moral health and opposed them to a principle of transcendent sincerity. Yet dissembling, Rousseau also notices, seems to be an inevitable
consequence of human social intercourse: theater leaches into social
life, making truth to self an unreachable ideal. "Perhaps," Barish concludes, "the antitheatrical prejudice reflects a form of self-disgust":
"Human existence can hardly avoid resembling in basic ways the experience of actors in the theater, and human consciousness can hardly
escape the tinge of bad faith this introduces in our actions, the incite-
ment it gives us to wish to be admired, stared at, made much of, attended to."[7]

Despite its encyclopedic reach and the broad range of its citations
Barish's book tends to treat the antitheatrical prejudice as an aberra-
tion; when the "giants" of philosophy indulge in it, they nod and reveal
themselves to be "mole-eyed" in spite of themselves. While Barish ac-
knowledges that the traditional defenses of theater are feeble and repetitive (just as the attacks themselves tend to be repetitive if by no means
feeble), he nonetheless exempts playwrights from the influence of antitheatricalism. *Hamlet*, in Barish's reading, amounts to a defense of
theater by theatrical means, and it is not until he reaches modern
dramatists and thinkers like Bertolt Brecht and Jean-Paul Sartre that he
detects antitheatrical sentiments among playwrights themselves.

But expressions of distaste for theater are common in the Renaissance and neoclassical drama as well as in the modern drama: like Hamlet, numerous characters refuse to be known by their actions and repudiate the theatrical means of their display. "Theatre has mimesis, not

as its method, but as its subject matter," David Cole has argued.[8] When a character like Viola or Prince Hal complains about being misread, misunderstood, misrepresented by malicious gossip, by the way that "every man thinks," by "common" perceptions, the whole enterprise of theatrical representation is called into doubt. That the characters' complaints that they run the risk of being perceived as actors are voiced by actors complicates the critique. To a high degree, the expression of antitheatrical sentiments by characters in plays can be seen as a playwright's critique of the medium's particular kind of mimesis, its reliance upon actors. Internalizing and echoing the strictures of antitheatrical moralists against both the corrupt lives of actors and the misleading nature of theatrical representation, Shakespeare, Molière, Henrik Ibsen, and a number of other playwrights of the early modern and modern periods are particularly engaged in this critique. The problem they engage is that an "own self," to which one can be true and then not false to any man, as Trilling and Polonius would have it, is a theatrical impossibility, a mimetic conundrum.

Playwrights write for actors, and as a result they know well that their characters are in some sense hostages to the actors who play them. Hamlet's instructions to the Player epitomize his dilemma as a character who is also a playwright. Recent criticism has led to acknowledgment of the widespread practice of collaboration in the early modern theater, but it is important to avoid romanticizing such collaboration. Clowns do speak more than is set down for them, and the relationship between playwright and actor is not always a harmonious one.[9] Ben Jonson's complicated interaction with the "loathed stage," whose actors he felt repeatedly marred his texts, is exemplified by the fact that he nonetheless printed their names in the 1616 folio of his *Works*.[10] Hamlet, too, feels he must remonstrate with the Player about the fourteen lines or so of script he has given him. "Suit the action to the word, the word to the action," he urges the Player, who patiently bears his instructions. "I hope we have reformed that indifferently with us, sir," the Player ventures to respond to Hamlet's complaints about overacting. "O, reform it altogether," Hamlet urges, expressing something like the zeal of antitheatrical polemic (3.2.17–18, 36–38). As characters give voice to antitheatrical sentiments, the playwright's dilemma — reliance upon a notoriously unreliable means of production — echoes through the texts of plays themselves.

Hamlet's mistrust of actors, like his insistence upon sincerity and integrity to self, is characteristic of the great seventeenth-century attacks upon theater in England and France. It is also characteristic of what has been called the discovery or "invention" of subjectivity in Michel de Montaigne, Shakespeare, and Rousseau. New historicist critics have lately written much about the relationship of antitheatrical discourse to emerging subjectivity in the early modern period, for the most part locating it within seventeenth- and eighteenth-century religious debates. Equally, at the other end of the political spectrum, Harold Bloom has celebrated Shakespeare for the "invention of the human."[11] "By positing the existence of a newly crucial space for personal decision, where the deepest forms of feeling, understanding, and self-direction were understood to intersect, the European era of religious struggle seems to have created the very privacy it sought sometimes to violate, sometimes to guard," Michael Goldman puts it.[12] But the privileging of inwardness, while it is certainly central to English Puritan and recusant and French Jansenist and Jesuit tracts, is ubiquitous in Western culture from the Renaissance through the modern period.

Barish's signal work makes this point inescapably: every actor, every playwright, and everyone who works in the theater functions in an atmosphere of stifling antitheatricalism. The mimetic problem of staging the inner self — by definition unplayable — extends through the whole context of European early modern and modern drama. The great characters of this drama, like Hamlet, Alceste, and Hedda Gabler, repudiate the falsity of the worlds they inhabit and arrogate to themselves sole power to be judges over themselves. Hedda and Hamlet demand to be judged not by what they do, but by what they are. This demand is antitheatrical, but it is also central to the high value that Western civilization places on sincerity, authenticity to one's own true self.

New historicist and feminist critics alike have attacked this high valuation of the true self. Stephen Greenblatt will have little truck with the Platonic idealism of antitheatrical thinking but instead stresses that the process of self-fashioning in the Renaissance has little to do with modern ideas of sincerity and authenticity. "The word Person is latine," declares Thomas Hobbes in a passage from *Leviathan* that Greenblatt has cited more than once, "as *Persona* in latine signifies the *disguise*, or *outward appearance* of a man, counterfeited on the stage; and sometimes more particularly that part of it, which disguiseth the face, as Mask or Visard: And from the Stage, hath been translated to any Representer of speech and action, as well in Tribunalls, as Theaters. So that a *Person* is the same that an *Actor* is, both on the Stage and in common Conversation." "There is no layer deeper, more authentic, than theatrical self-presentation," Greenblatt comments on this passage. "Identity is only possible as a mask, something constructed and assumed, but this need not imply that identity so conceived is a sorry business," he hastens to add. "In our culture, masks are trivial objects for children to play with and discard, and theatrical roles have the same air of pasteboard insubstantiality. But this is not always and everywhere the case; a man who lived in the shadow of Shakespeare might have had a deeper sense of what could be counterfeited on the stage or represented before a tribunal." Hobbes, "in the shadow of Shakespeare," is presumably more in touch with a notion of personality as performance than we moderns are. Greenblatt, by this deft move, suggests that if we sense any antitheatricalism in Hobbes's definition it is somehow the fault of "our culture" and its failure to take masks and roles seriously.[13] Thus for Greenblatt, early modern moralists attack players as hypocrites because for early modern "persons" there is nothing available but the mask.

The absolute gulf that Greenblatt envisions between "our culture" and the culture that grew up "in the shadow of Shakespeare" depends for its existence upon a discontinuity, a rupture between the claims of the self made by Hamlet and the antitheatrical divines of the seventeenth century and the claims made by Rousseau and his disciples in the eighteenth century. Antitheatricalism, however, provides the evidence of a continuous privileging of the inner life and derogation of performance (social performance as well as theatrical performance) in favor of the greater truths imagined to inhere in sincerity, truth to one's own self. Greenblatt's work is strongly influenced by the social scientist Erving Goffman, whose landmark book *The Presentation of Self in Everyday Life* gives rise to the notion of social life as performance. Greenblatt declares that equating social performance with bad faith is ahistorical, a feature of our culture which distorts early modern ideas of the self. Antitheatrical polemic in the early modern period itself, however, insists that performance on stage and in real life is an instance of hypocrisy, that social masking as well as theatrical playing hides and distorts a true self.

Goffman himself has been charged with approaching role-playing from just such a vantage point. Bruce Wilshire argues that Goffman is a closet believer in an authentic self: "He construes as manifest appearance, as one real thing, the character played by the actor, whereas the actor himself must be another particular thing, just momentarily hidden by the character he plays," like the profound heart that Viola conceals from the fangs of malice. Given his premises, Goffman "must see the actor's artistry as a kind of deceit. Inevitably, then, he must construe role-like activity offstage as a kind of deceit."[14] Hypocrisy is a constant feature of human existence. Social performance is as bad as acting: bad faith, what Sartre calls "the refusal to be what one is," contaminates all human relations.[15]

Feminist scholars have also examined the equation of hypocrisy with acting and its opposition to sincerity. Nina Auerbach resists a simple feminist binarism, although "it is tempting to personify as female the theatricality that is my subject," she declares.[16] Certainly the antitheatrical polemicists of the modern period often enough enact that equation themselves, painting the theater as a gaudy whore. The playing of women's roles by boys and men on the early-seventeenth-century English stage also brought gender to the forefront of attacks upon the institution. Scriptural authority supported the divines at least in their distaste for cross-dressing. "The anti-theatricalists and antifeminists conceive of an inner, 'real' self, which is too often profoundly private, and an outer self which, though it should express the reality within, too often conceals or distorts it," Katharine Eisaman Maus argues. She deplores both antitheatricalism and antifeminism because they share an essentialism that would "[uncover] the truth by laying bare, by stripping away, until the splendid and multifarious levels of deception have been forced aside."[17] Maus's feminist celebration of the actress's splendid and unsettling theatricality links her with Greenblatt and the new historicists. She ironizes the idea of a "real" self and embraces the notion of all social life as indistinguishable from theatrical performance.

The poles of debate — essentialist versus antiessentialist, conservative versus feminist and new historicist — remain strikingly similar to those established in the seventeenth and eighteenth centuries. To cherish sincerity and prize the inner self is to reject theater; to embrace theater is, cynically or enthusiastically, to ascribe inauthenticity to all social performance. While it is easy to reject simplistic and brutal antitheatricalism like Prynne's, we may nonetheless still prize some of the privateness that Prynne claims theater violates. Similarly, it may be difficult fully to embrace the antiessentialist model of all human action as performance, with its attendant inability to distinguish hypocritical from sincere performance. Must we throw out the baby of sincerity with the bathwater of antitheatricalism? Must we embrace mean-spirited antitheatricalism before we can acknowledge a secret sense of an own self?

There have been some attempts at finding a middle ground. "Having trifled with theater's idiom, some social scientists find themselves drawn into the rather tangled coils of its aesthetic," Clifford Geertz writes, noticing the kind of bind Goffman's disciples have landed in.[18] Elizabeth Burns is one social scientist who has struggled with Goffman's vision of social life as performance, and she, too, focuses her attention on the emergence of the idea of the true self in the early modern period. "For different reasons," Burns puts it, "the godly and the godless were committed in the sixteenth and seventeenth centuries to the development of character and individuality." "In their most highly valued relationships and preoccupations," she continues, "people like to think of themselves as free of all the attributes of the actor."[19]

Rousseau, in the *Letter to D'Alembert*, charges that in thinking of themselves this way people are lying to themselves. Acting and posing are conditions of living in modern society: "Rousseau's indictment of the acting and posing that develop in society is not limited to a denunciation of deception, hypocrisy, or false representation," David Marshall argues in a new historicist critique of the *Letter*. "People become actors — and this acting is problematic — from the moment they are aware that they must represent themselves for others." Self-exposure is necessarily false because the self cannot be exposed.[20]

Burns, however, attempts to erect a distinction between hypocrisy and acting that challenges Rousseau's traditional, antitheatrical identification. She does so by insisting upon a radical difference between the conditions of life inside the theater and outside: "Outside the theatre, where there is neither dramatist nor script, the same creativity in the field of ordinary behaviour is commonly unrecognised, or, when recognised, regarded as bizarre, perhaps disreputable, presumptuous, in any case deviant. The moral value placed on spontaneity and sincerity in personal relations has produced a dichotomy between 'natural' and 'theatrical' behaviour." To Goffman's claim that "an honest sincere performance is less firmly connected with the solid world than one might at first assume," Burns counters vigorously: "But, if sincerity is impossible, degrees of insincerity are controllable. Hypocrisy is recognised for what it is when roles in real life are overplayed, especially on occasions that are set and produced as if they were theatrical."[21] Burns offers a sliding scale of theatricality between the antitheatrical polemicists' determination to purge real life of the contamination of the theater and Greenblatt's resignation to the impossibility of such purgation. Some social performance is authentic, some hypocritical, insofar as it approaches overplaying; "rigidity and repetitiveness" become the "dangers of theatricality" (*Theatricality*, 232). Theater is ritual and formulaic in its nature, and social behavior is theatrical to the degree that it approaches the formulaic.

"The most beneficial edict the theatre could issue," says Charles Marowitz, "would be a thirty-year ban on the use of the words *real life* — until such time as all could agree to the same definition (which would be never) or up to that point where the majority of actors, writers, and directors might grudgingly concede there is no such thing."[22] Burns's attempt to mediate, to stress the distinction between the circumscribed world of theatrical performance and the social world, finds little sympathy here. Marowitz is probably exaggerating when he declares there to be no such thing as real life, but his vexation comes from a venerable source. The distinction between real life — spontaneous, sincere, authentic — and the hypocritical falsehoods of the actor is a constant thread in the antitheatrical polemic. So constant are the fangs of malice, Viola reminds us, that we can swear by them as easily as by the profound heart.

In a further paradox, many of the antitheatrical writers of the early modern period published their tracts in quasi-dramatic form: sometimes as dialogues, like Jeremy Collier's *Essay upon Gaming* (1713), and sometimes divided into acts and scenes, like Stephen Gosson's *Plays Confuted in Five Actions* (1582). Prynne's *Histriomastix* presents its argument act after act, scene after scene. In the study that follows, I have adopted this strategy. This prologue introduces three acts, and each act is divided into scenes. Linking them all, and linking them back to the original problem of identifying acting as hypocrisy and stigmatizing actors as hypocrites, is the idea of slanders against actors, slanders that particularly privilege the value of sincerity and set it in opposition to performance of all kinds. Among antitheatricalist writers, it is common to strike broadly and boldly against the actor. So each of the three acts rehearses one of the most persistent and potent slanders against actors — "They dress up"; "They lie"; "They drink" — as these slanders appear in the antitheatrical literature, in plays themselves, and in contemporary critical controversy about the plays. Through these slanders we can glimpse the complex interaction of our three highly charged terms — *hypocrisy, sincerity,* and *acting* — as characters and critics engage these issues. The slanders also reach out metaphorically into larger thematic concerns related to acting and to drama: impersonation through changes of clothing, false and misleading speech, and demonic intoxication and possession. Despite the radical social and political differences among the numerous contexts touched upon here, ranging from sixteenth-century England to twentieth-century America, antitheatricalism functions as a constant challenge to early modern and modern drama. Antitheatricalism — as expressed by pamphleteers, dramatic characters, and contemporary critics — offers a unique vantage point on modern Western culture's prizing of sincerity, of truth to the own self. Actors hold a mirror up to nature, Hamlet says; the slanders against them offer windows to the soul.

Fangs of Malice

Act One

THEY DRESS UP

Theophilus Lucas, in his *Memoirs* of 1714, recounts the story of how Major Clancy, an Irish "sharper" or confidence man, came to discover his true occupation. Clancy began as a valet, a "sort of page to Monsieur Mancy in Paris":

> One day Major *Clancy* being at his Exercise of Brushing, he locks the Chamber-door, lays apart each Suit of Cloaths, with all that belong'd to it, and putting on the finest of them, struts up and down like Crow in a Gutter, then goes to the Looking-glass, where he was so startled at first that he stept back, hardly knowing who it was in such a Habit; but finding at last, after part of his Wonder was over, that it was himself, he begins to propose to himself how happy and how fortunate should he be if he could order Matters so as to keep this Finery by which he was so alter'd, that he might appear to all others, as to himself in the Glass.[1]

Putting on his employer's fine clothes transforms Clancy the valet into Major Clancy, who can then pursue his notorious career. Dressing above his class, performing before the mirror, Clancy is an actor who takes costume and imposture off the stage and into real life. Sumptuary laws during the early modern period sought to limit the possibility of such misleading misuse of costume, but actors, who often purchased the clothes of aristocrats from valets who inherited or stole them, acquired whole wardrobes that they were not entitled to wear.

Rousseau, like many other antitheatrical writers, cautioned that theater tends to break down sumptuary laws. If clothing reflects social station, and if it is deemed necessary that all citizens should wear clothes that indicate their particular stations, then certainly the wearing of costumes by actors immediately transgresses such codes. Marjorie Garber rightly notes that while much recent scholarly attention has been dedicated to the ways in which sumptuary laws attempted to regulate gender, such "legislation was overwhelmingly concerned with wealth or rank, and with gender largely as it was a subset of these categories." Sumptuary laws mainly prohibited the wearing of certain fabrics by certain members of the population — cloth of gold, for example, being limited to "earls and above that rank and Knights of the Garter in their purple mantles." Simple fabrics, limited to the lower classes, were also identified with honesty: Berowne, in *Love's Labor's Lost*, rejects "Taffeta phrases, silken terms precise" by equating them with "maggot ostentation," promising instead to adopt a language of "russet yeas and honest kersey noes" (5.2.407, 410, 414).[2] While this donning of coarse domestic fabric is metaphorical, more extremely, King Gustav III introduced legislation in Sweden at the end of the eighteenth century mandating the wearing of national costume, designed by the king, in order to prevent the aristocracy from imitating the fashions of France.

In this act I address costume as a moral problem on the early modern stage. First I consider the professional status of the "boy-actress" on the English stage in the pre-Restoration period by concentrating on Viola's anxious meditations on her own problematic attire in *Twelfth Night* and then move to the metamorphosis that occurs as Viola comes to be played by actresses after the Restoration. Next Jeremy Collier's strictures in *A Short View of the Immorality and Prophaneness of the English Stage* against English comic authors, who "must ridicule the Habit as well as the Function, of the Clergy," focus attention upon stage clerics and friars.[3] The problem of true and false piety, as stirred up by the controversy in the 1660s about Molière's *Tartuffe*, has far-reaching implications: championing the cause of high moral seriousness in Restoration comedy, decrying those who see the plays as frivolous, recent scholars like Aubrey Williams and J. Douglas Canfield continue the debate in much the same terms as those in which Bishop Louis Bourdaloue excoriated Molière. Finally, I turn to fashion's most slavish adherents, the late-seventeenth-century fops, emblems of theatricality, despised for their monstrous similarity to actors. By the very beginning of the eighteenth century, however, dramatists have come to treat fops as human beings, inviting audiences to analyze their feelings and even to sympathize with their predicaments. Cross-dressing, putting on clerical garb, and foppery all come together as indices of iniquity in the curious career of Charlotte Charke, the youngest daughter of Colley Cibber. She herself often wore men's dress and not only played the foppish roles her father made famous but also produced a revival of Elkanah Settle's *The Female Prelate, or, the Tragedy of Pope Joan.*

Scene One

AS SECRET AS MAIDENHEAD

When Duke Orsino speaks to Viola, disguised as Cesario, of his attractions in *Twelfth Night*, it is in a language loaded with suggestion:

> Diana's lip
> Is not more smooth and rubious; thy small pipe
> Is as the maiden's organ, shrill and sound,
> And all is semblative a woman's part.
>
> (1.4.31–34)

Modern audiences immediately understand what is happening here: the duke is unconsciously responding to the sexual potentiality visually represented to us by a sexually mature actress wearing boy's clothes. The key to Viola's virgin mystery (she describes her history as "[a] blank, my lord" [2.4.110]) lies in visualizing the woman's body wrapped in inappropriate costume: one kind of "worm i'th'bud" (2.4.111). Her "growing to perfection" (2.4.41), like the unfolding of a rose, is an unclothing. Wistfully, Viola seems to recognize that her blooming as a woman necessarily implies the violation and end of her virginity — again represented in terms of costume by those "maiden weeds" (5.1.255) whose recovery is blocked by Malvolio's suit against the captain at the end of the play. Orsino's refusal to kiss Viola until she dresses appropriately in "other habits" (5.1.387) suggests a kind of stalemate.

But the emphasis on costume and the theatricality of the bawdy phrase "woman's part" should lead us to wonder how Viola's blossoming into womanhood would strike an audience used to seeing women's roles enacted by boys. What the actor playing Viola will himself blossom into is not a woman at all, but a man. "For they shall yet belie thy happy years / That say thou art a man," Orsino says (1.4.30–31). The histories of the boy actors Nathan Field and Edward Kynaston indicate that these apprentices could grow up to play adult lovers and tyrants or could grow up and continue to play women. Thus the actor playing Viola, a boy figuring a woman disguised as a boy on the Elizabethan stage, stands poised at a critical moment in a professional progression from "woman's part" to "man's estate."

"Let the usurping actress remember that her sex is a liability, not an asset," Harley Granville-Barker remarked as he coined the expression "boy-actress."[4] Granville-Barker's nostalgia for an idealized "celibate stage" finds some interesting echoes in recent feminist criticism. Stripped of its misogynist language, Granville-Barker's idea that the boy-actress's lack of what he called "feminine charm" could be an "asset" anticipates Juliet Dusinberre's assertion that Shakespeare and his fellow dramatists were "freed" by the convention of cross-dressing in the theater and in the plots of plays to "explore . . . the nature of women untrammeled by the customs of femininity."[5] "Obliged to convince the audience of the boy actor's femininity even when he looked, because of his disguise, exactly like the boy he was, Shakespeare and his fellow playwrights created a femininity to outlast the boy actor's changes of costume" (*Shakespeare*, 257). Thus both Dusinberre and Granville-Barker in their different ways suggest that the institution of the boy-actress provides a key to understanding Shakespeare's women. But Granville-Barker failed to follow through on this idea in his actual discussions of the plays, and Dusinberre's declaration of "Shakespeare's feminism" offers little help in deciphering the multiple sexual ambiguities that crown the Illyria of *Twelfth Night*.[6]

For psychoanalytic critics, these ambiguities are seen as comprehensible in terms of adolescent development. "The sexual ambiguity of this stage," says W. Thomas MacCary, "reflects itself in sexual ambivalence, all of which Shakespeare figures in his use of transvestitism." For Coppélia Kahn, this confusion is shared by the audience: "We experience the state of radical identity-confusion typical of adolescence when the differences between the sexes are as fluid as their desire, when a boy might feel more like a girl than a boy, or a girl might love another girl rather than a boy."[7] But neither MacCary nor Kahn addresses the physical fact of the boy-actress's own adolescence: the androgyny of figures like Viola or Rosalind remains for them confined to the play's written texts. Joel Fineman recognizes the importance of theatrical convention: "A playwright such as Shakespeare, whose psyche assembled around and responded to polarities, doubling negations, structures of distributive reciprocity, had available to him a theater whose forms and conventions gave flesh to just such structures."[8] Rosalind's epilogue in *As You Like It* is an unmasking: when "the actor who plays Rosalind shows himself a boy, he accomplishes with the nakedness of his masculinity a final unmasking, pointing thereby to the play's last disguise and to the conditional that is the premise of the play itself" (*Representing Shakespeare*, 92). Shakespeare's use of disguise in *Twelfth Night* is special, Fineman argues, because "disguise by itself constitutes the play's problem" (79). For Fineman, though, the problem remains in Shakespeare's "psyche." *Twelfth Night* ends with no such unmasking: Viola remains trapped in her boy's clothes; the boy-actress remains trapped in the role.

Anthropological approaches to Shakespeare have also engaged the vision of adolescence that Viola embodies. Her desire at the beginning of the play not to "be delivered to the world, / Till I had made mine own occasion mellow, / What my estate is" (1.2.42–44) suggests to Marjorie Garber and Edward Berry that the whole play is in some way a rite of passage from childhood to maturity.[9] Berry has linked the Elizabethan institution of apprenticeship with rites of passage in other cultures as a process by which a boy becomes a man and achieves a place in society through the mastery of a trade. Stephen Greenblatt has argued that "characters like Rosalind and Viola pass through a state of being men in order to become women," in a society in which both boys and women are perceived as incomplete men.[10] The positive androgyny seen in Viola by feminist critics, the fluid adolescent sexuality seen by psychoanalytical critics, and the magical liminality seen by anthropological critics are all aspects of the real adolescent playing the role. At this phase of his career, the boy-actress is neither male nor female, fish nor fowl; his ability to play both boy and girl may signify the beginning of his acting career as a man or the end of his acting career as a woman.

More recent discussions of the boy-actress on the Renaissance English stage have gone further and disclosed this figure to be transgressive in a number of ways. In the process, they vigorously embrace the antitheatrical slander that the desire the boys provoked in male audience members was homosexual desire. One of the most famous and most frequently cited examples comes from Phillip Stubbes's *Anatomie of Abuses*. When the plays are done, Stubbes claims, "everyone brings another homeward of their way very friendly, and in their secret conclaves, covertly, they play the sodomites or worse." Prynne, as Stephen Orgel notes, endorses Stubbes, "citing this passage as a proof of the specifically homoerotic character of the stage":

> The assumption here is first that the basic form of response to the-ater is erotic, second that erotically, theater is uncontrollably excit-ing; and third, that the basic, essential form of erotic excitement in men is homosexual — that, indeed, women are only a cover for men. And though the assumption as Prynne articulates it is clearly patho-logical, a *reductio ad absurdum* of antitheatrical commonplaces, it is also clearly related both to all the generalized anxieties attendant upon the institutionalization of masculinity within the culture, and to the sanctioned homoeroticism that played so large a role in rela-tionships between men.

Orgel argues that theater frighteningly blurs a line between the sexes that is historically blurry in the Renaissance.[11] Anatomically, women were men whose development had been arrested; and the process could be reversed. For Bruce R. Smith, "Shakespeare sees in cross-dressing just what his Puritan detractors did: a particularly volatile symbol of liminality, a relaxation of the social rules that hold man's animal pas-sions in check."[12] Orgel follows Barish in describing the antitheatrical tracts as pathological, but he joins with them in finding the boy actor to be what Marjorie Garber calls "a sign of the homoerotic subtext of Renaissance theater." "In Shakespeare's plays, Stubbes and his kind may have good reason for their suspicions," Smith agrees.[13]

"Gender *is* performance," Laurence Senelick has declared. Alisa Solomon has argued that female impersonation is "originary" to West-ern theater: because gender identities only exist in and through per-formance, "acting is bound up with 'femininity.' And," Solomon con-tinues, "because patriarchal culture has sustained an ideal of the artificial, malleable, and changeable woman, 'femininity' is bound up with acting." The threat of this kind of binding could be expressed in physical, anatomical terms, as Orgel suggests. Seventeenth-century English antitheatrical writers, according to Laura Levine, shared a "fear — expressed in virtually biological terms — that theater could structurally transform men into women."[14] Levine argues that neither the essentialist notion of an unchanging own self nor the new histori-cist assertion of the self as wholly socially constructed can account for this fear. Yet her answer — that at this historical moment "a cultural prejudice burgeoned into a personal symptomatology" — is likewise evasive. Antitheatrical writings reveal a problem representing and staging gender in the early modern period, but it is a problem, as Solomon points out, that has always been and is still part of Western humanistic discourse.

Marjorie Garber, too, advocates a transhistorical look at the ubiquity of such models. "[W]hat if that 'boy' were to be taken seriously as what it most disturbingly represents: the figure of the transvestite? Rather than appropriated, erased, or wished away, rather than taken primarily as a role model for female empowerment or gay — male or female — homoerotic play, this 'boy' is a provoker of category crises, a destabilizer of binarisms, a transgressor of boundaries, sexual, erotic, hierarchical, political, conceptual. The changeling boy." For Garber, transvestitism is category crisis, and it emerges from an original concern with clothing as a social marker. Her wide-ranging argument rests on the assumption that transvestitism is usually "looked through rather than at in critical and cultural analyses," noting "how often, indeed how insistently, cultural observers have tried to make it mean something, anything, other than itself." And it is also based upon the somewhat dubious assumption that the "changeling boys" of the Renaissance stage were themselves, in some essential way, transvestites. It might be useful to turn Garber's formulations around a bit. If the Renaissance boy-actresses provoke cultural anxiety by disrupting sexual and social binarisms, it might be possible to argue that they do so not because they are transvestites but because they are actors. What actors signal is a permeability of boundaries, in Michael Goldman's terms, a reciprocal joining of "Self and Other, actor and character, we and they, comedy and tragedy, what is outside the boundary and what within." [15] The category confusion and boundary crossing that Garber celebrates in transvestitism and Goldman in all aspects of theater prompts the panic of antitheatricalists. They revolt from the blurring of boundaries.

But Viola shows that boundary-crossing of another sort is at work in *Twelfth Night*. She not only is representative of a disturbingly androgynous "poor monster" (2.2.34) but also participates in a metatheatrical language that throughout the play identifies her as a "changeling boy" of a special kind: an actor at a decisive moment in his career. It is as an actor-in-training that Viola first presents herself to Olivia. Confronted with two veiled female figures, Viola — one of the two "ladies" of the play — repeatedly insists upon identifying the "honorable lady of the house" (1.5.164) before delivering her speech, afraid that it might be "cast away" upon the wrong person (168–69). The nautical language here and in Maria's attack — "Will you hoist sail, sir?" (198) — suggests an identification between the shipwrecked Viola and the speech itself. "I have taken great pains to con it," she says; and as Olivia presses her with the question "Whence came you, sir?" she insists upon her lack of improvisatory skill: "I can say little more than I have studied, and that question's out of my part" (170, 173–75). While Viola's adoption of the part of Cesario bespeaks great skill in improvisation — "Are you a comedian?" asks Olivia — boy performers on the Elizabethan stage were not given the company's fool's freedom to range beyond the scripted part. "You might do much," says Olivia after Viola's passionate rendition of the "willow cabin" speech (271). Her assessment of Viola as a performer moves into a social interest: "What is your parentage?" Viola responds in character as a young professional: "Above my fortunes, yet my state is well. / I am a gentleman" (272–74). Of course, Cesario is a "gentleman" insofar as Viola was born a lady; the boy-actress is both lady and gentleman only insofar as he is a "comedian." A full member of an Elizabethan theater company might, like Shakespeare, aspire to (and gain) the status of "gentleman": a first step on the way for an apprentice would be aspiration to full membership in the company.[16]

What in the first exchanges between Olivia and Viola seems sexual rivalry might then also be construed as professional rivalry, for both "ladies" enjoy the same marginal status in the company of which they are apprentice members. "Excellently done," says Viola, "if God did all" (231) when Olivia unveils. And the play's interest in social mobility — Malvolio's desire to be Olivia's "fellow" (3.4.78) is seen by the others as madness — has a special resonance here. Viola does receive an invitation to marry above her station; Olivia, played by the boy-actress who remains constant to the part of the lady, is married to Sebastian, who is of her own social rank.[17] The identity suggested by the anagrams Viola and Olivia is challenged by Viola's superior virtuosity.

"I would you were as I would have you be!" Olivia blurts in their second important duet (3.1.142). "Would it be better madam, than I am? I wish it might be, for now I am your fool" is Viola's curious reply. It is Olivia who is here making a fool of herself; but the play suggests throughout a connection between Viola and Feste, the professional Fool. As Cesario, Viola claims that she is no comedian. Although in the first act she proposes herself as a singing "eunuch" in "service" to Orsino (1.2.56, 59), when Orsino requests a song of her in 2.4 it is Feste "that should sing it" (9). The central scene of the play is the dialogue between Viola and Feste, in which the two improvisers play with words. "They that dally nicely with words may make them wanton," Viola observes sententiously; "I would therefore my sister had no name, sir," responds the clown (3.1.14–16). In the scene immediately preceding this, Malvolio has construed his name from the letters "M. O. A. I."; in the scene before that, Viola has told the story of her sister's history — "a blank, my lord." Malvolio's social climbing, Viola's strategy of "concealment," and the Fool's nihilistic dexterity become linked. And the scene has professional overtones again. "Now Jove, in his next commodity of hair, send thee a beard," says Feste, receiving a coin. "By my troth, I'll tell thee, I am almost sick for one — [aside] though I would not have it grow on my chin," Viola replies (3.1.44–47). Among its other associations — some quite aggressively bawdy — the beard can symbolize coming of age in the company. Viola's sickness can be seen not only as sexual desire but also as professional ambition, and her anxiety about beards as the boy-actress's worry at the peak of his career. Viola's commentary on Feste's skill — "This fellow is wise enough to play the fool, / And to do that well craves a kind of wit" (59–60) — reflects an awareness of a kind of folly radically different from the idiocies of the Illyrians. Robert Armin's identity with the role of Feste has traditional authority; as a skilled improvisatory artist he commands the boy-actress's respect. And as a vengeful and cruel punisher of Malvolio he insists upon the stability of rank.

Feste's song at the end of the play, then, may invoke not merely a grim "Drunkard's Progress" from boyhood to perpetual hangover but an invocation of the actor's life with its many perils.[18] The "changeling boy's" sexually undifferentiated foolishness gives way to "man's estate" with its accompanying (and threatening) "knaves," "thieves," and "tossposts." "By swaggering could I never thrive," sings Feste: heroic roles are not the Fool's province; nor does Viola distinguish herself in the manly art of combat. The song's persistent quibbling suggests all sorts of sexual confusion: "gate" commonly refers to women, and the Fool's wife seems unimpressed by his swaggering. The traditional associations of impotence and sexual voraciousness with foolishness animate not only the song but the whole social world of Illyria.

That world in many ways seems to be a theater, in which actors are matched and mismatched to their parts. "Insofar as the play has a norm," Marilyn French points out, "it is Viola, but she represents an absence, the searching, uncertain part of the self."[19] Looking at rather than through — or here, perhaps, into — Viola permits a rearrangement of this formulation: the searching and uncertainty of Viola are those of the boy-actress at the height of his career, wondering whether his next part will be male or female and if the breaking of his voice will mean the end of it all. Alone among the characters in the play, Viola chooses to be disguised (there is no reason for her not to introduce herself to Orsino, a friend of her father, from the very first), but the part she takes — Cesario, the singing eunuch who refuses to sing — expresses itself in a language of negation and passivity. "O Time, thou must untangle this, not I," she protests in her soliloquy. "It is too hard a knot for me t'untie" (2.2.40 – 41). This is radically different from the resourceful self-help of Rosalind in *As You Like It* ("Believe then, if you please, that I can do strange things" [5.2.57–58]). The stalemate for Viola is represented by her inability to improvise, to venture beyond the part set down; her passiveness and emptiness are preconditions of her femininity.

Rosalind's magical inventiveness is learned from a profound magician; Portia relays the deliberations of Belario. These instances not only figure the marginality and liminality of female adolescence; they also figure the passiveness of the puppetlike boy-actresses. "The feminist revision of Ophelia," Elaine Showalter has recently suggested, "comes as much from the actress' freedom as from the critic's interpretation": this kind of professional freedom is precisely what the apprentices in the acting companies lacked. The "newly powerful and respectable Victorian actresses," Showalter says, were able to "invent a story" for Ophelia.[20] Without status or power in their own right, bound to a marginal and powerless company of actors dependent upon government whim, the boy-actress — unlike the all-licensed fool — could only do what he was told.

The magician whom Rosalind invokes and the Belario who passes his judgment on to Portia both represent a shadowy authority in the background. These avuncular and patriarchal presences untie the knots of the plot: the playwright prompts the heroine and extricates the play from its plight. Viola in her play is provided with no such support: her willingness to play on in her part is characterized as an act of faith. "Prove true, imagination, O, prove true," she breathes at the mention of her brother's name. "That I, dear brother, be now ta'en for you" (3.4.377–78). In metatheatrical terms, she hopes to recognize in her baffling situation elements of the predictable substitution-plot of *A Comedy of Errors*. But she is not sure, any more than the apprentice actor could be sure of a continuing role in the company after reaching a certain age. Only the playwright holds the key to the plot; only the shareholders hold the key to the actor's career.

"You know he brought me out o' favor with my lady about a bear-baiting here," Fabian complains about Malvolio (2.5.7–8). The line establishes the theatrical environment of Malvolio's gulling, for the bear-baiting pit stood hard by the old Globe. Like Viola, Malvolio is caught between roles; his punishment is to be cozened into costuming, tricked into performing, and humiliated. As the transformed steward struts and smiles in front of Olivia, she is appalled, and her language metatheatrically invokes Shakespeare's greatest comedy of transformation: "Why, this is midsummer madness" (3.4.58). Malvolio's torment is equally an actor's nightmare: to be deprived of the audience for whom he desires to perform is to be deprived of every vestige of the actor's freedom. "Come, we'll have him in a dark room and bound," says Toby (3.4.137–38). There he is forced to endure, as audience, the clown's virtuoso performance as both himself and Sir Topas. Yet like Viola Malvolio reaches out to the Fool as in some way a model: "I am as well in my wits, fool, as thou art" (4.2.88), and the scene as a whole demands comparison to Viola's scene with the Fool (3.1).

Malvolio denies the "cakes and ale" (2.3.114–15) of Toby's "uncivil rule" (122). Yet while he insists upon "respect of place, persons [and] time" (91) when he rebukes the revelers, his social climbing belies this insistence upon degree. His performance of his vision of social mobility, in yellow stockings and cross-gartered, is a puppet-show, manipulated by Maria. Like Viola, Malvolio is an actor without freedom: he is a baited bear, a lunatic. "They have propertied me," he complains, no propertied gentleman but a theatrical prop (4.2.91). Playing out his most secret dream, he wins no libidinal liberty but the dark room. Since he cannot admit of play, all his enactment must be utterly in earnest. "But tell me true," asks the Fool, "are you not mad indeed? or do you but counterfeit?" (114–15). "Believe me, I am not," Malvolio replies. "I tell thee true." Viola is acutely aware of her blankness, her unripeness, her deceptive imposture. Malvolio's language of negation denies the possibility of imposture. "You can say none of this," he charges

Olivia as he confronts her with the forged letter (5.1.334) and challenges her to deny her hand. The possibility of forgery has never occurred to him: for Viola, nothing but costuming and imposture exist.

"The devil a Puritan he is," says Maria, "or anything constantly, but a time-pleaser" (2.3.146–47). The counterpart to Malvolio's futile, time-serving search for a role is the passivity Viola ascribes to her sister: "She sat like Patience on a monument, / Smiling at grief. Was not this love indeed?" (2.4.114–15). Like Malvolio's love, this love is indeed disfiguring, and his yellow stockings demand identification with the sister's "green and yellow melancholy" (113). "Not black in my mind, though yellow in my legs," Malvolio quips (3.4.27–28); costume and role are bafflingly confused. Malvolio, male, adult, and puritan though he may think himself to be, is Protean and theatrical despite himself; his desires confound and disfigure him.

Olivia, like Orsino, abandons propriety, fiercely wooing Cesario as Malvolio would be wooed, casting aside all thought of social station. "Have you not set mine honor at the stake / And baited it with all th'unmuzzled thoughts / That tyrannous heart can think?" (3.1.118–20) she asks, and the language of baited bears and tyrannous hearts is an odd conflation of Orsino's and Malvolio's excesses. Orsino's image is of himself as Actaeon, a hart pursued by "my desires, like fell and cruel hounds" (1.1.21). The miscasting of which Malvolio is the most grotesque and Viola the most affecting emblem is endemic to Illyria's unmuzzled lovers: violently setting their sights on inappropriate mates, Orsino and Olivia throw themselves, without knowing it, as Viola does, upon the mercy of the playwright.

One of Barish's most delightful quotes, illustrating the venerable tradition of the actor as Proteus, is from Robert Burton's *Anatomy of Melancholy*; it is all too common, Burton complains,

> To see a man turn himself into all shapes like a Chameleon, or as a Proteus transform himself into all that is monstrous; to act twenty parts & persons at once for his advantage, to temporize and vary like Mercury the planet, good with good, bad with bad; having a several face, garb, & character, for every one he meets; of all religions, humours, inclinations; to fawn like a spaniel, with lying and feigned obsequiousness, rage like a lion, bark like a cur, fight like a dragon, sting like a serpent, as meek as a lamb & yet again grin like a tiger,

weep like a crocodile, insult over some, & yet others domineer over him, here command, there crouch, tyrannize in one place, be baffled in another, a wise man at home, a fool abroad to make others merry![21]

We never know who this person really is: there is no denoting this fawning liar truly. According to Barish, the figure of Proteus recurs as an emblem of the actor's freedom to transcend social barriers and take on the costumes and signs of different professions and ranks. As "poor monster" (2.2.34) thrown up by the sea, Viola not only embodies Bruce Smith's myth of "The Shipwrecked Youth" but is also an Old Man of the Sea, Protean in the evasiveness of her outer shape.[22] Her inner truth, again like Proteus's, can only be fathomed when she is grasped and held, a consummation that the play leaves for Orsino's pleasure offstage. Malvolio (his name suggesting both ill will and a pun on Male-Viola) seeks Protean social liberties in his brutally stage-managed performance. The revenge the Fool takes on him is a literal enforcement of his own insistence to the revelers upon propriety and degree. As Viola recognizes (and Malvolio does not), only the Fool's role admits of improvisation, and even there improvisation consists of anticipating "their mood on whom he jests, / The quality of persons, and the time" (3.1.62–63).

Viola's problems with Olivia result in part from her own problems as an improviser. "I see you what you are: you are too proud," she says in the first interview (1.5.245); no professional Fool would be caught in such a bald statement. Better is her more profoundly foolish observation when in their second meeting Olivia demands, "I prithee, tell me what thou think'st of me." "That you do think you are not what you are," Viola gnomically replies (3.1.138–39). Both instances bear witness to her discomfort not so much with the role she plays as with role-playing itself. Remembering the glee with which Rosalind kits herself out as a man and takes the opportunity the love-struck shepherds offer to "prove a busy actor in their play" (*As You Like It*, 3.4.57), we should be struck by the distaste and philosophical discomfort that Viola expresses.

Portia, too, embraces the opportunity to play "a thousand raw tricks of these bragging Jacks" (*Merchant of Venice*, 3.4.77) in her men's clothes; Viola, in contrast, begins her play — in the very scene of her decision to take on the eunuch's costume — with a sententious meditation on the falsity of outward looks. "There is a fair behavior in thee, Captain," she tells her rescuer:

And though that nature with a beauteous wall
Doth oft close in pollution, yet of thee
I will believe thou hast a mind that suits
With this thy fair and outward character.

(1.2.47–51)

Viola is here disavowing a suspicion that the Captain might prove a hypocrite, a seemer filled with pollution. In choosing to place her faith in him, she decides categorically — "I will believe" — that in his case, at least, the inward being suits the outward show. This decision is hurled back at her by Sebastian's rescuer when he is arrested trying to save her. "Thou hast, Sebastian, done good feature shame," Antonio cries from the Officer's clutches:

In nature there's no blemish but the mind;
None can be called deformed but the unkind.
Virtue is beauty, but the beauteous evil
Are empty trunks, o'erflourished by the devil.

(3.4.369–72)

Like the worm in the bud, this image of emptiness tricked out suggests a hollowness beneath clothing that Malvolio and, in a different way, Sir Andrew and Sir Toby most plainly represent.

What is troubling in the play is Viola's sense of her own identity with the worm-eaten bud and, in the scene with Antonio, her acknowledgment of Sebastian ("Yet living in my glass" [3.4.382]) as model for her deceptive outer part. Especially troubling is the sententious (and misogynist) apothegm at the center of her soliloquy:

Disguise, I see thou are a wickedness
Wherein the pregnant enemy does much.
How easy is it for the proper false
In women's waxen hearts to set their forms!

(2.2.27–30)

Editorial glosses to the contrary, "pregnant enemy" suggests less the resourcefulness of the devil than the idea of a woman concealing her pregnancy with a disguise of loose robes (a situation which biographical critics of Shakespeare like the Stephen Dedalus of James Joyce's

Ulysses would find evocative of the bard's own wedding). The sexual overtones of the phrase "does much" and the reference to Elizabethan doctrines of the ways in which both the conception of the idea of love and the conception of literal offspring take place fill these four lines with a heavy burden of ambiguity. Viola's identification of her disguised self as Olivia's (and womankind's) "pregnant enemy" suggests a very female fear of the social tragedy of unwed pregnancy and casts maleness as an invading and embossing force that sets and fixes female fluidity. Yet at the same time Viola sees the "waxen hearts" of women as regrettably frail. In her "proper false" disguise she yearns for the fixity that only male power can impose.

Viola's confused desire for and fear of the "forms" that men set in women's hearts (and set women in) works in tandem with her expressions of conventional antitheatricality to offer a composite image of the actor's and the woman's social marginality. The play's emphasis on her male body links the status of woman with the status of apprentice — or at least performs that linkage for women who are, as Viola is, unpregnant. Olivia's state of being both "maid" and "made" (as self-sufficient lady of the house) is also one of being "mad" (for the house is in wild disorder as she extravagantly grieves over her dead brother and then shifts her extravagant attentions to Viola), as befits the relatively more stable status of the actor who plays her part, no more or less than that of "lady" in the play.

Shakespeare's ordinary comic practice of juxtaposing a conventional lady with a lively, boyish, and more self-conscious counterpart speaks in this play to the dangers of acting — not simply in the sense that social role-playing (as in Malvolio's case) is a specialized and theatrical skill, but also in professional terms. The fixity of the role of "lady" which Olivia plays is one possibility open to Viola — the names enforce this. So too is the radically different license of the improvising Fool, like so many of the characters of this play a cipher but, unlike them, self-aware. There is also the mad role-playing of the socially anomalous Malvolio, a male Viola whose waxen heart takes the form set in it by Maria's counterfeit writing. All of these possible roles are fraught with danger — as would be, in the Elizabethan world, the role of maid on the threshold of marriage, "to die," as Viola puts it of roses and maidens, "even when they to perfection grow" (2.4.41).

Bringing to completion through violation and death figures the maid's experience of sex and entrance into the new world of marriage. But equally the apprentice actor dies when brought to perfection: it takes a certain amount of time to train a boy as a virtuoso performer (even only of what is set down) and during the time of his training the boy must also inevitably approach the threshold of manhood. G. E. Bentley finds that there seems to be no set term for the indentures of boys in the acting companies; one explanation might be that boys develop at different rates. But becoming fully accomplished as a "lady" would not necessarily lead to full accomplishment as a player of male roles: it is conceivable, but not necessary, that Rosalind might grow up to play Orlando, Viola to play Sebastian.[23] Or the boy could grow up to specialize in women's parts. Colley Cibber tells a curious anecdote about Kynaston: King Charles II, arriving early at the theater, was told that a slight delay was inevitable, because "the Queen was not shav'd yet." "The King, whose good Humour lov'd to laugh at a Jest as well as to make one, accepted the Excuse, which serv'd to divert him till the male Queen cou'd be effeminated."[24] It is equally possible that the boy-actress's growth to perfection might lead to theatrical death: exclusion from the company as no longer valuable due to a surplus of young men.

But even full membership in the company betokens only marginality: as Feste sings at the end, "the rain it raineth every day," and the actor's freedom is only the freedom to "strive to please you every day." Just as Viola takes the risk of marrying a tyrant when she agrees to marry Orsino, the actor runs the risk of incurring the wrath of a tyrannical audience or a government censor. The play ends not with an image of completion, but with a song of contingency.

In her moments of antitheatrical sententiousness, Viola reminds us of the actor's reputation for duplicity and hypocrisy. Antonio's attack on her hurts because he accuses her of being a mere seemer and a gorgeous empty trunk. She is, perhaps, like Hamlet in his instructions to the actors, naive in her understanding of the extent to which actors can or cannot shape their own roles. From the very first, Viola cannot merely speak what is set down; she must respond to the enigmatic audience of the two veiled ladies. Where Hamlet as university student and apprentice playwright is particularly angered by the improvising of clowns, Viola as apprentice actor admires Feste's skill. But his freedom, like his all-licensed role, is sharply circumscribed by social rules. Feste, Viola, and the theater in which they perform are all part of a larger social order, in which the all-powerful minority of great ones at court sponsor activity which a large proportion of the community sees as impious and unlawful.

Viola's and Malvolio's antitheatrical strictures speak the language of this body of opinion. As Jean Howard, Smith, Orgel, Garber, Levine, and others have argued following Barish, Puritan invective against the institution of theater and its employment of boy-actresses went beyond recitation of the biblical strictures against cross-dressing and suggested with Stubbes that the actors and audience members sexually abused their apprentices.[25] Rosalind, offering "if I were a woman" to "kiss as many of you as had beards that pleased me," seems, as the actor who plays the "lady," to be promising to continue to play the role offstage. Female actresses in the Restoration promised forbidden backstage delights in prologues and epilogues.

Viola, however, repudiates any such linkage. In her first dialogue with Olivia, she professionally insists upon the difference between her role-playing and her secret self. "What I am and what I would are as secret as maidenhead," she tells Olivia (1.5.210–11). In the play's story, her secret is the virginity she shares with Olivia; and, in the play's language of acting, her secret is also her identity with Olivia as an accomplished and yet untested actor. The play's multiple infatuations are both homosexual and professional, like Shakespeare's "celibate stage"; Viola's mystery — so trade guilds described the skills in which apprentices were initiated — is her growing mastery of the acting trade.

The "natural perspective" (5.1.216) of Viola and Sebastian presents to the eye not merely a comic substitution that relieves the strain of sexuality in parentless Illyria but an image of the way that the theater can mirror and replenish itself — Viola can come to play Sebastian or even Feste, Olivia to play Orsino. But the play's puns on Male-Violas remain elusively unfulfilled even as they seem fulfilled: Malvolio holds the key to the costume room.

"Prynne was right," said the Victorian novelist and social reformer Charles Kingsley in "Plays and Puritans," one of his historical essays: "to make a boy a stage-player was pretty certainly to send him to the Devil. Let any man of common sense imagine to himself the effect on a young boy's mind which would be produced by representing shamelessly before a public audience, not merely the language, but the passions, of such women as occur in almost every play." And he cautions his readers against overvaluing the English drama of the early modern period, by "remembering ever that the golden age of the English drama was one of private immorality, public hypocrisy, ecclesiastical pedantry, and regal tyranny, and ended in the temporary downfall of Church and Crown." "Poetry in those old Puritans? Why not? They were men of like passions with ourselves," he concludes. "There was poetry enough in them, to be sure, though they acted it like men, instead of singing it like birds."[26] Kingsley rather oddly anticipates new historicist critics like David Kastan as he embraces the manly antitheatricalism that literalized the tropes of theater in actual regicide.

Kingsley's version of Puritanism, rather than Malvolio's mere time serving, closed the theaters, and with their reopening came the abolishment of the institution of boy-actresses. "For as much as many plays formerly acted doe conteine severall prophane, obscene, and scurrulous passages," read the royal patent issued to Thomas Killegrew after the Restoration,

> and the women's part therin have byn acted by men in the habit of women, at which some have taken offence, for the preventing of these abuses for the future . . . wee doe likewise permit and give leave, that all the woemen's part . . . may be performed by woemen soe long as their recreacones, which by reason of the abuses aforesaid were scandalous and offensive, may by such reformation be esteemed not onely harmless delight, but useful and instructive.[27]

One measure of the extent to which the profession of boy-actress died when it grew to perfection is our own difficulty — as readers, as Kingsley's men of common sense, or even as audiences at the rare performances of Shakespeare-in-drag — in responding to the convention. Granville-Barker envisions it as some sort of public-school harmless delight. "When Shakespeare's heroines came to be played by women instead of boys," says Elaine Showalter in her essay on Ophelia, "the presence of the female body and female voice, quite apart from details of interpretation, created new meanings and subversive tensions in these roles."[28] As apprentice to a trade that was itself next door to vagrancy, the boy-actress, too, embodies tensions at the heart of the highly marginal institution to which he did and did not belong.

It is not simply that modern audiences can no longer look at Viola without seeing through her to an adult female actor. *Twelfth Night*'s responsiveness to the whole world of antitheatrical discourse and the close parallelisms between its Illyria and the controlled chaos of professional playing are historical phenomena as well. An indication of the historical circumscription of this kind of playing can be seen in Viola and Olivia as they reappear, greatly altered, in William Wycherley's *The Plain Dealer* after the Restoration. Partly adapted from Molière's *Misanthrope* as well as from *Twelfth Night*, Wycherley's play conflates in its Olivia the coquette of Molière's comedy and the self-absorbed character of Shakespeare. Wycherley's Olivia is a false prude, too, and tolerates the fops Plausible and Novel. The Viola figure, Fidelia (following Manly in man's dress because she admires his frankness), charms Olivia, whose attempted seduction of Fidelia is interrupted by her husband, Vernish. Fidelia refuses to draw her sword: "O hold, Sir, and send but your Servant down, and I'll satisfie you, Sir, I cou'd not injure you, as you imagine. . . . I am a Woman, Sir, a very unfortunate Woman." "How!" exclaims Vernish. "A very handsom Woman I'm sure then: here are the Witnesses of 't, too, I confess — [Pulls off her Peruke, and feels her breasts.] (Well, I'm glad to find the Tables turn'd, my Wife in more danger of Cuckolding, than I was)," he chuckles, aside.

While language evokes and constructs Viola's femininity in Shakespeare's play, Wycherley's, less than eighty years later, strips and exposes the actress's female body to the audience's view. Fidelia urges Vernish to let her go: "A pair of Breeches cou'd not wrong you, Sir." But he has other plans: "Well, Madam, if I must not know who you are, 'twill suffice for me only to know certainly what you are: which you must not deny me. Come, there is a Bed within, the proper Rack for Lovers; and if you are a Woman, there you can keep no secrets, you'll tell me there all unask'd. Come."[29] There is no mystery here about the "changeling boy's" secret. The offstage bed that Stubbes fears and Smith romanticizes will reveal "what you are": "who you are" is a matter of indifference to Vernish.

Viola's language constructs her as a boy-actress at the cusp of his career; Fidelia is a female actor whose boy's costume functions primarily to show the audience her legs. Given the amount of theory-rich ink that has been spilled upon the Renaissance boy actors, it is remarkable how little comment the Restoration "breeches part" has excited. Between 1660 and 1700, according to John Harold Wilson, 89 of 375 new plays contained breeches parts.[30] This is almost 24 percent: and the women not only played parts in which their characters dressed as men but also played male characters. Tom Fashion, for example, in *The Relapse*, was first played by the "minor actress Mary Kent." Moll Davis, according to one strand of stage tradition, played the role of Hippolito, the man who has never seen a woman, in John Dryden and William Davenant's adaptation of *The Tempest* and went on to become Charles II's mistress. Nell Gwyn, too, "was especially adept at such parts," J. L. Styan notes.[31]

"Men's clothing was favored, it appears, both by prostitutes, and courtesans," Garber remarks of a custom in sixteenth-century Venice, and surely many of the actresses in the English Restoration began their careers as prostitutes or orange-wenches. "Playhouse flesh and blood," as Katharine Eisaman Maus points out in an article of the same name, is a phrase that refers to prostitutes; she argues that the actresses of the period are threatening to the social order because they are working women. "Women and actors, the agents of this disruption, do not themselves fit easily into the productive social hierarchy," she notes; antifeminist and antitheatrical tracts share "an inherent association of role-playing with female sexuality."[32] For Maus, the cross-dressed actress figures a kind of category crisis, not transhistorical as in Garber's *Vested Interests*, but specific to the Restoration period's own anxieties about social hierarchies and their all too recently experienced vulnerability to massive upheaval. Kristina Straub links the phenomenon of the cross-dressed actress to the larger problem of the construction of binary gender in the eighteenth century: "A slightly guilty pleasure in the sexual and gender confusion embodied in the cross-dressed actress is balanced against recuperation of her gender bending within dominant sexual ideologies." Vernish's interrupted rape of Fidelia reinforces a repressive patriarchal order which the cross-dressed actress threatens.[33]

Metaphorical stripping, in the case of Viola, becomes physical stripping on the Restoration stage. By removing one level of artifice — by permitting women to take the women's parts — the Restoration stage suggests that femininity resides in the female body. "The sight of women dressing as men," argues Lesley Ferris, "considered a threat to society twenty years earlier, had now become a sexualised theatrical commodity." The commodification of the actress, which Angelo anticipates in his appropriative gaze at Isabella, places women on stage in a kind of double-bind, according to Ferris: "[T]o work in the theatre, they must be experts in disguise, but because they are women, disguise is not seen as artistic creation, but rather as a natural part of that sign called 'woman.' . . . With no distancing device between role and self,

the male-controlled female role takes dominance over the tenuous, uncharted notions of the female self." For Ferris the wearing of masks by
the ladies in the audience figures the only escape from this dominance:
"But one can easily imagine that it must have been tremendously liberating to walk the streets of London with one's identity voided by the
simple black mask." There is a lingering essentialism in Ferris's nostalgia for "the tenuous, uncharted notions of the female self" that contradicts the social constructionism that otherwise propels her argument.[34]

The tenuous self that the boy-actress's role both conceals and reveals
through Viola, as we have noticed, is in the play's language set in dynamic relationship to the boy's professional status in the company.
While antitheatricalists like Stubbes may have seen the boys as commodities of a sort, the feminist discussions of the Restoration actresses
go further and declare actresses — because they are women — to be
nothing but commodities. Women's acting is natural because women
are naturally hypocritical: "The hypocrisy of women, and the hypocrisy
of players, cannot be morally neutral" to Prynne and his ilk, Katharine
Eisaman Maus reminds us.[35] In the induction to *Taming of the Shrew*
Shakespeare offers a joke that reinforces this notion of women as naturally players: the Lord advises that the Page might need an onion to
provoke tears:

> And if the boy have not a woman's gift
> To rain a shower of commanded tears,
> An onion will do well for such a shift,
> Which in a napkin being close conveyed
> Shall in despite enforce a watery eye.
> (Induction.1. 122–26)

A real woman would not need the onion: women weep on cue anyway.

The antitheatrical identification of acting with hypocrisy, and of
hypocrisy with femininity, as constructed in the early modern period
wins a curious kind of assent in the arguments of feminist critics like
Ferris and Maus. Ferris's idea that mask-wearing on the streets is
"tremendously liberating" because the mask voids "one's identity," like
Maus's insistence that acting is "necessarily insincere," succumbs to the
antitheatricalist line that actors lose their identities to the roles they
play, that playing is essentially dishonest, a betrayal of a secret self.

But the Restoration actresses set their personal identities into more
complex interaction with the roles they played. From Nell Gwyn boldly

declaring in a mock epitaph that "she liv'd a Slattern" to Jane Rogers fighting off the advances of an intoxicated George Powell during the Worthy and Berinthia scene in *The Relapse*, they laid claim to public identities that sometimes conflicted with and sometimes complemented the roles they played. The elusive goal of respectability which some of the actresses (like Anne Bracegirdle) sought is premised upon a sense of personal integrity that Ferris, Straub, and Maus, joining with the antitheatricalists they decry, deny to the women themselves. The character of Viola insists on such an integrity in her sententious antitheatricality, and we can track an identification of what is tenuous and uncharted in her notion of self with the tenuousness of the boy's acting career. Contemporary feminist and new historicist criticism, collapsing role into self, voiding identity in mask, declaring actresses to be commodities, embraces antitheatricalism and often relies upon analysts like Stubbes and Prynne for guidance. The occasional nod in the direction of the actor's freedom — like Showalter's recognition that the role of Ophelia changed as strong-willed actresses demanded more to do — does not alter the overwhelming bleakness of this criticism.

Those who see the Renaissance boys and the Restoration women as subversive forces in the theater, deconstructing gender and empowering women, and those who see this subversion as wholly contained in a hegemony of binary oppositions look at actors and see transvestites or prostitutes. Feminists and new historicists alike adopt the vocabulary of the antitheatrical divines, but so, too, does Viola in her anxiety about disguise and so, too, do the rare defenders of theater in the early modern period. So powerful is this vocabulary that what is left, what Viola clings to and identifies with the profound heart, seems particularly powerless: a blank, a secret, a mystery, Patience on a monument.

Scene Two

PUTTING ON THE CLOTH

"Art thou a churchman?" Viola asks Feste (*Twelfth Night*, 3.1.3); "I would I were the first that ever dissembled in such a gown," Feste says as he costumes himself for his baiting of Malvolio (4.2.5). In an utterly different context, Søren Kierkegaard also points to the way that preaching and acting tend to blur into each other. "To be appropriate to you, the alternatives must naturally be bold," writes the ethical man, B, to the aesthetic man, A, in *Either/Or*: "either a pastor — or an actor." The opposition is as extreme as B can imagine. "Here is the dilemma," B continues:

> Now all your passionate energy is aroused; reflection with its hundred arms seizes the idea of being a pastor. You find no rest; day and night you think about it; you read all the books you can find, you go to church three times every Sunday, make the acquaintance of pastors, write sermons yourself, deliver them to yourself; and for half a year you are dead to the whole world. Now you are ready; you can speak with more insight and seemingly with more experience about being a pastor than many a one who has been a pastor for twenty years. When you meet them, it arouses your exasperation that they do not know how to expectorate with a completely different eloquence. You say: Is this enthusiasm? Compared with them, I, who am not a pastor, who have not dedicated myself to being a pastor, speak with the voice of angels. That may very well be true, but you nevertheless did not become a pastor. Now you conduct yourself the same way with the other alternative, and your enthusiasm for art almost exceeds your ecclesiastical eloquence.[36]

B's concern is with his friend's inability to choose, to settle. He illustrates that with an example of a contrast that is as "bold" as possible:

between a pastor and an actor. He does not describe the zeal with which A might throw himself into the art of acting; but he does not have to. For the process of becoming a pastor, we notice, is described by B as a rehearsal process. A is throwing himself into the role of pastor, and A's complaint that the real preachers lack "enthusiasm" is an actor's critique.

Himself a parson, Jeremy Collier differed in *A Short View of the Immorality and Prophaneness of the English Stage* from other seventeenth-century antitheatrical diatribes by devoting a substantial chapter to "The Clergy Abused by the Stage." He apparently considered any portrayal of organized religion a slap in the face to the clergy, for he cites, in addition to a number of parson-scenes from comic drama, the "swaggering against Priests in [Dryden's] *Oedipus*."[37] Collier was particularly distressed by the appearance on stage of actors dressing as priests performing ceremonies or of actors playing characters who then dress as priests and perform ceremonies. Blurring the boundaries between ritual and performance, such mock rituals struck him as blasphemous.

A long tradition in English antitheatricalism identifies Roman Catholicism with imposture and "masquery." In early modern England the theater "caught up into" itself the iconographic richness of the old religion, and the Protestant commentators expressed unease and distaste for the "gay gazing sights" it offered.[38] Any kind of priesthood, as Collier makes plain, could be interpreted to represent established religion, and the ease with which true religion could be distorted into stage playing is cited again and again in antitheatrical literature. John Rainolds, recalling the "profane and wicked toyes of *Passion-playes*" in the days of the old religion, denounced "*Popish Priests*": "as they have transformed the celebrating of the Sacrament of the Lords *supper* into a *Masse-game*, and all other partes of the *Ecclesiastical service* into *theatricall sights*; so, in steed of *preaching the word*, they caused it to be played; a thing put in practise by their flowres, the *Jesuits*, among the poore *Indians*."[39] Not only do the Papists transform worship into ridiculous performance, but they impose the hollow shows of the mass upon the hapless victims of colonialism.

Perhaps the most famous imposture associated with the clergy, however, is not an imperialist exercise. The priestly impostor is Tartuffe, and no one knows exactly what kind of garb the hypocrite wore on the occasion of the play's first performance. The controversy about the original costume of Tartuffe circles around a vacancy. The unanswerability of this question inheres in the invisibility of a lost costume, the irrecoverability of a suppressed and since substantially revised text, the evanescence of the whole occasion of the festival of the *Plaisirs de l'Ile enchantée*. This has not prevented scholars from arriving at positive conclusions on the matter, however. "It is common ground," argues John Cairncross, that "Tartuffe was dressed in 1664 as a priest or at any rate like a pious layman who affected clerical garb."[40] Cairncross and the scholarly consensus he invokes rely upon Molière's defense of *L'Imposteur* — a play in which he replaced Tartuffe with the character of Panulphe — for this common ground. Describing the suppression of this ill-fated substitute in the second *Placet* appended to *Tartuffe*, Molière bewails his enemies, who insisted that the forbidden *Tartuffe* and the new play were the same:

> In vain did I bring it out under the name of *The Impostor*, and disguise the character under the fashions of a man of society: in vain had I given him a little hat, a big wig, a wide collar, a sword, and lace trimmings all over his suit; softening him up in so many places; removing with care everything I thought capable of offering a shadow of a pretext to the famous originals of the portrait I would have wanted to paint: None of this worked at all.[41]

Making Panulphe's clothes fashionable suggests that Tartuffe's clothes were not: the big wig, the wide collar, and the gentleman's sword all must be items not worn by the original Tartuffe. Cairncross even adduces this absence as proof that in the 1664 version of the play the second act, with the proposed marriage of Mariane to Tartuffe, did not exist: "It follows there could be no question of a marriage between Tartuffe and the daughter of the house" (*New Light*, 36), since the hypocrite was clearly a postulant for holy orders.

"Somber, austere, pious, but not the costume of a priest," argues Herman Prins Salomon, describing the famous 1669 engraving of Tartuffe.[42] As Cairncross suggests, the pious laymen who "affected clerical garb" were themselves impostors of a sort, wearing small collars — the *petit collet* — without being clerics. An early dictionary definition explicitly links this item of clothing with hypocrisy.

> A *petit colet* man, or simply *un petit colet*: These words are used to refer to men of the Church, who for reasons of modesty wear small collars, whereas men of the world wear large ones decorated with

needlework and lace. They also refer to a man who enters into the way of piety and reform (*disciplinae severioris cultor*), and sometimes *petit colet* is used with a negative connotation to refer to hypocrites who affect modest manners, especially wearing a small collar.[43]

Jean-Marie Apostolidès confidently asserts that the appearance of Tartuffe, "the man in black," in the multicolored environment of Orgon's household conveyed a visual shock to the original audience.[44] It may well have been a shock of recognition: according to Molière's own theory, expressed in his preface to the play, hypocrites recognized themselves in Tartuffe and were consumed with rage. At any rate, the play's opponents generally recognized that Tartuffe was taking on the function of lay director of conscience in Orgon's household. This institution was precious to the divines who engineered *Tartuffe*'s suppression.

But *Tartuffe*, as I have argued elsewhere, is remarkable for the way in which it encapsulates within its story the dynamics of its own suppression and public release.[45] In Tartuffe, Molière unleashed on the stage a figure that devours roles just as fast as the plot can generate them: he is a pious counselor, an amorous libertine, an outraged householder in turn before being exposed by the king's officer as a notorious criminal. Tartuffe embodies an uncontrollable virtuosity of impersonation that has no need to be convincing — no one really believes in his piety, for example, except the play's fools — in order to achieve its desires. He represents a Protean acting force that threatens to unseat the order of his world until he is finally, and miraculously, exposed and reined in by the king. The exposure of Tartuffe as a vagabond and thief enacts the necessary fate of the acting profession without royal protection: the action of the play, then, is to some degree antitheatrical. To restore order to Orgon's house and to his kingdom, the king in the play must expose acting as what it is without his royal license, an extended confidence trick. Outside the theater, as Elizabeth Burns has argued, acting is hypocrisy.[46]

The debate about *Tartuffe* sparked a high degree of serious consideration of the nature of hypocrisy itself in French sermons and moralizing tracts. The first flush of opposition saw the play as an endorsement of libertinism and a scandalous mockery of pious behavior and dress. According to this line of thought, the play represented as ridiculous conduct that the church endorsed as contributory to one's salvation. "Hang up my hairshirt and my scourge," Tartuffe instructs his lackey Laurent upon his famous first entrance. As Salomon has demonstrated, Tartuffe's hairshirt and scourge, along with his insistence that Elmire suspend her visits and Dorine cover her décolletage, are characteristic of reformist attitudes current in the seventeenth-century French church.[47] The play revealed fissures within the church on larger doctrinal matters: Tartuffe's use of Jesuitical casuistry in his seduction scenes with Elmire might have pleased Jansenists, except that no Jansenist could approve of the general principle of exposing vice through a play.

Many divines agreed that the hypocrite and the pious person are the same in appearance and explored the difficulty of discovering what distinguishes them in secret. Bishop Bourdaloue, in his sermon against hypocrisy, probably delivered in 1691, adverted to St. Augustine's notion that hypocrisy could not easily be distinguished from authentic piety. Only God knows what drives the heart, and people lack the capacity to distinguish true from fake piety. In fact, the argument continues, hypocrites could perform a useful social service by displaying pious behavior and therefore encouraging others to imitate their imitations of piety. One of the most effective ways of pretending to be virtuous is to do good deeds. The antitheatrical notion that actors ran the moral risk of becoming like the bad characters they imitated, infected by the bad actions they performed, has a counterpart in the sermons against Molière's *Tartuffe*. Hypocrisy can itself work the opposite way: performing good actions in order to seem virtuous can habituate the performer to good action and gradually lead to true piety. Molière's crime, according to this line of argument, was grossly heightening Tartuffe's criminality. Hypocrisy, for many a first step on the road to piety, is painted in such unattractive colors as to confound those who would wish to approach virtue by imitating the virtuous.

Barish argues that one consequence of such arguments by divines from both sides of the controversy, Jesuits like Bishop Bourdaloue and Jansenists like Pierre Nicole, "was implicitly to exonerate the actor from the charge of hypocrisy."[48] Instead, actors really experienced the passions they played and became infected by them. Like hypocrites being secretly imprinted with virtue by degrees through habituation, actors were imprinted with vice. The scorn that libertines showered upon the pious, Bishop Bourdaloue contended, was an inadvertent homage.[49] Bourdaloue anticipates La Rochefoucauld's famous maxim — "Hypocrisy is the homage vice pays to virtue" — and speaks of a world in which all social interaction is performance and in which virtue receives a grudging kind of respect in the attempts of the vicious at least to appear good. "Sincerity comes from the heart" runs another of La Rochefoucauld's maxims. "One finds it in very few people; what one usually finds is but a deft pretense designed to gain the confidence of others." La Rochefoucauld's world of masks is one in which those capable of sincerity must stand aloof from the herd of hypocrites pretending to virtue, imitating qualities of honesty they do not possess. Barish finds in La Rochefoucauld an opposition between theater and self: "If the self is to come into its own, the theater must be discarded."[50] The theater he refers to is not just the stage, but the theater of the world, and there is an aspect of pathos in La Rochefoucauld's portrayal of the world as a network of masks. If the actor is exempt from the charge of hypocrisy, it is only because everyone is acting.

The debate about *Tartuffe*, too, reveals how problematic separating the world from the stage can become. The reputation of the play changed as the reputation of the court changed in the mid-1680s. Secretly married to Madame de Maintenon, Louis XIV converted and persuaded his courtiers likewise to eschew brilliant costume and to engage in pious activities. "Libertines yesterday, dressed in black today," the courtiers found themselves in a situation in which Tartuffian displays of mortification, far from being ridiculous, became a necessary means to social advancement.[51] It was before this newly reformed court that Bishop Bourdaloue offered his sermon on hypocrisy in 1691, arguing that hypocrites, imitating pious actions for the wrong reasons, might well become truly pious by habit.

"Behold what they [the libertines] claimed as they exposed on the stage and to public ridicule an imaginary hypocrite, or even, if you will, a real hypocrite," Bourdaloue thundered:

> transforming in this character the most holy things into objects of ridicule — the fear of the judgments of God, the horror of sin, practices most worthy of praise in themselves and most Christian. Behold what they achieved, putting into the mouth of this hypocrite Religion's maxims, feebly defended at the same time that they imagine them to be most forcefully attacked; making him reproach the scandals of the age in an extravagant manner; representing him as conscientious to the last delicacy and scruple on the least important

matters, when all the time he ought to have been conscientious as he perpetrated the most grievous crimes; showing him with the visage of a penitent, which only served to cover his infamies; giving him, following their whim, a reputation of most austere piety.[52]

Bourdaloue preaches that Molière and the party of libertines to which he assigns him had no intention of reform: rather, by presenting so exaggerated and grotesque a view of piety, they subjected the truly pious to suspicions of false piety. Hypocrisy here becomes a site of partisan strife: libertines are able to advance their cause and make the most sacred practices ridiculous because they share the universal human inability to read others' secret motives. What the bishop deplores, as he addresses Louis XIV's reformed and pious court, is the misreading of motives that their pious display might inspire. *Tartuffe* encourages uncharitable speculation about motives that can only be judged in some way that is not theatrical and that, indeed, is not social.

Critics find themselves confronted in *Tartuffe* with a play whose own history calls its author's motives into question. Not only did the play invite charges of bad faith from its critics from the very inception, but modern critics, too, find themselves in trouble sorting out the play's structural problems from its textual problems and from the difficulties proposed by its notorious ending. Formalist critics argue for an aesthetic coherence to the play that takes its *rex ex machina* ending as a necessary concession to comic form. New historicist critics discover in the final moments a movement of the subversion and containment paradigm they champion. The seventeenth-century debate about the play reveals that the play struck a nerve, and the uncertainties it inspires in contemporary criticism suggest that there is still something irritating about it. Is Molière flattering the monarch in that final act just to get the play on the stage? Are Molière's claims that his play endorses true piety by exposing false piety convincing?

In the first *Placet* addressed to the king in 1664, Molière insists that there is nothing "équivoque" about his presentation of the hypocrite in *Tartuffe*: "[T]he better to preserve the esteem and respect one owes to true *dévots* . . .," he writes, "I discarded everything that could confuse good with evil and only used in this portrait the special colors and essential traits that permit recognition, from the very first, of a true and frank [*véritable et franc*] hypocrite."[53] In the 1669 preface to the play Molière uses a vocabulary drawn from theatrical convention, declaring the hypocrite to be a recognizable stage type, like any other group of traditional victims of comedy. "The *marquis*, the *précieuses*, the cuckolds, and the doctors have peacefully submitted to being represented [on stage], and they have made an effort to appear to enjoy, along with everyone else, these portrayals of themselves; but the hypocrites have no understanding of mockery: from the first they became enraged, and they found it strange that I might have the courage to stage their grimaces and to wish to denounce a profession in which so many honest people find themselves embroiled."[54] For Molière, hypocrites differ from other kinds of comic butts in refusing to play along: all the other types find themselves forced to laugh with the rest of the audience in the theater at their own follies. Hypocrites just don't get it. If a foolish marquis can pretend to be entertained by the spectacle of a foolish marquis on stage, a hypocrite should have no trouble making this kind of effort, too. But instead they react, Molière avers, like confidence tricksters whose profitable scams are being exposed: the play inhibits their ability to pass among others, to trap the honest in their snares. By portraying hypocrites in the 1669 preface as a political party or interest group, Molière anticipates Bourdaloue's difficulties in the 1691 sermon, in which he must address a court party whose reputation, certainly among the worldly Parisians, was for hypocrisy.

The hypocrites in Molière's preface are not in the last analysis the poor dissemblers he suggests them to be by contrast to the *marquis*, the *précieuses*, the cuckolds, and the doctors. Rather, they feign a pious indignation which covers their malign political purposes. "They did not take care to attack it [my play] for the way in which it hurt them; they are too politic for that, and know too well how to live to expose the depths of their souls." An apparent failure to play along with the joke masks a deeper self-preservative drive. "Following their laudable custom, they covered their interests with the cause of God; and *Tartuffe*, in their mouths, is a play that offends piety."[55] Draped in priestly robes, mouthing piety, the hypocrites are themselves Tartuffes and like him are following an agenda of removal and dispossession.

For Molière goes on to insist that he has fought so hard for his play against this party because of his own noble motives. "I would concern myself very little about what they can say, were it not for the scheme they have of making enemies of those I respect and of precipitating into their party true people of worth [*véritables gens de bien*], whose good faith they deflect aside and who, because of their zeal for the affairs of heaven, are open to receiving the impressions people want to give them."[56] Credulous in their zeal, good people are too easily misled.

While there was indeed a party of religious reformers — the Compagnie de Saint-Sacrement de L'Autel — that opposed *Tartuffe*, the play itself does not propose that Tartuffe is a member of such a secret order.[57] The exposure at the end of the play makes it clear that Tartuffe is an opportunist working alone. Denouncing Orgon to the king, Tartuffe exposes himself as *un fourbe renommé* — a famous confidence trickster — well-known to the king under another name. The pun on *renommé* and *sous un autre nom* (5.7.1923–24) insists on the fluidity of identity invoked here. Tartuffe can attempt to rename and recreate himself, but his identity is fixed in the king's knowledge of his past and his dossier of past actions. While *marquis*, cuckolds, *précieuses*, and doctors appear most often in multiples in Molière's plays, Tartuffe is a solitary predator; he stalks Orgon alone, singling him out in the church. Molière's insistence in the preface that Tartuffe is a type like other comic types is undercut by the king's forceful arrest of him at the end. More boldly, Molière suggests that organizations like the Compagnie de Saint-Sacrement de l'Autel are themselves fronts for confidence tricksters and hotbeds of treason.

The play's oscillation between private and public interests, which comes to a head in its ending, begins in its portrayal of Orgon's household as an analogue, in little, to the kingdom. With its memory of recent civil strife — the notorious black box which Tartuffe brings to the king — the house embodies the kingdom, but in a state of carnivalesque inversion: Mme. Pernelle calls it "la cour du roi Pétaut" (1.1.12).[58] Tartuffe functions best, however, as a private menace, a threat to property; when he takes his crimes public, by denouncing Orgon to the king, he reveals himself to be a notorious fraud. Molière's contention in the preface that hypocrites work in groups and are dangerous as a party does not find support in the play. Tartuffe may be a public menace, but his history of crimes is uniquely his own.

Molière develops the hypocrite as type pointedly in *Dom Juan*, in which the central figure becomes a hypocrite in the fifth and final act as the culmination of his career. Vowing a "a sudden change of life," Dom Juan promises his father that he will henceforth strive toward piety. To that end, he continues, he will seek someone to function as a "guide, under whose direction I might walk straight on the road which I have just entered" (5.2[214–15]).[59] Hypocrisy, for Dom Juan, is explicitly the kind of partisan activity that Molière describes in the preface to *Tartuffe* but denies to that protagonist. "There's no shame in that now," Dom Juan assures Sganarelle once his delighted father has left the scene. "Hypocrisy is a fashionable vice, and all fashionable vices pass as virtues. The character of a man of worth is the best of all characters one could play these days, and the vocation of hypocrites has wonderful advantages." The word he uses, *profession*, carries the suggestion of holy orders; he has enlisted in what is, in a sense, a faction that is both theatrical and religious: those who play the role of the "man of worth." "All other vices of men are exposed to censure," Dom Juan continues, "and everyone has the right to attack them vigorously: but hypocrisy is a privileged vice, which with its hand stifles the mouth of the whole world, and enjoys in repose a sovereign immunity." Hypocrisy is a kind of censorship, and it is immune to prosecution, as the sovereign is in an absolutist society. The society of hypocrites, silencing censure with "grimaces," makes it certain that those who are truly moved by the spirit ("véritablement touchés") will be absorbed into its body and misinterpreted.

Joining this club is merely a matter of donning the right clothes: "How many do you think I know who, by means of this stratagem, have deftly refitted the disorderly conduct of their youth, making a shield for themselves from the cloak of religion, and, in this respected habit, have license to be the worst men in the world?" Molière conflates in Dom Juan's tirade a number of motifs from the preface to *Tartuffe*, but here he is especially explicit in linking the idea of the cabal to the idea of clothing. The secret society that misleads people of goodwill and true zeal is one that hides itself in costume, that plays the character of the "homme de bien." In short, just as Tartuffe at the end of his play is an actor deprived of his royal license to perform and returned to the state of confidence man, the hypocritical cabal is a conclave of performers, duping the well-meaning, and erupting in cries of impiety and blasphemy when exposed. Molière invokes the language of antitheatricalism in both instances. The "profession" followed by Tartuffe and the cabal is a kind of vocation, a kind of cult, a kind of work that sets its practitioners apart from others. The word *profession* carries that weight, and Molière's use of *métier* to characterize the hypocrites' calling in the preface also stresses that they are artisans of a dubious sort. The moral of each play is clear: Tartuffe is ruthlessly exposed and punished; Dom Juan utters his outrageous embrace of hypocrisy as the current fashion only moments before the statue arrives and takes his hand. In each instance Molière sits in judgment upon a rival kind of acting — acting that is not professional, not licensed by the king, not circumscribed by the theater. Where antitheatrical divines blurred the distinction between the kind of acting that happens in theater and the kind of role-playing people do in society, seeing the two as equally evil and theater as the mechanism for the propagation of both, Molière designates hypocrisy as a false profession, a *métier* that is socially destabilizing and worthless, while insisting on the integrity of his own craft. After defending the morality of *Tartuffe* in the preface, Molière indicates that he knows what is at stake: "The play of *Tartuffe* must be approved, or all plays in general must be condemned."[60]

Revising *Tartuffe* in 1717, Colley Cibber translates the idea of a faction of hypocrites literally into the figure of his *Non-Juror*. Written explicitly as an attack upon Jeremy Collier, Cibber's play transforms the title character into the non-juring Doctor Wolf. Like Molière's hypocrites, but unlike the character of Tartuffe himself, Doctor Wolf is an emissary from a secret society. To Sir John Woodvil — the Orgon of the play — Heartly is no fit suitor for his daughter Maria because Dr. Wolf has reported rumors that "he is a time-server, one that basely flatters the government, and has no more religion than you have."[61] While Heartly and his friend Colonel Woodvil, the Damis of the play, attend the "Establish'd church," Sir John, under Dr. Wolf's pernicious influence, questions their sincerity. "I would first have him be sure he is a Christian," he urges the Colonel of Heartly. "A Christian, Sir!" fumes the Colonel. "Ay, that's my question, whether he is yet christen'd? I mean by a pastor, that had a divine, uninterrupted, successive right to mark him as a sheep of the true fold?" (268).

Cibber casts the young lovers as true English patriots, confronted with a comic opposition that is political as well as religious. To Sir John, the younger generation are wastrels congregating at coffeehouses like Button's, surrounded by "fine company indeed, Arians, party-poets, players, and Presbyterians." "That's a very unusual mixture, Sir," replies the Colonel (270). Sir John's demonization of the clientele of the coffeehouse marks him as under Collier's influence, indiscriminately lumping heresies and play-acting together in a contemptuous hodgepodge.

Where Tartuffe, at his first entrance, bids his attendant "hang up

[his] hair shirt," the entrance of the non-juring Dr. Wolf (played by Cibber) is prepared in terms of a more repellent abuse of costume. "This sanctify'd rogue," Colonel Woodvil avers, "is carnally in love" with his stepmother. To this end, Dr. Wolf has forbidden "assemblies" in the Woodvil house: "Nay, at the last masquerade this conscientious spy (unknown to her) was eternally at her elbow in the habit of a cardinal." Worse yet: "She lost one of her slippers 'tother day, (by the way she has a mighty pretty foot) and what do you think was become of it?" the Colonel asks his friend Heartly, who replies, "You puzzle me." "I gad, this lovesick monkey had stole it for a private play thing, and one of the house maids, when she clean'd his study, found it there with one of her old gloves in the middle of it." Upon this sensational revelation, Dr. Wolf enters, bidding his attendant bring down "half a dozen more of those manual devotions that I compos'd for the use of our friends in prison" (278–79).

Tartuffe's famous offstage hairshirt is elaborated into Dr. Wolf's cardinal's habit and his "private play" with the fetishes of Lady Woodvil's slipper and glove. Cibber's pun on "manual devotions" leaves little of Dr. Wolf's offstage conduct to the imagination. At the end of the play, Dr. Wolf is exposed: "Here are affidavits in my hand that prove him under his disguise a lurking emissary of Rome," thunders Colonel Woodvil, "that he is actually a priest in Popish orders, and has several times been seen, as such, to officiate public mass in the church of *Notre Dame*, at *Antwerp*." Tartuffe is exposed as a confidence trickster who affects the pseudo-clerical garb affected by the pious layman — which later became the fashion of Louis XIV's reformed court. Dr. Wolf is exposed as a priest "under his disguise" (353). By exposing Tartuffe and the hypocrites who decried the play as actors in bad faith, unlicensed performers who muddy the distinction between the theatrical and social world, Molière sought to vindicate his own craft. Cibber, using a traditional English vocabulary that conflates theatricalism with popery, degrades his own profession by this association.

In his *Apology* Cibber argues that the institution of theater is a moral calling, "where to excel requires as ample Endowments of Nature as any one Profession (that of holy Institution excepted) whatsoever." "Look into *St. Peter's* at *Rome*," Cibber continues, warming to his theme, "and see what a profitable Farce is made of Religion there! Why then is an Actor more blemish'd than a Cardinal? While the Excellence of the one arises from his innocently seeming what he is not, and the

Eminence of the other from the most impious Fallacies that can be impos'd upon Human Understanding?"[62] As so often happens in the *Apology*, Cibber protests too much, and the resulting confusion suggests that good acting is like bad religion.

Molière, by identifying the faction of hypocrites in his audience with bad acting, avoids falling into Cibber's error. By reenacting in the 1669 version of *Tartuffe* the play's earlier history of suppression and release, Molière wittily disguises whatever the original play might have been. The ambiguities of the "petit collet" — emblem of piety or uniform of a faction of hypocrites — dissolve in the mists of revision and recision.

Kierkegaard's B proposes pastor and actor as the boldest possible contrast, a polarity that founders as he imagines A approaching the task: preaching and acting mingle in the discipline of performance and rehearsal. To a new historicist, this muddling is inevitable, because dressing up and performing are necessary aspects of social life. But the demonizing of pious frauds by Molière and in his cruder way by Cibber and the demonizing of actors by Bishop Bourdaloue suggest a refusal to accept this simple distinction or its equally simple erasure. Chiding certain kinds of behavior as inauthentic presumes some notion of authentic behavior. What might be the markers of that authentic behavior? Not Tartuffe's hairshirt or Dr. Wolf's cardinal costume; not the "petit collet," the affectation of clerical garb by the pious.

Unlike Molière's play, Cibber's play does attempt to wrestle with the other side of the conundrum, to find a reliable indicator of authenticity. When Mariane and Valère in *Tartuffe* dissolve into mutual mistrust in the *dépit amoureux* of act 2, Dorine resolves their difficulty; they provide a comic distraction, and their squabble is seen as merely silly. Cibber inflates the roles of the young lovers, Maria and Heartly, and provides Anne Oldfield, who played Maria, with an opportunity to display her skill as a coquette. Where Valère and Mariane stumble into misapprehensions, Maria manufactures them. Heartly's passion and jealousy overwhelm him as she pretends to take seriously Dr. Wolf's offer of marriage:

MARIA: [Affectedly smiling] Am I not a horrid, vain, silly creature, Mr. Heartly?
HEARTLY: A little bordering on the baby, I must own.

MARIA: Laud! How can you love one so then? But I don't think you love me though — do you?

HEARTLY: Yes, faith I do, and so shamefully, that I am in hopes you doubt it.

MARIA: Poor man! he'd fain bring me to reason.

[Smiling in his face.]

HEARTLY: I would indeed, nor am ashamed to own it — nay, were it but possible to make you serious only when you should be so, you would be the most perfect creature of your sex.

MARIA: Oh, lud! he's civil —

HEARTLY: Come, come, you have good sense, use me but with that, and make me what you please.

MARIA: Laud! I don't desire to make any thing of you, not I.

HEARTLY: Don't look so cool upon me, by Heaven I can't bear it.

MARIA: Well now you are tolerable.

[Gently glancing on him.]

HEARTLY: Come then, be generous, and swear at least you'll never be another's.

MARIA: Ah! laud! now you have spoil'd all again; beside, how can I be sure of that before I have seen this t'other man, my brother spoke to me of?

(274–75)

Heartly's demands that Maria be "serious," show "good sense," and be "generous" are met with light ridicule. Throughout the play she teases him, educating him out of his jealousy and possessiveness.

It is not to Heartly, indeed, but to Charles, the serving-man attendant upon Dr. Wolf, that Maria exposes her true feelings. Charles confesses to Maria that he has been working secretly to defuse Dr. Wolf's plans and alludes to his own "stronger motive to it, than barely duty." Acknowledging her commitment to Heartly, Maria lets him down gently: "and to show my particular good opinion of you, I'll do you a favour, Mr. Charles, I never did any man since I was born — I'll be sincere with you." "Is it then possible you can have lov'd another, to whom you never were sincere?" Charles gasps. "Alas!" chides Maria, "you are but a novice in the passion — sincerity is a dangerous virtue, and often surfeits what it ought to nourish; therefore I take more pains to make the man I love believe I slight him, than (if possible) I would to convince you of my esteem and friendship" (318–19). Left alone, Maria ponders Charles's attractive modesty: "Lord! how one may live, and learn! I could not have believ'd, that modesty, in a young fellow could have been so amiable a virtue; and though, I own, there is I know not what of dear delight in indulging one's vanity with them; yet, upon serious reflection, we must confess, that truth and sincerity have a thousand charms beyond it" (321). At this moment of confronting her own vanity Maria vows to overcome her reluctance to show her "real inclination" toward Heartly.

Cibber's Maria enjoys both a degree of self-consciousness and an independence of means denied to Molière's Mariane: she has a fortune of her own, and her father's threats of disinheritance amount to only a few thousand pounds. The limits to her father's power transform the household from Molière's absolutist environment, in which Orgon's whims can utterly devastate his children, to an environment in which certain checks and balances prevail. While Cibber's transformation of Tartuffe into a non-juror is patriotic in a plainly partisan way, the rational polity of Sir John Woodvil's home speaks of rule by reasonable persuasion. Subverted by the modest and sincere Charles, the deed of gift to Dr. Wolf never poses a real threat. Sir John abases himself at the end: "Let it suffice, I see my errors with a conscious shame; but hope, when I am justly weighed, you'll find those errors rose but from a ductile heart, not disinclin'd to truth, but fatally misled by false appearances." "Whoever knows your private life, must think you, Sir, in this sincere," echoes his son (356).

The emphasis on sincerity and on the "ductile heart" in the play places Cibber's *Non-Juror* in a wholly different moral universe from *Tartuffe*. Cléante's famous commonsense declaration that he knows right from wrong and can easily determine the falsely pious from the truly pious by their conspicuous display does not receive support from the play; he is impotent at the end, just as are Tartuffe's dupes. Only royal intervention can save the day. In Cibber's play, too, the monarch guarantees stability and his royal pardon reunites Charles with his long-lost father; but in the main plot the "filial virtues" of Maria and Colonel Woodvil work to save their father from his own weakness. Just as Maria eventually must reveal her true inclination to Heartly, Sir John's own inclination (or lack of disinclination, as he puts it) toward truth will prevail.

Cibber's play celebrates as particularly English a kind of moderation and good sense as well as certain specific guarantees of legal rights to children represented in Maria's private fortune. Cibber also insists, in the dedication of the play to the king, upon the good intentions of actors. "Your comedians, Sir, are an unhappy society, whom some severe heads think wholly useless, and others dangerous to the young and innocent. This comedy is therefore an attempt to remove that prejudice, and to shew, what honest and laudable uses may be made of the *Theatre*, when its performances keep close to the true purposes of the institution." Among these purposes, Cibber continues, theater can "divert the sullen and disaffected from busying their brains to disturb the happiness of a government, which (for want of proper amusements) they often enter into wild and seditious schemes to reform." Here is a curious reversal of the antitheatrical claim that theater encourages seditious gatherings and presents images of subversion to an unruly public. The unruly public envisioned by Cibber gathers at coffeehouses (as Sir John accuses his son of doing) and foments discontent. Going to plays would distract the disaffected from such evil enticements and cement them in ridiculing the "follies" of opposition. "Our labours have at least this glory to boast," Cibber maintains, "that since plays were first exhibited in *England*, they were never totally suppress'd but by those very people, that turn'd our *Church* and *Constitution*, into *Irreligion* and *Anarchy*" ([263]).

Invoking the dark days of the Civil War, Cibber echoes Molière, in a curious way. *Tartuffe* takes place against the backdrop of the successful suppression of the Fronde, and Molière identifies civil unrest with unlicensed theatricality, a carnivalesque upsetting of roles. Cibber, by reminding his king of the Interregnum, verges on the tactless; after all, "those very people" not only closed the theaters but executed the king. Theater, Cibber suggests, is an important part of the English Constitution, its restoration equivalent to that of the monarchy in 1660. The king's authority and the feebleness of the opposition, Cibber concludes, are revealed nowhere more effectively than in the playhouse: "there being no assembly where people are so free, and apt to speak their minds, as in a crowded *Theatre*; of which your Majesty may have lately seen an instance, in the insuppressible acclamations that were given on your appearing to honour this play with your royal presence" ([264]). The king's authority is legitimized by applause; and Cibber seems (no doubt inadvertently) to be hinting that malcontents and non-jurors in the audience would not have been shy about showing their displeasure and showering the king with catcalls.

Cibber's play figures a model of a moderate monarchy, in which theater and king validate each other's existence. This image of mutuality stands in stark contrast to Molière's vision of a theater dependent upon the monarch for protection against its enemies. Only the king can see through Tartuffe, and only the king has the dossier that reveals Tartuffe's history as a criminal. In Cibber's play the young men of good sense — Colonel Woodvil, Heartly, and Charles — can all work together to expose Dr. Wolf and, in the process, to reunite the Woodvil family and to reunite Charles with his father. The king pardons Charles for his seditious actions while in Dr. Wolf's employment, but he does so at his father's importunity. There is no special royal dossier. Insisting upon sincerity and honest intentions, forgiving the ductility of Sir John's heart, the play identifies Englishness with a theater in which the very actors, spurred by their loyalty and devotion, call upon the king to witness the depth of their patriotic feelings.

The Non-Juror enjoyed revivals coincident with Jacobite activity through the early eighteenth century. Deeming its satire too topical, Isaac Bickerstaff revisited the play and adapted it as *The Hypocrite* in 1792. "The TARTUFFE is usually esteemed the *chef d'oeuvre* of MOLIERE," Bickerstaff's prefatory remarks declare: "It is in truth a masterly display of the sullen hypocrisy of the Churchman; and the traces of the character have only been effaced in France by the Revolution. COLLEY CIBBER applied it to the Nonjuror, a being now utterly forgotten — Among the audiences of the present day the Cantwell of this piece will be variously attributed through the whole circle of fanatics, as one sect or another may have become obnoxious to the spectator."[63] Bickerstaff's adaptation closely follows Cibber, but without Cibber's edge. As Bickerstaff suggests, instead of particular or pointed satire against a specific sect the new play offers generalized cynicism against any sect the spectator may find "obnoxious." The reference to the extirpation of Tartuffian hypocrisy in France by the Revolution picks up the echoes of the Fronde in *Tartuffe* and of the Civil War in *The Non-Juror*.

But in the play itself the peril is minimized. Dr. Cantwell, the Tartuffe of the play, is exposed but merely in his machinations against the family (now named the Lamberts). The coquette, Charlotte, is as self-conscious in her torture of her intended as Cibber's Maria, but she takes an even more active role in the unmasking of the impostor. And it is to her that the play gives its final words. Sir John Lambert, freed from his bondage to Dr. Cantwell, vows: "from henceforward I renounce all pious folks; I will have an utter abhorrence for every thing that bears the appearance — " Charlotte must interrupt him:

> What! because a worthless wretch has imposed upon you, under the fallacious shew of austere grimace, will you needs have it every body is like him? confound the good with the bad, and conclude there are no truly religious in the world? — Leave, my dear Sir, such rash consequences to fools and libertines. — Let us be careful to distinguish between virtue and the appearance of it. Guard, if possible, against doing honour to hypocrisy. — But at the same time, let us allow there is no character in life greater or more valuable than that of the truly devout — nor any thing more noble, or more beautiful, than the fervour of a sincere piety. (99)

Charlotte's speech reiterates the complacency of Cléante's assertion: "My only knowledge and my only art / Is this: to tell the true and false apart" (*Tartuffe*, 1.5.353–54).[64] What is put to the test in Molière's play is here enunciated as the concluding moral of the piece. Cibber's *Non-Juror* evoked considerable controversy: as one biographer notes, "Attacks came from every quarter hostile to Cibber or the government."[65] Bickerstaff, in contrast, points out that no one has taken offense at his play. "Happy is the writer to say," he notes in the preface, "that he does not imagine any one can be found, who will liken this odious being to any MEMBER of our liberal and enlightened National Church." While *Tartuffe* struck at the heart of seventeenth-century debates about theater and religion and *The Non-Juror* provoked hostile rejoinders to its partisanship, *The Hypocrite* neutralizes Dr. Cantwell by permitting audiences to identify him with any sect they find obnoxious.

Bickerstaff further neutralizes Dr. Cantwell's threat by furnishing him with a ridiculous dupe, Maw-Worm. Responding to a call from the Doctor, Maw-Worm preaches at street corners, suffering ridicule for his pains. While he is out, the Doctor visits his wife. *Bell's British Theatre* illustrates the play with an engraving of "Mr. Fawcet Junr., as Maw-Worm," accompanied by a line which must have been one of the comic sensations of the original performance: "And between you and me, Doctor, I believe Susy's breeding again" (44). The amorous drives of Tartuffe and Dr. Wolf are confined to the stepmother of the house;

Dr. Cantwell is apparently well provided with alternatives. Seeing a vision of a devil "with a great big pitchfork" (96), sponsoring the revelations of the denouement, Maw-Worm and Old Lady Lambert (the Madame Pernelle of the play) deflect any sense of menace into low comedy.

In *The Hypocrite*, then, good sense and sincerity prevail; Dr. Cantwell, far from being a virtuoso threat like Tartuffe or a dangerous subversive like Dr. Wolf, is a simple comic butt, relegated, like Maw-Worm and Old Lady Lambert, to ridicule. The play, in other words, responds to Collier's critique and to concerns about the appearance of clergy on stage by making sure that Dr. Cantwell is seen as an utterly illegitimate figure, representative of all sectarians in general rather than of any particular sect. That there is a concomitant loss of comic potential in the figure along with the loss of menace is suggested in Bickerstaff's invention of Maw-Worm as a victim who does not make any call upon the audience's sympathy.

Cibber's and Bickerstaff's English *Tartuffe*s point to the powerful influence of Collier's *Short View* on eighteenth-century English drama. Cibber satirizes Collier directly in the person of Dr. Wolf; Bickerstaff appeases anxiety about the appearance of a clergyman on stage by ridiculing Dr. Cantwell's nonconformism. In another instance, Cibber reports that a revival of John Vanbrugh's *The Provoked Wife* in 1725 necessitated some revisions. The actors, "in keeping the Stage clear of those loose Liberties it had formerly been charg'd with," had neglected the play "for some Years." For the revival, "Sir John Vanbrugh, who was conscious of what it had too much of, was prevail'd upon to substitute a newly written Scene in the Place of one in the fourth Act, where the Wantonness of his Wit and Humour had (originally) made a Rake talk like a Rake in the borrow'd Habit of a Clergyman: To avoid which Offence, he clapt the same Debauchee into the Undress of a Woman of Quality." Cibber goes on to assess the relative offensiveness of this imposture: "Now the Character and Profession of a Fine Lady not being so indelibly sacred as that of a Churchman, whatever Follies he expos'd in the Petticoat kept him at least clear of his former Prophaneness, and were now innocently ridiculous to the Spectators."[66]

Cibber's notion that the transvestite comedy of the scenes is more "innocently ridiculous" than the satire against the clergy points to a different sense of transgression from that which motivates contemporary criticism of cross-dressing in plays. Where Lord Rake proclaims that

Sir John in clergyman's garb is "like a bishop going to the Holy War," the comparisons in the revised scene allude to the long tradition of Amazons and warrior-women on the English stage: "He looks like a queen of the Amazons," says Lord Rake; later on Sir John identifies himself as "Bonduca, Queen of the Welchmen" as he hurls himself against the watch (*The Provoked Wife*, appendix B, 127–28).

In suggesting that the scene is generalized satire against "Women of Quality" instead of clergymen, Cibber fails to notice the appropriateness of Sir John's metamorphosis in the context of the play. (The same may be said of the play's twentieth-century editor, Curt Zimansky, who proclaims the new scenes "patently absurd" [124].) It is far from irrelevant that the package of clothes Sir John hijacks from the tailor in the revised scene is destined for Lady Brute herself, the much provoked wife of the title. "The robe of my wife," Sir John effuses, "with reverence let me approach it. The dear angel is always taking care of me in danger and has sent me this suit of armor to protect me in this day of battle. On they go!" (127). Assaulting the watch and insulting the Justice in the two scenes, Sir John offers a portrayal of a lady of quality that appalls the officials: "Indeed, lady, I'm sorry he has such a wife," says the Justice as Sir John identifies himself as Lady Brute. Sandwiched between the two scenes of transvestite transgression are scenes in which Heartwell and Constant arrange and then carry out an assignation with Bellinda and Lady Brute, and the first scene of Sir John's trouble with the watch (4.1) follows a long discussion between Bellinda and Lady Brute in which Lady Brute confesses her attraction to Constant and warns that "the garrison begins to grow mutinous." "The sooner you capitulate, the better," Bellinda urges (3.3.115–16). "Why, you saw her husband beat her," Heartwell reminds Constant right after the scene in which we see Sir John, in his wife's clothes, beat the watchmen (4.2.26). The reversal played out here, as Sir John assaults decorum and disparages the role of a "Lady of Quality," powerfully reinforces the terrible bind in which Lady Brute finds herself. Her plight — married to a violent drunkard, unable to seek a divorce, besieged by the importunate Constant — resonates in Sir John's Amazonian attack upon the officers of the court. The violence that Sir John unleashes in his wife's garb points out her own entrapment in the marriage and emphasizes the ineluctability of her bondage. Lady Brute cannot take up Amazonian arms and defy her condition; instead, she proposes herself as a martyr to the marriage when Sir John finally returns home after his long night out. "For heaven's my witness," she says of his wounds, "I had rather see my own blood trickle down than yours." "Then will I be crucified," snarls Sir John. "'Tis a hard fate, I should not be believed," she replies. "'Tis a damned atheistical age, wife," he growls (5.2.30–34). In short order, Sir John will *burst open the door* (69 [stage direction]) of Lady Brute's closet and find Constant and Heartfree huddling within.

Sir John's critique of the "atheistical age" would ring as broad, general satire if his earlier garb was that of a clergyman; but when it comes after his assuming in Lady Brute's dress a freedom to transgress which she denies herself, it points to a wide gulf between marriage as a sacrament and marriage as practiced in the Brute household. Sir John's claim in his own person to be a martyr to the marriage reinforces an audience's sense of Lady Brute's powerlessness and entrapment. Cibber's disclaimer to the contrary, the replacement of clerical garb by Lady Brute's dress heightens the play's conflicts and sharpens its characters' bitter reflections upon marriage.

Michael Cordner has found an exchange of letters in the *Athenian Mercury* which suggests that Sir John Brute's imposture of a clergyman had its imitators in real life. *"There is a Young Man of my acquaintance,"* the correspondent writes, *"who resolves to put on* a Clergyman's Habit, and *commit all manner of* Extravagances *therein* as Picking up Women, Drinking, Quarrelling, &c. On purpose to render the Clergy Odious. He has made me acquainted with it, and I have represented the immorality of such an Action, and used all my endeavour to divert him from it, tho' without success, he being still resolv'd to go on; — the Consequences whereof are so ill, that I desire your advice what further Method I may take to prevent it?"* [67] Here the transgressions which were contained by the institution of the theater in Vanbrugh's play — and in the series of plays running from *Tartuffe* to *The Hypocrite* — threaten to unleash themselves upon society. The young man's plan is theatrical — he intends a performance in real life that will *"render the Clergy Odious."* He arrogates to himself an actor's freedom that the institution of theater reserves for actors on the stage. Molière's *Tartuffe* offers a stage version of the destabilizing and blasphemous possibilities inherent in unrestrained and unlicensed acting in the social sphere, and the Young Man's acquaintance, fearing for the "Consequences" to his soul, is troubled by the difficulty of sorting out performed from actual blasphemy in his friend's theatricalized plan. To what extent is performing improvisationally the role of a

blasphemous clergyman itself a blasphemous act? Does the player of
Tartuffe or Doctor Wolf or Sir John Brute run a personal risk of damnation? Molière's and Cibber's insistence upon their own piety and integrity forces to the front the gulf between actor and role enforced by
the institutional discipline of the theater. Professionals know how to
avoid the taint. What is troubling about the Young Man, then, is that
he intends to perform a degrading vision of a clergyman in the social
arena: unlicensed, unsupervised, and amateur. In the process, he sets
his own soul at risk.

HUMANIZING THE FOP

"Seest thou not what a deformed thief this fashion is?" Borachio marvels at the ease by which Claudio can mistake Margaret for Hero in *Much Ado about Nothing*; "I know that Deformed," mutters Seacoal of the watch (3.3.123). Like the watchmen who arrest Sir John Brute in either of his disguises, as priest or as lady of fashion, these watchmen are confronted by a performance that they do not understand. Borachio is commenting homiletically upon the way dressing up and showing up at the wrong window can be misread by the spectators. *Fashion* stands in as shorthand for all kinds of imposture: getting it wrong, of course, the watch gets it right.

Borachio's sententious identification of fashion with monstrous deformity reaches a kind of apogee in the career of the Restoration comedy fop. From the deformities of fashion come even greater deformities. Fops are often presented in these plays as monsters. The Elder Worthy brother in Colley Cibber's *Love's Last Shift, or, The Fool in Fashion* rages that Hillaria humiliates him "by fastning on a Fool, and caressing him before my Face, when she might have so easily avoided him."[68] When his younger brother asks, "But, prithee, who was the Fool she fasten'd upon?" the Elder Worthy obliges with a full character of Sir Novelty Fashion:

One that Heaven intended for a Man; but the whole Business of his Life is, to make the World believe he is of another Species. A Thing that affects mightily to ridicule himself, only to give others a kind of Necessity of praising him. I can't say he's a slave to any new Fashion, for he pretends to be Master of it, and is ever reviving some old, or advancing some new piece of Foppery; and tho' it don't take, is still as well pleased. because it then obliges the Town to take more Notice of him: He's so fond of a public Reputation, that he is more extravagant in his Attempts to gain it, than the Fool that fir'd Diana's Temple to immortalize his Name. (1.1.249–56)

Sir Novelty, a compendium of foppish traits assembled by Cibber as a means to augment his own "public Reputation," is a highly derivative fop. Worthy's satirical diatribe, however, insists that his conventional comic vanities and affectations must be taken seriously.

It is not enough for him to scorn Sir Novelty: what he does in this speech is to utterly dehumanize him. Sir Novelty is of indeterminate species; framed to be a man, he is instead a "Thing." Not only is he uncertain of species, he also is a radical mishmash of social strata: Elder Worthy cannot tell whether Sir Novelty is a slave to fashion or its master. His ignominious attempts to gain public attention deserve as little notice as the sacrilege of Herostratus, whose effort was rewarded by the passing of a law in Ephesus forbidding the mention of his name. This last detail links the fop's indeterminacy with violent impiety. The fact that the temple involved is Diana's adds to the crime an aspect of rape.

Sir Novelty is also characterized in theatrical terms. "Oh! Mr. Worthy," teases Hillaria (whose condescension to the fop has occasioned Worthy's jealous outburst), "we are admiring Sir Novelty, and his new Suit: Did you ever see so sweet a Fancy? He is as full of Variety as a good Play." Here Sir Novelty's outrageous dress is conflated with the extravagances of dramatic construction. He creates problems of genre as well: "He's a very pleasant Comedy indeed, Madam, and drest with a great deal of good Satyr, and no doubt may oblige both the Stage and the Town, especially the Ladies," Elder Worthy replies (2.1.104–11). Worthy's point is that Sir Novelty is ridiculous, a walking comic stage hit; but the pun on *satyr* pushes again in the direction of the fop's freakishness.

Sir Fopling Flutter, in George Etherege's *The Man of Mode*, establishes the convention of introducing the fop with a satirical portrait before he appears. He, too, is introduced into the conversation at Dorimant's morning toilet in language that places him at the theater and links him with clothes. "No man has a better fancy in his clothes than you have," Young Bellair assures Dorimant. Medley points out: "There is a great critic, I hear, in these matters lately arrived piping hot from

Paris." Sir Fopling was sighted "yesterday at the play, with a pair of gloves up to his elbows, and a periwig more exactly curled than a lady's head newly dressed for a ball."[69] Sir Fopling Flutter's affectations are newly acquired in France: "He went to France a plain, bashful English blockhead," Dorimant tells Harriet, "and is returned a fine undertaking French fop" (4.1.345). Sir Fopling's French adventures are literary rather than theatrical, though he shows a wholly theatrical frame of reference in his failure to catch Harriet's joke in this exchange:

> SIR FOPLING: I was well received in a dozen families where all the women of quality used to visit; and I have intrigues to tell thee more pleasant than even thou read'st in a novel.
> HARRIET: Write 'em, sir, and oblige us women. Our language wants such little stories.
> SIR FOPLING: Writing, madam, 's a mechanic part of wit. A gentleman should never go beyond a song or a billet.
> HARRIET: Bussy was a gentleman.
> SIR FOPLING: Who, d'Ambois?

"Not d'Ambois, sir, but Rabutin — he who wrote the loves of France," Harriet is forced to explain (4.1.269–81). Sir Fopling exposes both an ignorance of the tattle of fashionable France and an excessive familiarity with the dated repertoire of the pre-Restoration theater.

The clothes of the fop can sometimes take on a life of their own. Colley Cibber tells a story of an encounter between the periwig he wore in the role of Sir Novelty and Henry Brett. Brett, the patentee, came backstage not (as one might ordinarily expect) in pursuit of "the Charms of our Theatrical Nymphs" but rather because of "a more sincere passion he had conceived for a fair full-bottom'd Perriwig which I then wore in my first Play of the Fool in Fashion in the year 1695," Cibber reported. In Cibber's anecdote, the fop's periwig undergoes a seduction of sorts:

> In a Word, he made his Attack upon this Perriwig, as your young Fellows generally do upon a Lady of Pleasure, first by a few familiar Praises of her Person, and then a civil Enquiry into the Price of it. But upon his observing me a little surprized at the Levity of his Question about a Fop's Perriwig, he began to railly himself with so much Wit and Humour upon the Folly of his Fondness for it, that he struck me with an equal Desire of granting any thing in my Power to oblige so facetious a Customer. This singular Beginning of our

Conversation, and the mutual Laughs that ensued upon it, ended in an Agreement to finish our Bargain that Night over a Bottle.[70]

Young Brett's embarrassment at Cibber's surprise so charms Cibber that the two become friends. But the item of costume becomes a kind of indeterminate creature. Cibber's friendship, cemented by mutual laughs and sealed over a bottle, is won in the narrative. But the encounter covers much theatrical ground. From seeking the periwig rather than an actress, Brett moves to inquiring its price, like a whore's; Cibber takes the periwig's place or perhaps, as he seeks to please the facetious customer, becomes its pimp. As the relationship progresses through the evening, Cibber's periwig has metonymically metamorphosed from fop's wig to whore to actor as shifting object of young Brett's desire.

Confining her attention to "the main-line vestimentary fop, the one obsessed with clothes, accessories, or at least with the appearance he makes in the mirror," Susan Staves, in a beguiling article, offers "A Few Kind Words for the Fop." Noting the fop's susceptibility to sliding into gender indeterminacy, Staves reminds us that fops are "asexuals, who like to spend their time with the ladies. As connoisseurs of fashion, they have interests in common with women." It is this expertise, along with the "lack of strong sexual appetite," that allows the fop, "in the increasingly polite mind of the eighteenth century," to be identified as "female or effeminate." Far from being homosexual, Laurence Senelick argues, elaborating on Staves's article, the fop is "most definitely focused on women as sexual object as well as decorative possession. His interest in them is so strong that it is projected onto women's appurtenances, such as fine lace and the mysteries of toilette."[71]

To Staves, the fop's fixation with clothes is less a matter of fetishism than an extension into the later seventeenth century of attitudes about clothing expressed in the sumptuary laws. During the seventeenth century, she argues, we witness the breakdown of an equation of clothing with social status and with individual worth: by the nineteenth century, "Renaissance ideals of magnificence and dressing well have finally expired. The less vital the connection between dress and human worth, the less seriously the culture may be expected to take foppery, which will increasingly seem less a blasphemy and more a whimsical if stupid eccentricity" ("A Few Kind Words," 427). Thus foppery flourishes at the particular historical moment of Restoration comedy of manners and dissipates into farce by the end of the eighteenth century. At the same time, Staves notes, many of the characteristic features of the fop are absorbed into the mainstream idea of the man of feeling. Nonviolent, not obsessed with personal honor, not sexually rapacious, this benevolent being represents a softening of the paradigm of the Renaissance gentleman. "The so-called effeminacy of these old fops was an early if imperfect attempt at the refinement, civility, and sensitivity most of us would now say are desirable masculine virtues," she concludes (428).

Staves's insistence that we take the fop seriously as a new kind of man is perhaps tongue in cheek. While harmless to the ladies and fascinated by fine needlework, Sir Fopling Flutter is no role model, no matter how much we may be appalled by Dorimant's libertine ways. But the scorn which Cibber allows the other characters in *Love's Last Shift* to shower upon his creation Sir Novelty Fashion is directed not only at his lack of predatory manliness but also at his theatricality. Sir Novelty's likeness to an actor makes him despicable. In Cibber's anecdote about the periwig, the shifts by means of which Brett's inquiries about the price of the whorish wig develop into a successful negotiation over a bottle suggest an equation between the actor and his famous piece of costume.

A fop's relation to his costume is often metatheatrical, as his costumes take on lives of their own. Tailors appear in Restoration comedies to assemble the fop before the audience's eyes in conventional scenes of dressing. Most fops' levées derive from the scene in Molière's *Le bourgeois gentilhomme* in which Monsieur Jourdain receives his new suit. The shoes hurt, M. Jourdain complains. "Not at all, sir," replies the Tailor. "What do you mean, not at all?" cries the poor gentleman. "You're imagining it," the Tailor assures him.[72] Thus comforted, M. Jourdain is dressed in his new outfit to music: "Such outfits require ceremony," the Tailor declares. These scenes of outfitting the fop bring onto the stage the rituals of costuming that normally reside backstage. "The act of dressing in a Restoration comedy might be considered to be not unlike that of preparing for dramatic performance itself," J. L. Styan observes of the scene in which Lord Foppington is dressed in Sir John Vanbrugh's sequel to *Love's Last Shift*, *The Relapse*.[73] Like M. Jourdain, Lord Foppington disregards the evidence of his senses in favor of the Shoemaker's expertise. "Your lordship may please to feel what you think fit, but that shoe does not hurt you," asserts the Shoemaker; "I think I understand my trade." "Now by all that's great and powerful, thou art an incomprehensible coxcomb; but thou makest good shoes, and so I'll bear with thee," declares the long-suffering fop.[74]

But Foppington's levée has a dimension more complex than simply garbing himself for a day of idle self-display before the town. He is watched throughout the process by his younger brother, Tom Fashion, who has come to call in hopes of borrowing a thousand pounds. As the famous periwig is brought in (Vanbrugh's Foppington is Cibber's Sir Novelty Fashion after he has purchased a title), young Fashion simmers angrily at his brother's indifference. "A very friendly reception from a brother after three years absence," he chafes in an aside to Lory, his servant. "Why, sir, it's your own fault," rejoins Lory. "We seldom care for those that don't love what we love. If you would creep into his heart, you must enter into his pleasures. Here have you stood ever since you came in and have not commended any one thing that belongs to him" (1.3.111–16). Tom's anger at his brother and Lory's prudent advice place Foppington within a context of human relationships that is rare in foppery and that requires a judgment of both Tom and Foppington as moral agents.

Brothers and relations to fops usually function to remind both the fop and his onstage and offstage audiences of his origins as a plain, bashful English blockhead. Brothers and relations are embarrassments that highlight the artificiality of the fop's newly constructed self. Vanbrugh provides Cibber's Sir Novelty with a younger brother as well as with a title: through Tom Fashion, Vanbrugh places Lord Foppington on trial as a human being. Snubbed by his brother, Tom learns from Coupler that he can take revenge by presenting himself as Lord Foppington and marrying Miss Hoyden before his lordship has a chance to make the journey from town to country. But Tom professes "a qualm of conscience" before embarking on this plan; "I have scruples," he tells Lory. "My conscience shan't starve me neither," he continues:

> But thus far will I hearken to it before I execute this project. I'll try my brother to the bottom: I'll speak to him with the temper of a philosopher; my reasons, though they press him home, shall yet be clothed with so much modesty, not one of all the truths they urge shall be so naked to offend his sight. If he has so much humanity

about him as to assist me, though with a moderate aid, I'll drop my project at his feet and show him I can do for him much more than what I ask he'd do for me. This one conclusive trial of him I resolve to make.

> Succeed or no, still victory's my lot;
> If I subdue his heart, 'tis well, if not,
> I shall subdue my conscience to my plot.
>   (1.3.290, 295, 298–311)

Tom Fashion's test of his brother's "humanity" is unique in the history of fops, and it differs significantly from the automatic scorn showered upon the type by gentlemen like Dorimant or the Elder Worthy.

"In Foppington," Lincoln Faller argues, "there is something attractive, even sympathetic, and this derives not only from his capacity for genuine wit, his real sense of humor, his almost imperturbable cool."[75] While Faller is certainly right that Vanbrugh has given Foppington a deeper and more complex character than Sir Novelty is allowed in Cibber's play, he is certainly wrong in the matter of Foppington's attractiveness. When put to the test by Tom Fashion, Foppington is brutally dismissive and assumes the worst of Tom's motives. Foppington is convinced that Tom has called in hopes that the blow he recently suffered after flirting too vigorously with Amanda has proved fatal. Foppington is edgy, nasty: for Helene Koon, Foppington marks a radical departure from the innocuous Sir Novelty Fashion: "He has all of Sir Novelty's flaws without the central redeeming virtue; vanity becomes pride, pretense is hypocrisy, and greed outweighs morality."[76]

On his way to a new play, Foppington urges Tom to make his point quickly. The interchange shows a highly unsympathetic Foppington, who jokes that Tom might as well "take a purse" in his desperate situation: "for if you succeed you are relieved that way; if you are taken — you are relieved t'other" (3.1.78–80). "I do not ask it as a due, brother," Tom ventures. "I am willing to receive it as a favor." "Thau art willing to receive it anyhaw, strike me speechless," Foppington rejoins (the unorthodox orthography reflects his affected nasal tones):

> But these are damned times to give money in: taxes are so great, repairs so exorbitant, tenants such rogues, and periwigs so dear, that the devil take me, I am reduced to that extremity in my cash, I have been forced to retrench in that one article of sweet pawder till I have

braught it dawn to five guineas a manth. Naw judge, Tam, whether
I can spare you five hunder paunds? (3.1.86–95)

Foppington's "imperturbable cool" (in Faller's words) drives Tom to
distraction: "Will nothing provoke thee? Draw, coward!" he cries in
frustration as Foppington shrugs off his insults (119).

Foppington's self-absorption, far from being sympathetic, makes
him instead a self-willed victim of Tom Fashion's stunt. "His lordship
has given me a pill has purged off all my scruples," Tom declares, urging Lory to saddle the horses for their country adventure (133–34).
Curt Zimansky finds that "Tom Fashion is hardly an object of pity and
his poverty is pretty clearly the result of his living beyond a modest
though possible income" and that for Vanbrugh, in staging an interview with Lord Foppington, "the opportunity for a comic scene was
probably as important as any moral consideration."[77] Tom Fashion's
claim upon his brother may indeed be irresponsible. But the fact that
Tom is a wastrel does not make Foppington's callous dismissal of his
claims any less odious.

Nonetheless, twentieth-century scholars of the play, including its
editor, find themselves worrying about the relative moral merits of
Tom Fashion's appeal and Lord Foppington's rejection of that appeal.
In deriving Lord Foppington from Cibber's earlier, more thoroughly
conventional Sir Novelty, Vanbrugh has changed the comic and moral
stakes of his enterprise. Zimansky, dismissing Tom as an "object of
pity," finds himself in powerful company. In *A Short View* Jeremy Collier vents his spleen against the moral of the play and focuses his wrath
upon the figure of Tom Fashion, the wastrel:

> His Moral holds forth this notable Instruction.
> 1st. That all Younger Brothers should be careful to run out their Cir-
> cumstances as Fast, and as Ill as they can. And when they have put
> their Affairs in this posture of Advantage, they may conclude them-
> selves on the high Road to Wealth, and Success. For as Fashion Blas-
> phemously applies it, Providence takes care of Men of Merit.[78]

Collier's critique of the play runs parallel to Faller's as well, for Collier
also finds Foppington's conduct more prudent than might be expected.
"'Tis true he was Formal and Fantastick, Smitten with Dress, and
Equipage, and it may be vapour'd by his Perfumes; but his Behaviour
is far from that of an Ideot," Collier expostulates (261). Troubled by

this plain violation of comic convention (fops should be "Ideots"), Collier is forced to conclude that Vanbrugh has become enamored of his fop: "Vanity and Formalizing is Lord Foplingtons [*sic*] part. To let him speak without Aukwardness, and Affectation, is to put him out of his Element. There must be some Gumm and stiffening in his Discourse to make it natural. However, the Relapser has taken a fancy to his Person, and given him some of the most Gentile raillery in the whole Play." Foppington, Collier insists, "flies out into Sense, and smooth expression" in the first scene with Tom Fashion; and in the second interview — in which he proposes that Tom take purses — "He relapses into the same Intemperance of good Sense" (271).

There is something strange about a fop who can provoke this kind of discussion. Collier is eager, of course, to demonstrate that Vanbrugh is incompetent, but the measure of his incompetence is that he has created a fop who is not utterly ridiculous. "Later on, as we see Foppington trussed up and tossed about by the clumsy country boobs, we cannot help laughing," Faller declares; "and yet, for we have come to feel almost fond of him, our laughter may be tinged with some slight distress." What to Collier is evidence of Vanbrugh's lameness as a dramatist is to Faller an indication that he has created a character "more complex and less easily digested than his antecedents in late seventeenth-century comedy," an amiable fop.[79] While Tom Fashion's test fails to reveal any benevolence in the heart of the fop himself, we are nonetheless encouraged to think of his brother's "humanity." Lory urges Tom to "creep into his heart" by pointing out that "[w]e seldom care for those that don't love what we love" (1.3.113–14). Lory's use of *we* suggests a humanity common to fop, servant, rake, and members of the audience. "We" are all encouraged to speculate on Tom's approach to his brother and to wonder whether Tom's spendthrift ways are responsible or not.

Collier's tract, Vanbrugh's play, and the Cibber play to which Vanbrugh was responding are all closely linked: they all seem to have something important to do with the emergence of "sentimental comedy" in the closing years of the seventeenth century. *Love's Last Shift* conferred upon Cibber the informal title of "father of sentimental comedy."[80] Cibber's celebration of Amanda's virtue is usually seen as a gesture in the new direction of sentimentalism, and Vanbrugh's *Relapse* as a curative rebuttal. "The strange popular reputation of these two plays suggests that they epitomize a clash — the first great 'sentimental' comedy debunked by one of the last true 'Restoration' comedies,"

Robert D. Hume declares. Vanbrugh's coarse cynicism in this narrative flicks aside the easy moralism of Cibber's play, through Loveless's almost immediate backsliding after his reunion with Amanda.[81]

Vanbrugh's *A Short Vindication of "The Relapse" and "The Provok'd Wife," from Immorality and Prophaneness*, however, seems to adopt Collier's strictures. Collier bluntly began his famous tract with some definitions: "The business of Plays is to recommend Virtue, and discountenance Vice; To shew the Uncertainty of Humane Greatness, the suddain Turns of Fate, and the Unhappy Conclusions of Violence and Injustice; 'Tis to expose the Singularities of Pride and Fancy, to make Falsehood contemptible, and to bring every Thing that is Ill Under Infamy, and Neglect." With leaden irony, Collier snarls: "The Design has been oddly pursued by the English Stage" (8). "I may be blind in what relates to myself," Vanbrugh puts forward in rebuttal, " 'tis more than possible, for most People are so: But if I judge right, what I have done is in general a Discouragement to Vice and Folly; I am sure I intended it, and I hope I have performed it." Vanbrugh argues that the story of Loveless is "a natural Instance of the Frailty of Mankind, even in his most fixt Determinations": "If indeed *The Relapse* is a play concerned with the frailty of man, whose hold upon happiness and virtue is tenuous to the extreme," Faller argues in commenting on this passage, "then it would appear that Vanbrugh had conceived the play in a spirit more akin to that of tragedy than of comedy." Vanbrugh and Cibber seem to be staking out a territory of generic insecurity, creating a new form that is comic but in the last analysis serious, an enterprise that will become widespread throughout the eighteenth century. Denis Diderot's *comédie larmoyante* and Richard Steele's "joy too exquisite for laughter" are lurking just beyond *Love's Last Shift* and *The Relapse*.[82]

In this narrative a comic monster like the fop becomes something of a problem. Because if Vanbrugh and Cibber are anticipating the generous tears shed by benevolent audiences of eighteenth-century sentimental dramas, Lord Foppington needs must become the attractive, amiable fool described by Collier. Furthermore, Collier's complaint that Foppington, because he is not an "Ideot," would never get into the situation of negotiating for a bride through a notorious confidence man like Coupler does indeed threaten to make a hash of Vanbrugh's plot. "The contrivance [of the double plot] is just as wise as it would be to cut a Diamond in two," Collier comments on the lack of proper subordination of main to subplot. "There is a loss of lustre in the Division. Increasing the Number, abates the Value, and by making it more, you make it less" (*A Short View*, 281). Collier's rabid antitheatricalism should not blind us to the fact that, to a high degree, he has taught subsequent critics how to read the play, how to interpret its relationship to Cibber's original, and how to discuss the problems it raises.

The play's broken-backed nature is proverbial, and many efforts have been made to discover in *The Relapse* a unity between its sentimental (almost tragic, to Faller) relapse plot and the comedy of the Tom Fashion plot. Some vote on the side of pure cynicism: "In *The Relapse*," James S. Malek argues, "virtue, though not condemned, is simply not taken seriously."[83] Collier would probably agree, though not in as value-neutral a way. For Frank McCormick, the play offers in Amanda and Tom Fashion "alternative 'right' ways of behaving, each successful in its own terms, each incompatible with the other." Amanda, "strangely compelling in her monumental intransigence, . . . is nevertheless clearly at odds with the society into which she has been cast."[84] This attempt to find a kind of harmony in the play leads toward generic reshifting: the degrading society that the play represents threatens all except the monumentally intransigent. For J. Douglas Canfield, the whole play puts virtue on trial through its frequent use of religious language (decried by Collier as blasphemous): "In the major religious metaphor of the play, virtue is often brought to 'trial' in this world, and sadly enough, most often it fails."[85] These efforts to demonstrate a coherence in the play, to find a meaning in it, to bring its "test of virtue" plot in line with its fop plot, all speak of desperation. Like Vanbrugh in his *Short Vindication*, all of these critics seek to counter Collier's identification of formal incoherence with moral uncertainty. For them, the play becomes coherent and moral; its action is tragic and Foppington's foolishness the pitiable vanities of a mortal man.

But this argument concedes Collier's main premise by finding moral clarity in formal integrity. The play only seems incoherent, but its plots function in tandem and its moral is grim but certain. Tom Fashion's rakish ways, Lord Foppington's extravagance, Loveless's susceptibility to sexual temptation, and the crude manners of the Tunbelly household all characterize a fallen world, willfully rejecting redemption. The difference between such twentieth-century "dark" readings of the comedy and Collier's censure is only that the contemporary critics do not fly into a rage and do not hold that the portrayal of the willful rejection of redemption on stage is itself evil. But they do agree with Collier that in creating a fop who is no "Ideot" Vanbrugh exposes the limits of the genre in which he chooses to work.

Cibber played the part of Sir Novelty Fashion in his own original play and of Lord Foppington in Vanbrugh's sequel. Later Cibber offered a third version of the character: Lord Foppington, appearing in *The Careless Husband*, becomes almost human. "Nay, don't despise him neither," Sir Charles Easy warns Lord Morelove when the latter learns that the fop is his rival. Foppington's self-absorption, Sir Charles assures Morelove, is excusable and self-protective:

SIR CHARLES: Have a care, I have seen him at Lady Betty Modish's.

LORD MORELOVE: To be laugh'd at.

SIR CHARLES: Don't be too confident of that; the Women now begin to laugh with him, not at him: For he really sometimes rallies his own Humour with so much Ease and Pleasantry, that a great many Women begin to think he has no Follies at all; and those he has, have been as much owing to his Youth, and a great Estate, as want of natural Wit: Tis true, he's often a Bubble to his Pleasures, but he has always been wisely vain enough to keep himself from being too much the Ladies humble Servant in Love.

LORD MORELOVE: There indeed I almost envy him.

(1.1.394–404)

Here indeed is a transformation: Cibber incorporates into this sketch of Lord Foppington the whole problem raised by Collier. Where Collier found Foppington's digressions into sense a violation of the generic rules according to which he should have been created and a sign of Vanbrugh's incompetence, Cibber creates here a complex psychological profile for the fop. By contrast, Elder Worthy's characterization of Sir Novelty Fashion as "a Thing" from "another Species" links the fop to a universe of discourse drawn from the theater. The fop is deplorable because he performs constantly, because he is always aware of his audience. Styan examines the way Foppington, before he is dressed, rehearses for his appearance later at court, greeting his "imaginary idolators on this side and that with a wave or a nod": "Comic distancing rarely achieves such precision."[86] But the discussion of the fop before his entrance in *The Careless Husband* is not satirical or distanced. Sir

Charles excuses Foppington's follies with a certain sympathy, and Morelove envies the fop's wise vanity.

Far from being a grotesque parody of elegant dress and fashionable chat, like his predecessors, Lord Foppington has become one of the Lady Modish's set. The ladies "laugh with him, not at him," and he has a history which can excuse his conduct. Somehow, in his journey from Sir Novelty Fashion through his incarnation in *The Relapse* to *The Careless Husband*, Lord Foppington grew up: his follies are relegated to his youth, and he is now "wisely vain," self-protective rather than self-absorbed. As the fop becomes less a monster, less a thing made by a tailor, and more a "Man of Sense" (for Sir Charles uses this phrase, too, to refer to Foppington [389]), audiences are urged to look at his qualities rather than his clothes and recognize the fellow human being within. Is it Cibber or Vanbrugh or Collier who marks this shift of sympathy? Or do all three participate in the same activity of humanizing the fop, treating him as having feelings, values, and a history, though seemingly taking opposite sides of the argument about the value of stage plays? Redeeming *The Relapse* as "an Instance of the Frailty of Mankind," as Vanbrugh does, or portraying Foppington as "wisely vain" in his indifference to love, as Cibber does, is conceding the field to Collier.

Humanizing the fop detheatricalizes him; and that enterprise runs closely parallel to Cibber's agenda in the *Apology* of insisting upon the respectability, the piety, and the good citizenship of actors.[87] The fop's claim to be seen as a person with feelings, with a self and a history, is repeatedly echoed in Cibber's autobiography. To become an actor is to expose oneself willingly, to put on display feelings which should remain private. Foppishness is an extreme example of this kind of exposure. Commenting on a humiliating episode in which a hostile claque berated an actor, Cibber marvels that anyone would take on the trade of acting:

> While these Sort of Distresses are so unavoidable, it is no wonder that young People of Sense (though of low Fortune) should be so rarely found to supply a Succession of good Actors. Why then may we not, in some measure, impute the Scarcity of them to the wanton Inhumanity of those Spectators, who have made it so terribly mean to appear there? Were there no ground for this Question, where could be the Disgrace of entring into a Society whose Insti-

tution, when not abus'd, is a delightful School of Morality; and where to excel requires as ample Endowments of Nature as any one Profession (that of holy Institution excepted) whatsoever? [88]

The "wanton Inhumanity" of the spectators here threatens the supply of actors for the stage. Who would strut and fret before such a restive and critical audience?

Cibber counsels the actor to adopt a "decent and unruffled Temper": the iniquities of self-exposure counsel a kind of stoicism. "While he is conscious, That, as an Actor, he must be always in the Hands of Injustice, it does him at least this involuntary Good, that it keeps him in a settled Resolution to avoid all Occasions of provoking it, or of even offending the lowest Enemy." Keeping a low profile is, in a way, adopting a philosophical attitude. The actor, Cibber continues, can be assured

> That, if he excells on the Stage, and is irreproachable in his Personal Morals and Behaviour, his Profession is so far from being an Impediment, that it will be oftner a just Reason for his being receiv'd among People of condition with Favour; and sometimes with more social Distinction, than the best, though more profitable Trade he might have follow'd could have recommended him to. [89]

Here is Lord Foppington, being laughed *with* rather than laughed *at* in the inner circle of Lady Betty Modish or Cibber sharing a bottle with Henry Brett on the occasion of the fair, full-bottomed periwig. The actor's is a respectable profession, and one that strengthens character, teaching the necessity for a stoical "settled Resolution." Only holy orders require as much of the aspirant in the area of natural endowments, and Cibber is careful to exempt the "profitable Farce" of Catholicism: "Why, then, is an Actor more blemish'd than a Cardinal?" Bad theater, "the Abuses of the Stage," "I give up to the Contempt of every sensible Spectator, as so much rank Theatrical Popery," Cibber concedes (80–81). As popery is to the true religion, immoral plays and dissolute actors are to the true theater; an actor of "irreproachable" morals can hope to rise high in society, "receiv'd among People of condition with Favour." But the suspicion of hypocrisy, like the taint of popery, lingers on in the anxious language of Cibber's striving.

Cibber's insistence that the philosophical and truly pious actor is best known by his unblemished personal morals confuses the respectability of the craft itself with the private life of the craft's practitioners. It is therefore a concession to the strand of antitheatrical polemic that deplores the private lives of actors. By conferring upon Foppington, with whom he strongly identified himself throughout his career, a private integrity which is tacitly recognized and admired by the social set to which he aspires, Cibber plays out his own struggle to present a respectable, "wisely vain," virtuous self to the world.

The conflation between the garb of the cleric and the costume of the lady of quality that Vanbrugh provided for Cibber in the revised scenes of *The Provoked Wife* points to a correspondence between putting on religious habits and cross-dressing that has been elaborated by Marjorie Garber.[90] One episode in Cibber's own domestic life crystallizes the correspondence. Charlotte Charke, Cibber's youngest daughter, recounts in her *Narrative of the Life of Charlotte Charke* a production of *Pope Joan*, with herself in the title role.[91] Estranged from her father, she remained on reasonable terms with her brother Theophilus and had just successfully performed the role of Young Bevil in Steele's *The Conscious Lovers*, with Theophilus Cibber as Tom and his daughter Jenny as Indiana. But "some of my DEAR FRIENDS," Charke writes, interceded with Colley Cibber and "prevailed on my Father to send his positive Commands to his Son to withdraw his Daughter, on pain of his Displeasure." The result of Jenny Cibber's withdrawal, Charke complains, was "a dreadful house."[92]

While *The Conscious Lovers* seems well within the normal repertoire, *Pope Joan* does not. As her playing of the role of Young Bevil suggests, Charke had by this time in her checkered career (1745) gained considerable fame as a performer of male roles. If the *Pope Joan* which Charke hoped would restore her to prominence on the professional stage was indeed Elkanah Settle's 1680 tragedy *The Female Prelate*, that play's crude anti-Catholicism mingles with an equally powerful misogyny. Joan, who has successfully concealed her female identity under her priestly habit, is introduced as "that gay effeminate Priest, John" in act 1 (4). "I have lived an undiscover'd Woman," she reveals, "Bred among Priests, high fed, hot-blooded Priests / Those long-wing'd Hawks at all the Female Game." Protected from this rapacious lot by her cassock, "John" advances steadily through the ranks, piling crime upon crime. The play's climactic moment comes when, during her coronation parade, she "miscarrie[s] in the Street." To guarantee that "Romes mitred head henceforth shall be a man," the play concludes in act 5, a "subtle concave" shall be placed in the "Coronation Porphyry . . . thro' which a reverend Matron's hand — " (71). Small wonder that Cibber, with his anxious desire to assert the dignity of the acting profession, found his daughter's excesses embarrassing. In a notice for the play (which Fidelis Morgan suspects is "quite clearly an advert which she placed to arouse interest in her one-off performance") a putative reader of the *Daily Advertiser*, "Q. Z.," remarks upon Charke's selection of the role of Joan: "I must confess it gave me pleasure when I read her name for a female character and take this public manner of congratulating her on her appearing in her proper sphere, and hope there will be a crowded audience to encourage her to persevere in the resolution of laying aside the hero and giving them the pleasure of her performance for the future as the heroine."[93] Dressed as a woman who, dressed as a priest, confounds Rome and ascends to the papacy, Charlotte Charke as Pope Joan ascends herself to her "proper sphere." But what is that sphere?

Charke entitles chapters of her autobiography "Her Adventures in Mens Cloaths, going by the name of Mr. Brown, and being belov'd by a Lady of Great Fortune, who intended to marry her" and "Her being Gentleman to a certain Peer." Just as "John" passes among the "hot-blooded" priests and escapes their hawking advances, so Charlotte claims she was able to pass as male and make a living for herself in the hard times when her father refused to acknowledge her. For Kristina Straub, Charke's narrative, like the cross-dressing of actresses in the eighteenth century, is "threatening to the construction of a stable oppositional relationship between male and female gender and sexuality."[94] Figuring the struggle of the lesbian in early modern England, Straub's Charke is a heroic figure, translating the gender uncertainties that were her father's specialty in his fop roles into a narrative of improvisation. Fidelis Morgan, noticing a strong current of misogyny in previous accounts of Charke's life and in the commentary that accompanies L. R. N. Ashley's edition of her autobiography, suggests that there is no necessity for the "wild" Charlotte Charke to be construed as a "frustrated lesbian." Instead, Morgan suggests, the adventures she encounters might well be understood as those faced by the strolling player; her marginality is that of an actor banished from the leading theatrical family of the age, finding her way in the byways of the profession. Rudolf Dekker and Lotte van de Pol, the historians of female transvestitism, argue that "it was not at all exceptional for women to take on the appearance of men as a solution to their personal problems" — which could include poverty or a desire to serve in the military as well as lesbianism, "unknown" in the early modern period.[95]

Charke's cross-dressed itinerant life is a constant reproach to her father. Her *Narrative* shadows Cibber's *Apology* with images of the actor's life that challenge his vision of the actor as a respectable citizen. While Cibber insists that the fop's periwig offers a kind of entrée to polite society, Charke inhabits the murky reaches where playing breeches parts on stage leads to serving as gentleman's gentleman. Cibber portrays himself as being laughed *with* rather than *at*: Charke's adventures make herself and her family ridiculous. Charke rehearses all the slanders of dressing up: she confuses gender, she puts on the cloth, she acts the part of the fop. Cibber, of course, wants to distance himself as much as possible from these slanders against actors by insisting that acting is a legitimate career, that performing can contribute to a pious, stoic resolve, that actors have feelings that can be hurt. To this poet laureate, so acutely aware of the ridicule showered upon him by sharp wits like Alexander Pope, Jonathan Swift, John Arbuthnot, and John Gay, Charke's wild embrace of life on the margins of theater must have been a constant trial. Every charge that the *Apology* counters Charke levels against herself; every claim that the *Apology* makes for acting as respectable, safe, and useful Charke's career makes ridiculous. Small wonder Cibber treated Charke as badly as he did: she was the return of the repressed.

And Charke's cross-dressing reiterates how widespread confusion of genders was in the English theater after the Restoration. To return briefly to Tom Fashion: Laurence Senelick takes issue with Susan Staves for her assertion that Coupler in *The Relapse* is "explicitly homosexual," chiding her for the use of this "anachronistic coinage."[96] Coupler's "taste for young men" is revealed in a scene in which he fondles Young Fashion. "Ha! you young lascivious rogue, you! Let me put my hand in your bosom, sirrah," wheedles Coupler. "Stand off, old Sodom!" exclaims Tom (1.3.181–83). What are audiences or readers to make of this moment? Tom Fashion was first played on the stage as a breeches part, by the actress Mary Kent. For this reason, Madeleine Bingham has contended that, on the plane of "the real," Coupler's advances are "the perfectly normal advances of a man towards an attractive woman."[97] While Staves and Senelick accept the play's fiction at face value and disagree on what its depiction of Coupler and his "Hephestion" (208) means, Bingham seems to find an assurance of normality in the actress's presence: since Tom Fashion is played by a woman, the scene is not sodomitical at all. "Ah, you young hot lusty thief, let me muzzle you. — [Kissing] Sirrah, let me muzzle you," Coupler insists. "Psha, the old lecher," Tom Fashion mutters, aside (264–66). Is this Mary Kent voicing her disgust at Benjamin Johnson, playing Coupler and noted for his "large, speaking, blue eyes"?[98] Is it Tom Fashion revealing his revulsion at the necessity that he play Coupler's Hephestion in order to win his trust and learn a way to outfox his brother? Is this another instance in which Garber insists that the figure of the "changeling boy" evokes "a primal scene" of cultural anxiety?[99]

Cibber's repudiation of his daughter, in the context of the kind of theater in which he first made his name, smacks of anxiety, too. Having begun as a fop, he retreats into respectability and denies aid to the daughter who cross-dresses and plays his own famous roles. Her barnstorming, masquerading, and Clancy-like imposture all bespeak an embrace of the actor's marginality that challenges Cibber's new status. Cibber's rejection of Charlotte Charke testifies to the power of Jeremy Collier's campaign to reform the stage in England at the end of the seventeenth century, however much Cibber might mock Collier in the person of the non-juror. Playwrights like Vanbrugh and William Congreve and critics like John Dennis joined Cibber and defended theater by conceding Collier's main point — that theater should be a morally improving institution — and then quibbling over whether particular plot-lines or particular references to the clergy were or were not conducive to this goal.

One play actually brings Collier himself onto the stage for special ridicule: Tom Brown's *The Stage-Beaux Toss'd in a Blanket or, Hypocrisie Alamode; expos'd in a True Picture of Jerry ———, a Pretending Scourge to the English Stage: a comedy* (never performed, 1704). Brown's play identifies Collier, who in the play appears as Sir Jerry Witwoud, as a member of the party of hypocrites: "But indeed the Stage has no Enemies but such as are Hypocrites and real Enemies to Vertue, because the Stage is a profess'd Enemy to them and their Darling Vices," Brown declares in his prefatory remarks.[100] Alluding to *The Plain Dealer*, Brown opens his play with a scene in which the sensible Eliza discusses Collier's book with Clemene, a prude whose habit of speech is "my Aversion of all Aversions, as Olivia says." Clemene now avoids the playhouse, "for Mr. *Collier* has prov'd the Poets a Company of strange, debauch'd Fellowes — who are furiously my Aversion" (p. 11). In the climactic scene, Brown's Sir Jerry strips off his robes. "But pray, by the way, why have you left off your Gown?" Clemene wonders as he approaches. "Because some Accidents may happen, Madam," replies Sir Jerry, "that may bring a Scandal to the Gown; and now whatever I say or do falls upon the Prophane Laity, and so I give Sir *John Brute* a *Rowland* for his *Oliver*." Unfortunately, Clemene is a real prude and doesn't get it. "Put, put off the Veil, I know you're a Hypocrite," cries Sir Jerry in frustration, attacking her. "Nay, now you begin to be Abusive, I vow I'll call out if you won't let me alone — A Hypocrite!" "Nay, I'm sure of it," Sir Jerry persists, "for almost all our Party are so" (57). His attempted rape stymied by the intervention of the true gentlemen, Sir Jerry exits: "Ah, no! — if the Hypocrites were expos'd, half the town wou'd go naked — and all the Stage Enemies, like me, go off with their Tails betwixt their Legs" (60).

The faction of hypocrites in Brown's play, as in Molière's *Dom Juan*, imperils public morality. His *raisonneur*, Dorimant, announces the flaw of Collier's book early in the play. The stage, Dorimant argues, is especially valuable because "[i]t ridicules Hypocrisie and Avarice, the first ruining Religion, the latter the State; so that the Stage is the Champion of Church and State against the Invasion of Two of their most formidable Enemies; and this is what renders it odious to those who cry against it. It is not that it is Lewd, Prophane, or Immoral; but because it exposes the Vices and Follies of a too prevailing Party, the Hypocrites, and the Misers" (*The Stage-Beaux*, 12). Hypocrites and misers are not only conventional comic butts; they are also a subversive political party. This is of course the way Cibber and Bickerstaff present the nonjuror and dissenting clergy in their adaptations of *Tartuffe*. Plays are not only expressions of loyalty but provide, through theatricality, the means to expose the hypocrites among us as the subversive partisans they are.

About a hundred years later, John Gardiner rose to address the Massachusetts House of Representatives on the matter of repealing "the illiberal, unmanly, and despotic act, which now prohibits THE-ATRICAL EXHIBITIONS among us." The new country is "by nature, intended for the cultivation of *sound reason* and for an enlightened, manly freedom." The act prohibiting plays shows instead the "detestable, canting hypocritic spirit" of "our renowned *puritan an-*

cestors." Extolling the stage, Gardiner rises to heights of eloquence: "There is seen the canting, crooked hypocrite, who values himself upon his cunning and duplicity, (equally false to GOD and *man*) whose face is harder than brass, whose soul is dark *as Erebus*, and whose heart is full of stratagems and spoils; *even here, upon the stage,* we behold this *detestable monster* stript, laid bare, and naked to the public eye; while abhorrent aversion is excited in every honest breast, as the scenes unfold, and the abominable wretch is traced through all his base intricacies, hell-born villainies, and unhallow'd impurities." Gardiner looks prophetically forward to a time when *"the dark, gloomy bigott must soon go off the* stage of life; *when a new set of* Actors *will appear, of more liberal ideas, and of a more refined taste, formed to enjoy the polished refinements of social life, and to delight in the rational entertainments of a* chaste *and* well-regulated Theatre." [101]

For Gardiner as for Tom Brown, defense of theater means antipuritanism. Both of them portray the puritan hypocrite as a terrible threat to the social fabric. Brown's hypocrite and miser threaten the central British values of church and state; Gardiner's manly United States has no place in it for bigots, and the "Actors" of his remarks are enlightened citizens. Kingsley sets the terms of the opposition in his essay "Plays and Puritans," and Barish echoes it in his chapter on "Proteans and Puritans." The figure of the puritan stalks this act: first in the shadow of antitheatrical polemic that attaches to Viola and to the festive world of *Twelfth Night* and then in the cabal of *dévots* who succeeded in suppressing *Tartuffe*. In Cibber's desire to make fops sympathetic characters and actors respectable citizens, Collier's kind of puritanism, with its insistence on sincerity, becomes part of the theatrical mainstream. Charlotte Charke, with a puppet stall out in the marketplace, passing herself off as a manservant, is an affront to this agenda of reform.

But Brown and Gardiner suggest that it is because the theater exposes the theatrical mechanisms of the puritan hypocrite that the detestable monster attacks it. Theater shows the social world to be itself playing; and the hypocrite, whose act is to decry acting and to lay claim to an antitheatrical sincerity, must be its enemy. Far more dangerous than fops — who might after all have their human qualities — or crossdressers or even fake clergymen are those who profess sincerity and move among us undetected. These are not coarse butts like Sir Jerry Witwoud, but rather deft players of the social game like Joseph Surface in Richard Brinsley Sheridan's *School for Scandal*. Sincerity is their stock in trade — which means it can itself be an act.

The affectation of sincerity is far more disconcerting to moral thinkers than dressing up. The cross-dresser, the fake clergyman, and the fop all deceive at a surface level. While sometimes these exterior shows might infect or contaminate the actor or the audience, they remain on a level of playing that identifies acting with disguise. Costume stands in metaphorically for the acting of social roles. Lying is a more insidious application of acting skills in the social arena. Hypocrisies of dress — foppery, cross-dressing, putting on the cloth — are susceptible to theatrical exposure. Costumes are meant to be read; and, while sumptuary laws and the dictates of fashion may be hard to enforce, clothing functions as a rudimentary social marker. But playing at sincerity — looking exactly like an honest person — is not a matter of disguise. It is far more insidious: hypocrites who play at not playing are dangerous not, as Molière suggested, because they opt out of the game of social performance and pretend to a bogus authenticity, but because their performance seamlessly repudiates theatricality.

Act Two

THEY LIE

"Is it possible there should be no Sincerity in the World, and that we dare not confide in anybody?" queries Jean Bellegarde at the beginning of his chapter "Of Imposture" in *Reflections upon Ridicule*. Bellegarde's treatise, published in France in 1696 and translated into English shortly thereafter, raises the specter of a society infiltrated and subverted by impostors. "Sincerity," he proclaims, "is the Soul of Commerce and Civil Society, and yet 'tis a very uncommon Vertue in so refining an Age as this we live in, 'tis an Art and a Trade to disguise the Sentiments; that pretended Openness of Heart, is only a Lure to attract the Confidences of Men; we find none Sincere but those that have not wit enough to play the Impostor." If, as La Rochefoucauld put it, hypocrisy is the homage vice pays to virtue, here the homage slides into substitution. Religious hypocrites, in Bellegarde, are themselves actors: "Their Life is one perpetual Comedy, and they seem always upon the Stage; they hardly ever pull off the Mask; their Vices don't at all discourage them, provided they are cover'd with a specious Appearance." Successful impostors boast of their sincerity and become "Tom-Doubles" indistinguishable from their hapless victims. "They put on the Mask of Sincerity," Bellegarde cautions, "and they affect an easy, natural, and undesigning Ayre. That concerted Sincerity is a subtle and delicate Deception, which leads People where they would have them, and betrays them without perceiving it."[1]

"These people," Bellegarde repeats in his chapter "Of Sincerity," "bear a great Resemblance to Comedians, who act several Characters in Masks, and change their Habits according to the Parts they play." Yet what is to be done? "If we banish Sincerity, we must renounce the World: for without it, civil Society is a kind of Kidnapping; we try all Practices to abuse, gull, and surprize the People we converse with"

(*Reflections*, 2:177). Fake sincerity is the worst kind of hypocrisy, as well as a kind of acting. Where Molière's hypocrites, in their clothes of pious black, set themselves apart from the world, Bellegarde's are everywhere around us. Instead of dressing up, they lie: their feigning runs deep and lies beneath the surface.

Richard Head, in a tract called *Proteus redivivus* (1675), gives a name to the art of those who pretend to sincerity: *The Art of Wheedling, or Insinuation*. His book exposes the techniques of "the Art of Insinuation, or Dissimulation, compounded of mental reservation, seeming patience and humility, (self-obliging) civility, and a more than common affability, all which club to please, and consequently to gain by conversation." Head's tract, like Bellegarde's, offers hints for survival in a highly theatricalized social world. The language of antitheatricalism becomes applied to the type of wheedler, who is an actor freed from the confinement of the stage. "They are like a fish called a *Polypus*," Head warns of the wheedlers among society, "of whom it is storied, that it hath the power of converting its colour into that which is nearest it, and most contiguous for self-preservation; these *Protei* of this loose age can turn themselves into any shape, so that the conversion of the form will produce any profit or advantage." What is troublesome about Head's wheedlers, as it is about Bellegarde's religious hypocrites, is that what they feign is sincerity itself. They prey upon the honest person's inability to feign. The honest person's passions, Head argues, "mutiny without our leave, and by an impression which they make in our countenance, they teach our enemies all that lies within our hearts, and invite the *Wheedle* to come, and banquet on our follies." [2]

Like the Proteus, the Polypus, and the porcupine, Mr. Wheedle has a sting. He haunts taverns, spas, and, of course, the theater:

He is very solicitous to get acquaintance with some of the Actors, not out of any respect he bears to their Ingenuity, but to gain so far an interest in them, as to be let into the house now and then *gratis*, and upon no other score, than to pick up a Bubble, or some unpracticed young Female, whom he pinches by the Fingers, and cries *Damme*, Madam, were you but sensible of that Passion I have for you, you could not but instantly show some pity to your languishing Vassal, this he utters at first sight, and if the first show him no countenance, the next he comes at shall have the same Compliment; having trim'd his Wigg and caress'd his Breeches, he cruseth to and fro the Pit, (not minding the Players who Act their parts so well on the Stage, that Ladies send for them to act in their Chambers) and never at quiet till he hath made prize of some or other, whom he tows off to a Tavern, and there rummages the Hold at pleasure. (204–5)

Head's indictment of Mr. Wheedle is a compendium of antitheatrical motifs. Wheedle's cruising of the pit engages the author's scorn because it competes with the performances of the ingenious actors: yet those performances themselves are reprehensible in their lewdness, tempting ladies to send for the players after the show. Stubbes's scenario of actors and audience members playing "the sodomites, or worse" afterward is brought up to date by Head's vision of Wheedle and his "Bubble" at the tavern.

The world of Head's and Bellegarde's tracts is composed of "us," the readers, innocently self-exposing, naively trusting, and the Wheedles, Tom-Doubles, and Protean hypocrites who take advantage of our inadvertent self-exposure and "banquet on our follies." Yet somehow such manuals of social survival suggest a lurking contrary: for when the readers learn the art of wheedling, or learn how to avoid ridicule, they themselves become sophisticates. What then distinguishes their self-conscious self-protectiveness from the cunning duplicity of the "enemies" they now can see through and can manipulate to their own advantage? Bellegarde's vision of "civil Society" as a "kind of Kidnapping" translates the language of antitheatricalism into the realm of social intercourse and transforms social interactions into gulling, cozenage, and abuse.

Head and Bellegarde anticipate the powerful distinction between private and public life and the privileging of private life that is most clearly associated with Rousseau. In this act, then, I consider first the private domestic violations of trust that hypocrisy entails, through discussion of Rousseau's antitheatrical strictures and some early modern plays, chief among them Sheridan's *School for Scandal*. Ibsen's *Hedda Gabler* offers a glimpse of a modern type recognizably derived from Rousseau: the self-deceiving hypocrite. Tom Brown and John Gardiner insist upon a public dimension of hypocrisy, the realm of the politician: following these suggestions leads me to a discussion of Shakespeare's Prince Hal and his representation in two film versions of *Henry V*.

Scene One

ROUSSEAU & THE CULT
OF SINCERITY

The most eloquent exponent of the desire to be simple, integrated, pure, virtuous, and sincere is Jean-Jacques Rousseau, whose *Letter to M. D'Alembert* is a key document in eighteenth-century antitheatrical polemic. Allan Bloom, who translated and edited Rousseau's letter for Agora Editions under the title of *Politics and the Arts*, identifies Rousseau with the Platonic tradition that Barish documents: "The only preparation for the writing of this book which we know Rousseau to have done is that he made a paraphrase of Book X of Plato's *Republic*, and its influence on the text is evident."[3] Bloom follows Plato and Rousseau in insisting that such an imperative is best followed in a world without theaters. For Bloom does not merely translate Rousseau's letter; rather he defends it and urges that it "points to the possibility of an alternative to the moderns which remains philosophic" (xxiv): "The moderns had forgotten nature, and nature teaches that human life has two poles at tension with one another: the life of the mind and the life of the city; this tension is an irreconcilable one, rooted in man's very existence, and it is the very core of Rousseau's thought." "Perhaps we moderns," Bloom concludes his introduction to Rousseau's letter, "have forgotten what the real problem of art is when we smile at the illiberal inconsistency which causes the poet-philosophers Plato and Rousseau to banish poets from their cities" (xxxviii).

In the *Letter to D'Alembert* Rousseau describes a community of mountain people, "perhaps unique on earth," in the vicinity of Neufchatel. In this utopia (utopian because there is no theater there) the farmers work hard and provide for themselves; but more important for Rousseau is the way they spend their leisure time. "In the winter especially, a time when the deep snows prevent easy communication, each, warmly closed up with his big family in his pretty and clean wooden house, which he himself has built, busies himself with enjoyable labors which drive boredom from his sanctuary and add to his well-being." Never idle and never bored, they invent and make useful instruments and entertain one another with the singing of psalms. Rousseau invites his readers to suppose that a theater is then established for the benefit of these good people: "Let us further suppose that they get a taste for this theatre, and let us investigate what will be the results of its establishment." He enumerates five "disadvantages": "slackening of work," "increase of expenses," "decrease in trade," "establishment of taxes" (to build roads and make up for trade deficits), "introduction of luxury." Here women will strive to outshine one another in dress, the sumptuary laws will fall into disregard, and husbands will be ruined.[4]

A number of recent critics have pointed out that discussion of Rousseau's *Letter* should avoid the temptation to see his argument as universal and recognize its concentration on the local problem of Voltaire's plans to introduce theater into Geneva. Rousseau does indeed draw a distinction between major cities like London and Paris with well-established theaters and small cities like Geneva (here likened to the idealized community of mountain folk). Allan Bloom, according to James F. Hamilton, "has provided a reasonable defence of Rousseau's dramatic theory by bringing the question of censorship into historical perspective." Hamilton argues that in Rousseau's theory of the development of human societies the arts play a major role, which he calls "conspiratorial." In the preface to *Narcisse*, he points out, Rousseau describes the way in which "the arts" corrupt societies: "They destroy virtue, but they leave behind the public image of virtue, which is always a beautiful thing. Politeness and discretion take virtue's place, and the fear of appearing evil is replaced by the fear of appearing ridiculous."[5] More highly developed societies (like Paris or like Rousseau's vision of Athens) have fully fallen victim to this infection of substitution. But simpler societies (like Geneva or like Rousseau's vision of Sparta) have not yet completely succumbed.

John Hope Mason likewise locates Rousseau's distaste for theater within the context of Geneva as a republic, although he stresses Rousseau's reliance upon classical republicanism in his view of inevitable decline: "For all republican writers the passage from frugality to luxury was a fatal step; once it had occurred, the republic was doomed." "To be at home in this new society it was necessary above all to be adaptable and to go along with the artifice. Lord Chesterfield wrote to his son: 'a man of the world must like the chameleon be able to take on every different hue.' And Kant observed in his *Anthropologie*: 'the more civilised men become, the more they become actors.'" Rousseau, Mason argues, has something in common with postcolonial theorists: "Far from being intolerant, he was here articulating what has in our century become familiar, the desire to resist what we now call cultural imperialism."[6]

To Rousseau, theater is an institution which must oppress one class for the luxury of another. He insists that theater will widen the gulfs between classes and add to the misery of the poor. Weeping at the misfortunes of others in plays permits us to think that "we have satisfied all the rights of humanity without having to give anything more of ourselves; whereas unfortunate people in person would require attention from us, relief, consolation, and work, which would involve us in their pains and would require at least the sacrifice of our indolence, from all of which we are quite content to be exempt." Worse, theater functions as a kind of regressive tax, unduly placing a burden on "the poor beyond their strength": "the modern theatre, which can only be attended for money, tends everywhere to promote and increase the inequality of fortunes."[7]

Rousseau's sense in *Letter* is that such inequities are inevitable. The process of Geneva's decline has already begun. In fact, as David Marshall has argued, for Rousseau theater "represents the fall from the state of nature"; "Rousseau's indictment of the acting and posing that develop in society is not limited to a denunciation of deception, hypocrisy, or false representation. People become actors — and this acting is problematic — from the moment they are aware that they must represent themselves for others." Social life is performance, and as Geneva develops into a modern society the Genevans will become "spectacles and actors" to one another.[8] In a sense, Rousseau turns the new historicist paradigm on its head: if to the new historicist the modern condition (traced back to its early modern antecedents) is performance, and social interaction is theater, for Rousseau theater is the modern condition. Displacing the state of nature as it inevitably must, theater forces men and women to abandon their natural roles, increases the gap between rich and poor, encourages false piety and empty expressions of sympathy for others, and mandates oppression and hypocrisy.

For Rousseau, the penetration of the theatrical problem of appearance into the social world is of special moment: actors, as Patrick Coleman puts it, "represent society's ideal of action for they deceive without being deceived. So if actors are despised, it is because they show only too clearly the degraded nature of that ideal, and not on simple moral grounds. For it becomes apparent that conformity to social norms of behavior is no more linked to virtue than deception is tied to evil intent. If intention is nothing, and surface behavior all, then morality is not so much threatened as dissolved."[9]

The breakdown of morality is introduced by the power of theater to effeminize culture in the *Letter to D'Alembert*. The establishment of a theater in Geneva, Rousseau argues, would lead to a collapse of public morals as women become their arbiters:

> Love is the realm of women. It is they who necessarily give the law in it, because, according the order of nature, resistance belongs to them and men can conquer this resistance only at the expense of their liberty. Hence, a natural effect of this sort of play is to extend the empire of the fair sex, to make women and girls the preceptors of the public, and to give them the same power over the audience that they have over their lovers. Do you think, Sir, that this order is without its difficulties; and that, in taking so much effort to increase the ascendancy of women, men will be the better governed for it ?[10]

Here the establishment of a theater in a free republic carries with it the threat of gender inversion, the "order of nature" perverted as women begin to make laws.

Rousseau participates in what Henri Peyre and a number of others have called a modern "cult of sincerity." Peyre argues that sincerity comes to be prized in the French seventeenth century as a result of the collapse of the traditional genres into the new mixed forms of drama that corresponded to the English sentimental comedy examined in Act One. Weeping comedies and middle-class tragedies mark "a revulsion against the twofold peril encountered by that age: that of politeness turned to social falsehood and grimaced masquerading" — the stuff of comedy — "and that of heroic tension and rigid sclerosis of the whole being through exalted will power" — the stuff of tragedy.[11] Social life seems to mimic the genres and to be rigid, sclerotic, and false.

For Rousseau and his tradition, paradoxically, acting is the modern condition, under the constant reproach of a notion of the natural, the sincere, and the authentic that social life necessarily belies. And being sincere, authentic, and transparent never seems quite to work out. Somehow, for Rousseau, being honest leads to being Protean, to becoming a wildly virtuosic performer of the type ridiculed in antitheatrical literature. "Nothing is more dissimilar from myself than I myself," he proclaims in *Le persifleur*:

> therefore it would be useless to try to define me otherwise than by that unique variability: so changeable is my mind that it occasionally affects even my feelings. At times I am a severe and fierce misanthrope; and at other moments I wax ecstatic amid the charms of society and the delights of love. Now I am austere and devout, and for the welfare of my soul I strive to make these holy inclinations last; but I soon become an arrant libertine, and as I concentrate then upon my senses rather than upon my reason, I constantly abstain from writing in those moments: it is good that my readers be sufficiently warned about this, lest they expect to find in these pages things which they will certainly never see. In a word, a Proteus, a Chameleon, a woman are less changeable beings than I am.

Rousseau exhibits here the paradoxical nature of the claim of absolute sincerity: he revels in his Protean changeability. Trying always to be true to oneself can lead to contradictions between a better self, austere and devout, and a libertine self which must be concealed from the readers. "One can be authentically many things, including authentically dishonest," comments Ruth W. Grant on the persistence of this problem.[12]

Furthermore, Rousseau portrays himself here as becoming a woman: Protean and changeable, women are always theatrical in Rousseau. Thus the presence of theater in the big cities leads to the dominance of women, where men are governed by women. But if, in attempting fully to express his own sincerity, his own transparency, Rousseau finds in himself some traces of woman, should he report it or should it be one of those things that readers "will certainly never see" in his pages? The notion of women as natural performers, by nature hypocrites, derives from their refusal to stay put in their roles; or, as Elizabeth Wingrove has put it, in Rousseau's *Letter* "the theater extends women's empire by challenging the roles of the sexual dynamic." The ascendancy of women in Rousseau's vision of the theatricalized social world makes life harder for men, who must learn to read the moment when "her eyes accord what her mouth feigns to refuse." Here "no" means "yes."[13]

Rousseau's vision of a feminized world of performance finds an echo in Nina Auerbach's portrayal of the anxiety with which the Victorians confronted the idea of theatricality. "'Theatricality' is such a rich and fearful word in Victorian culture that it is most accurately defined, as Carlyle uses it, in relation to the things it is not. Sincerity is sanctified and it is not sincere," she argues. "Reverent Victorians shunned theatricality as the ultimate, deceitful mobility. It connotes not only lies, but a fluidity of character that decomposes the uniform integrity of the self." Rejecting theatricality as a moral value, Auerbach notes, the Victorians nonetheless inhabited a world in which theatrical entertainments abounded, with their threats and lures more available to a mass audience than ever before. High culture, as represented by Matthew Arnold and Thomas Carlyle, set itself in opposition to the "dangerous potential of theatricality to invade the authenticity of the best self"; but for Auerbach the struggle is incessant: "The Victorian self refuses to stop becoming; its development produces only spectacular transformations." Auerbach's Victorians are caught up in a process of metamorphosis and display which they deplore but cannot escape. Rousseau's cult of sincerity was enshrined in a dominant culture in which, as Arnold would claim, only "high seriousness, the high seriousness which comes from absolute sincerity," redeems literature from the taint of theatricality.[14] Auerbach's anxious, antitheatrical Victorians inhabit a world prophetically imagined by Rousseau.

The pervasive bad faith, role-playing, and feminization of society in Rousseau's vision of society has led to the contention, among political philosophers like Ruth Grant, that Rousseau here laid the groundwork for modern, bourgeois society and also to the charge that, in laying claim to an absolute sincerity about himself, Rousseau is as guilty of bad faith as the world he envisions. The passage from *Le persifleur* suggests that for Rousseau himself, at least, a complete indulgence in sincerity, to the point of revealing libertinage, is not acceptable. "Some critics of Rousseau," declares Grant, "argue that, while claiming to teach sincerity, he provides only a 'cult of sincerity' that feeds the vanity of its adherents." For Grant, the type of the modern hypocrite who fakes sincerity is inseparable from Rousseau's political thought. "[T]he citizen of a liberal regime comes to be understood as a certain kind of hypocrite, the bourgeois," she states. "The bourgeois is alienated and inauthentic, never himself, never in public life what he would privately wish to be. Subjected to the pressures of modern life in commercial, liberal societies, he must create a phony self to satisfy his anxious concern to be pleasing, to be acceptable, or respectable in the eyes of others." It is not enough to be liked; you have to be well liked, Grant reminds us, with a note referring to Willy Loman in *Death of a Salesman*.[15]

Rousseau's struggle to preserve Geneva from theater is doomed because Geneva already offers social life, and social life is inauthentic performance. The idea of an essential self and the idea of the self as ridiculous performer on the stage of society are mutually interdependent. Thomas M. Kavanagh discusses at length a passage in the *Confessions* in which Rousseau describes his own visit to the theater at Fontainebleau on the occasion of the performance of his play *Le devin du village* on October 18, 1752. Rousseau determined to dress coarsely and casually as usual and not to shave. He presented himself "as someone acting outside social convention, as someone undetermined by recognized hierarchies, as someone capable of refusing all dictates devolving from the presence of king and court." Yet he was graciously received; tears flowed freely from the elaborately clothed and coifed audience. On this occasion, Kavanagh points out, Rousseau "presents himself as a noble savage," but paradoxically "Rousseau's nature . . . is everywhere derived from and dependent on the signifying systems of a pre-existing culture." Without the formulas and *politesses* of the court, Rousseau's ostentatious nonconformity would be meaningless.[16] This vision of Rousseau at the theater is rich with paradox.

"An excess of Sincerity," Bellegarde says, "is sometimes as dangerous, as a too effeminate and studied Complaisance. You become the Terror of all Companies, by the Liberty you take to tell all People, to their Face, your Thoughts of them" (*Reflections*, 1:19). Rousseau's reviling of the phony self in the *Letter to D'Alembert* reaches a peak in his famous misreading of Molière's *Misanthrope*. For Rousseau, Alceste, the terror of all companies, is admirable and heroic; Philinte comes to represent the insidious false friend. In the play Alceste decries Philinte's social performance in the opening moments, as he storms onto the stage with his friend in pursuit. What has enraged Alceste is Philinte's warm, cordial embrace of a virtual stranger: "Good Lord! You play a base unworthy role," Alceste fumes, "By stooping to betray your very soul" (1.1.25–26).[17] Philinte's plausible charm, his ease in society, enrages his friend, to whom his civility is the "shameful trade" ("commerce honteux," 68) of the hypocrite. Bellegarde, too, uses the language of commerce to describe the perilous world: "Instead of Honesty and Sincerity, we find nothing but Artifice, Disguises, and oftentimes Treachery in the Commerce of the World" (2:190).

Molière's joke in the play is to make the rigid, antitheatrical Alceste amorous: in love with the most theatricalized woman in the play, the coquette Célimène. Artifice and disguise are her mode of being. Philinte finds Alceste's preference a "strange choice" (1.2.214), especially considering the interest taken in Alceste by the prude Arsinoé and the sincere ("sincère" 215; translated by Frame as "candid") Eliante. For Molière, Alceste's excessive sincerity is comically undermined by his foolish passion for a female fop.

To Rousseau, however, this joke was unworthy of both Molière and Alceste. Rousseau characterizes Alceste as "straight, sincere, estimable, a true man of worth"; Molière, to cater to the audience of social climbers in his theater, must make this figure ridiculous and reinforce his audience's corruption and vanity. "Philinte is the wise man of the play," Rousseau snarls:

> one of those honest men of high society, whose precepts closely resemble those of confidence men; one of those sweet, temperate men who find that everything is going just fine because it's not in their interest for things ever to go any better; who are always pleased with everybody because they don't care about anybody; who, at the well-appointed dinner table, maintain that it's not true that the people are going hungry; who, with well-lined pockets, find speeches about the poor in bad taste; who, from their locked-up houses, would see the whole human race robbed, stripped, slashed, massacred, without a complaint: granted, God has blessed them with a most meritorious sweetness of disposition — to tolerate the misfortunes of others.[18]

Going along and getting along, for Rousseau as for Alceste, not only cheapens social intercourse but hardens the heart and imperils the soul.

In *Philinte de Molière* (1790), a curious play written as a sequel to *Le misanthrope*, the revolutionary and poet Philippe François Nazaire Fabre d'Eglantine (guillotined among the Dantonists during the Terror) follows Rousseau's lead. The play features a Philinte whose true friend Alceste works tirelessly on his behalf, in spite of his manifest insensitivity and indifference to the sufferings of others. "I tell you straight," Alceste confronts Philinte, "that to your hardened soul nothing, no affinity, no sentiment aligns me. I cast you from me; at a distance, among those cold beings who have lost the right to the good name of man. . . . *Honor, charitable deeds, fairness, candor, love*, and *friendship* cannot ever exist in a heart without *PITY*." "I was wrong," confesses Philinte, "confounded." Eliante, to whom Philinte is married in this play, weeps at the just reproaches of this "perfect friend." [19] In this play Philinte must confront the sufferings of others and make amends for his careless behavior. Rousseau's contempt for his social performance finds expression in a drama in which Philinte is given a chance to make amends, to do the right thing. What Rousseau found obnoxious in Molière's play, the holding up of Alceste's sincerity to ridicule, becomes in Fabre d'Eglantine's play the crux of the action: Philinte is forced to concede the sincerity, the virtue, the magnanimous zeal ("zèle magnanime!") of Alceste. In *Philinte* the tables have turned: Alceste's sincerity, far from being ridiculous, is noble, self-effacing, humane.

Rousseau and Fabre d'Eglantine turn against the worldly sophisticate the weapon of theatrical discomfiture. While Molière and satirists like Tom Brown delight in exposing prudes and self-righteous moralists, stripping off their costumes and abasing them in amorous intrigue, these puritanical antitheatricalists detect a hollowness, a coldness, and a profound inhumanity in the *raisonneurs* who inhabit the stage's social world. In creating Philinte, as Rousseau points out, Molière reinforced the prejudices and indifference of the court audiences of his era. Their callousness toward the poor, like Philinte's in Fabre d'Eglantine's play, is little short of criminal and, as Fabre d'Eglantine's subsequent career shows, awaited a deadly tribunal at the guillotine.

Scene Two

PLAYING JOSEPH SURFACE

In his discussion of the acting style of John ("Plausible Jack") Palmer, Charles Lamb raises a question that lurks in the drama rather than in ethical tracts: if hypocrisy consists in the transposition of the theatrical into everyday life, how is hypocrisy then to be represented on the stage? Lamb avers that "Jack had two voices — both plausible, hypocritical, and insinuating; but his second or supplemental voice still more decisively histrionic than his common one." This voice "was reserved for the spectator; and the dramatis personae were supposed to know nothing about it." Lamb recalls the performance of Palmer from the early days of his theatergoing: "When I remember the gay boldness, the graceful solemn plausibility, the measured step, the insinuating voice — the downright *acted* villany [*sic*] of the part, so different from the pressure of actual wickedness, — the hypocritical assumption of hypocrisy, — which made Jack so deservedly a favourite in that character, I must needs conclude the present generation of play-goers more virtuous than myself, or more dense."[20]

Here Lamb explicitly locates the problem in his, and the audience's, modernity, understood by Lamb as a condition of bringing the moral consciousness of real life into the theater, where (at least in terms of the comedies of the previous generation) it does not belong. "The times cannot bear them," Lamb declares of "The Artificial Comedies of the Last Century"; nineteenth-century spectators "see a stage libertine playing his loose pranks of two hours duration, and of no after consequence, with the severe eyes which inspect real vices with their bearings upon two worlds" (62). Lamb's vision is of the theater as an antitheatrical space: "The privileges of the place are taken away by law. We dare not dally with the images, or names, of wrong. We bark like foolish dogs at shadows. We dread infection from the scenic representation of disorder, and fear a painted pustule" (63). For Lamb, Plausible Jack Palmer's performance is no longer possible not because the acting style went out of fashion, precisely, but because of a fundamental change in the audience's consciousness — one that corresponds directly to Rousseau's and the moralists' conviction that the infection of social life with playing is not funny, not comical, but serious business. What happens in Lamb's essays on the theater is a transposition of this concern. To Lamb, audiences who bring the conscience of the real world into the theater, who "substitute a real for a dramatic person, and judge him accordingly" (62), can never experience the pleasure of escape "out of Christendom into the land — what shall I call it? — of cuckoldry — the Utopia of gallantry, where pleasure is duty, and the manners perfect freedom" (64).

Lamb famously elides Collier's strictures in this move, consigning the profane dramas that so unsettled the non-juror to the realm of cloud-cuckoo-land. The modern, bourgeois theater, with its moralizing, alienated audience, becomes an unsuitable venue not just for Restoration comedy, in Lamb's criticism, but for Shakespeare as well. Watching *Lear* leads this audience to feelings of middle-class guilt: "We want to take him into shelter and relieve him. That is all the feeling which the acting of Lear ever produced in me," Lamb confesses (96). When Lamb and the audience that he imagines bring the real world into the theater, it is a world where the less fortunate require gestures of benevolence and cuckolds are more to be pitied than censured.

"Poor Jack has passed from the stage in good time, that he did not live to this our age of seriousness," Lamb proclaims with mock wistfulness. "We must love or hate — acquit or condemn — censure or pity — exert our detestable coxcombry of moral judgment upon every thing. Joseph Surface, to go down now, must be a downright revolting villain — no compromise — his first appearance must shock and give horror — his specious plausibilities, which our fathers welcomed with such hearty greetings, knowing that no harm (dramatic harm even) could come, or was meant to come of them, must inspire a cold and killing aversion" (67). There is no denying the playfulness of this essay, for it celebrates a playful way of playing: Plausible Jack's Joseph Surface was "*acted*" (128), his hypocrisy comically telegraphed to the audience.

As Michael Cordner has pointed out in a recent edition of Sheridan's plays, "[t]wentieth-century actors have rarely attempted a reading of Joseph as a 'downright revolting villain.'" Instead, we have had "dandyism," "shallowness," "no depth at all," according to a sample of commentators quoted by Cordner.[21] Lamb's strictures thus seem to apply to a nineteenth-century audience who simply cannot allow Joseph Surface to be funny, just as Rousseau cannot allow Alceste to be the butt of Molière's cruel humor. Joseph's utterance of sentiments was telegraphed to the audience in Palmer's performance, according to Lamb, in which the actor "was playing to you all the while that he was playing upon Sir Peter and his lady" (66): but what Lamb envisions in his present is a theater in which such double-edged acting is not permitted.

But is Joseph Surface a villain? And are his abuses of trust to be taken seriously? One stage tradition holds that the famous screen scene should be played for pathos: Cordner cites reviews of productions that leave Lady Teazle in "hysterical grief" and confront an audience with a "marriage momentarily in ruins" ("Introduction," xxxiii). Sheridan is ingenious in recasting the comic stripping of the hypocrite as an unveiling of his intrigue: and, as James Morwood has pointed out, Sheridan draws upon his audience's familiarity with *Tartuffe* — Cibber's and Bickerstaff's versions as well as the original and its first English adaptation by Matthew Medbourne — in crafting the screen scene. For Morwood, this stage shorthand allows Sheridan to cloak Joseph in "an aura of menacing evil which is in fact altogether absent from his characterization. The whiff of sulphur clings to Molière's Tartuffe."[22] The extent to which Joseph Surface's manipulations are akin to those of his predecessors allows audiences to take him seriously, in Morwood's view, even though his own efforts are comically undercut by his asides to the audience and by his ineptitude in plotting. Morwood's Joseph Surface, in his "self-aware and humorous soliloquy," reminds us of Plausible Jack: "Sincerely, I begin to wish that I had never made such a point of gaining so very good a character, for it has led me into so many cursed rogueries that I doubt I shall be exposed at last" (2.2.241–44).

It is clear from Lamb's comments on Palmer's performance and from Morwood's reading of the text that Joseph Surface is not meant to be seen as a successful Tom-Double or Mr. Wheedle. His performance is marred by a certain kind of overplaying that allows not only the audience but certain members of the social group depicted in the play, especially the good-hearted Rowley, to see it as performance. Joseph's exposure in the screen scene, too, is not exactly of a piece with the exposures of hypocrites in *Tartuffe* and its derivatives. In order to keep Sir Peter quiet, Joseph must expose himself by inventing the fiction of the French milliner: "Though I hold a man of intrigue to be a most despicable character, yet you know it doesn't follow that one is to be an absolute Joseph either" (4.3.244–46), he quips at Sir Peter's glimpse of a petticoat behind the screen. In response to Charles's goading — "I suppose he would as soon let a priest into the house as a girl" (365–66) — Sir Peter determines to have a good laugh at the "man of sentiment" and let Charles in on the "best of the jest," the "little French milliner" (360, 381–82). As Joseph reenters, of course, Charles pulls down the screen and reveals Lady Teazle.

The effect is richly comic. Charles's remarks have allowed audiences to identify the space behind the screen as a kind of priest-hole as well as the shelter of a troublesome prostitute. The primary irony, once the screen is down, is of course Joseph's exposure and humiliation, but it is Lady Teazle who is frozen before the wondering audience of Charles and Sir Peter. While his shame is a comic topping to his earlier admission of hypocrisy in concocting the story of the French milliner, hers comes from her conflation with that image while she hides behind the screen. Not just Joseph's guilty secret, she is a moral agent in her own right and has contrived, with Joseph's help, her own shame. The dynamic of self-exposure is yet more complex, for behind the screen Lady Teazle has learned of Sir Peter's generous plans to provide her with an independent income. So while Joseph is doubly exposed as a comic hypocrite, and Lady Teazle is humiliated and exposed in her novice intrigue, Sir Peter passes a theatrical test and exposes his good nature as Lady Teazle witnesses his generosity from behind the screen. "[Y]our own arts have furnished her the means," she tells Joseph of her recovery of her senses in her final speech in the scene:

> — Sir Peter, I do not expect you to credit me; but the tenderness you expressed for me, when I am sure you could not think I was witness to it, has penetrated to my heart. And, had I left the place without the shame of this discovery, my future life should have spoke the sincerity of my gratitude. As for that smooth-tongue hypocrite, who would have seduced the wife of his too credulous friend, while he affected honourable addresses to his ward, I behold him in a light so truly despicable, that I shall never again respect myself for having listened to him. (437–47)

The screen plays multiple roles as it functions to expose both Joseph's duplicity and Sir Peter's integrity.

For Lady Teazle, her reduction to French milliner and butt of Charles's and Sir Peter's coarse jokes provides a kind of sentimental education. She learns from this school what traps the urban social world sets for her innocence. Moral education takes place in the screen scene, not through the undercutting of the already undercut pieties of Joseph's sentimental utterance, but through Lady Teazle's exposure to Sir Peter's benevolence. In this way, Sir Peter's experience mirrors Charles Surface's when — put to the test by his uncle Oliver in the guise of "little Premium" the broker — he inadvertently reveals his good nature and gratitude by keeping back Oliver's picture from the sale of ancestors.

All three Surfaces inhabit, as their name insists, a highly theatricalized social world in which all play roles that shield their private selves from scandalous gossip. Joseph ports the sentimental mask to conceal his plots; Charles plays the role of prodigal, deflecting scandal by flouting it; and Sir Oliver, in his testing roles as Premium and Mr. Stanley, the distressed relative, seems to feel that concealment of his true identity is a necessary prerequisite to reentry into this world. That good nature triumphs through its inadvertent self-exposures marks the boundary between the play-world of *The School for Scandal* and the real world of the moralists, in which self-exposure provides a banquet of follies for Mr. Wheedle.

The multiple exposures in *School for Scandal* allow audiences to laugh at the sentimental language of Joseph Surface. As a sentimentalist, he is a late comic parody of the type of virtuous character first glimpsed in Cibber's and Steele's comedies of the early eighteenth century. (It is difficult, however, to know how seriously to take the sentimentalists of these plays: after all, Charlotte Charke played the role of Bevil Junior in *The Conscious Lovers* with great success.) To the complexities of the screen scene compare a scene of exposure and humiliation from Cibber's *The Careless Husband*. The play's seventh edition (1731) features a frontispiece that illustrates act 5, scene 5. Here Lady Easy discovers her husband, Sir Charles Easy, *"without his periwig"* (stage direction; in the illustration the periwig lies on the floor by his chair), sleeping in one armchair and her maid, Edging, in another. She knows what to make of this scene; but *"unable to speak"* for some time, she hesitates. Perhaps, she finally decides, she will "wake him in his guilt, / And barefaced front him with my wrongs"; upon better consideration, however, she decides to leave him be and let "heav'n" be the judge. The periwig's absence, though, gives her pause: perhaps "heav'n, offended, may o'er-take his crime, / And in some languishing distemper, leave him / A se-vere example of its violated laws" (5.5.7–8, 20, 23–25). So that Sir Charles will not take a chill, she removes her "*steinkirk off her neck*" and places it on his head. Another engraving from the period indicates her solicitous care in close-up. When he awakens, he is justly shamed and marvels at her virtue.

This is the kind of scene that Paul E. Parnell finds most characteris-tic of what, in an influential article, he calls "The Sentimental Mask." Lady Easy's solution to her problem is not just a dramatic visual re-minder to her husband of her knowledge of his sin and her forgiveness. Through the means of the steinkirk, the white lace neckcloth that she takes from her neck and places on his head, she transforms him into a kind of bride with a lace veil and reaffirms her own chastity by expos-ing her bosom like an unmarried girl. Instead of showering him with reproaches, she stages a scene in which his own self-reproach is the only possible response. Such a strategy leads Parnell to embark on an attack not only upon characters in the sentimental comedies of Cibber and Richard Steele but also upon Steele himself. To Parnell, Steele and the sentimentalists he created for the stage are of a piece: "Steele, like most sentimentalists, is playing a double game," says Parnell of a letter that Steele wrote asking for a job: "he wants to think of himself as continu-ously virtuous, and he wants to get the job too." This involves the sen-timentalist, according to Parnell, in a continuous process of redefini-tion and rationalization that works toward "its designed effect: a clear-ing of his conscience and a conviction of his own sinlessness and altru-ism." "Thus," Parnell concludes, "sentimental thinking is balanced del-icately between hypocrisy and sincerity, simplicity and duplicity, self-consciousness and spontaneity."[23] Lady Easy's gesture, like Steele's job letter, shows the sentimentalist to be communicating his or her virtue to the object of that virtue. But, and this is what troubles Parnell, the sentimentalist also communicates the belief that his or her virtue is unassailable — and, indeed, in Cibber's play Sir Charles Easy does reform.

The term *sentimental* is a vexed one, and late-eighteenth-century dramatists like Sheridan and Oliver Goldsmith sought to distance themselves as much as possible from the charge of sentimentalism. But there is much in common between the demonstrations and exposures of virtue and hypocrisy in *School for Scandal* and *The Careless Husband*.

Such demonstrations, Ann Jessie Van Sant has recently argued, have much to do with the rise of scientific exploration of the nature of sensation and feeling in the period. Van Sant has sought to disentangle the threads linking sensibility to sentimentalism. "Both were important terms in the general shift of the foundation of moral life from reason and judgment to the emotions," she explains, while *sensibility* tended to refer to the body and *sentiment* to thought and verbal expression. "This alignment of moral thought with feeling was sometimes regarded as spurious and was the source of satire on both sentimentalism and sensibility."[24] Sensibility she defines as "an organic sensitivity" that inheres in body, brain, and nerves: this kind of acuteness of feeling cannot be feigned, although it may be temporarily concealed (as Charles Surface conceals his goodness of heart beneath a veneer of rakishness). But the expression of this kind of acuteness of feeling in moral sentiments — the generalizations that characterize Joseph Surface's discourse and animate the sober sentimental interview in Goldsmith's *She Stoops to Conquer* — is widely open to parody and ridicule.

Parnell, while he links himself with this tradition of satirizing the sentimentalist and ridicules Cibber and Steele, insists upon an important difference between his figure and the figure of the hypocrite. "The sentimentalist spends half his time justifying his morally ambiguous actions and the other half exclaiming over the beauties of Christian virtue, including his own. But, although the process of rationalization is more or less conscious, the sentimentalist is so determined to convince himself, and so successful, that he cannot be called a hypocrite. He may share with the hypocrite a determination to keep his opportunism intact; but, unlike the person of conscious duplicity, he feels obliged to wear at all times the sentimental mask" ("The Sentimental Mask," 535). Parnell here contrasts a "naïve" hypocrite, Joseph Surface, who conceals behavior which he knows to be wrong, to another kind of hypocrite, Parnell's sentimentalist, who, like Lady Easy, is not conscious of any duplicity: she simply knows her own moral superiority to her husband. She puts the steinkirk on his head not to shame him or embarrass him: rather she convinces herself that she is doing it for his own good, so that he will not catch a chill and become a casualty of his careless behavior. Both types coexist in the early modern period. Joseph Surface, who knows he is vicious but pretends to be virtuous, has his roots in Tartuffe. Lady Easy's decision to indicate her knowledge of his adultery indirectly to Sir Charles and (through the steinkirk) to communicate to him her forgiveness in advance marks her within the context of Cibber's play as wholly virtuous. But to Parnell the act reeks of bad faith.

The classic hypocrites pretend to be good while knowing themselves to be evil, the early modern preachers remind us. But they, too, were worried about the problem of hypocrites who did not know what they were doing, who were dishonest not only to others but also to themselves. Bishop Bourdaloue, in his sermon on hypocrisy, struggled with the problem of self-deception; and Bishop Joseph Butler, in his sermons, determined "internal hypocrisy" of this kind to be the result of self-absorption or self-ignorance.[25] Joseph Surface, as played by Jack Palmer in Lamb's account, is an external hypocrite, like Tartuffe; the screen scene exposes his hypocrisy both before (in the tale of the little French milliner) and after the falling of the screen. An internal hypocrite, of Butler's type, is exposed in the scene, too: Lady Teazle is caught in her own self-deception. Embroiling herself in Joseph's intrigue is less shameful to her than lying to herself about it.

"Bad faith" in Sartre's terminology is of a piece with Bourdaloue's and Butler's notions of internal hypocrisy, a kind of lying to oneself, "hiding a displeasing truth or presenting as truth a pleasing untruth."[26] For Parnell, the protagonists of the sentimental comedy, in their demonstrations of their superior virtue, epitomize this kind of bad faith; Steele himself is guilty of the crime of lying to himself about himself. In *School for Scandal* Lady Teazle's motives for coming to Joseph's rooms are put into question. She is troubled by her husband's suspicions of her, yet her visit raises questions about her "consciousness of [her] own innocence." The phrase is comically highlighted in Joseph's seduction speech:

> Ah, dear madam, there is the great mistake. 'Tis this very consciousness of innocence that is of the greatest prejudice to you. What is it makes you negligent of forms and careless of the world's opinion? Why, the consciousness of your innocence. What makes you thoughtless of your conduct and apt to run into a thousand little imprudences? Why, the consciousness of your innocence. What makes you impatient of Sir Peter's temper and outrageous at his suspicions? Why, the consciousness of your innocence. (4.3.61–70)

"'Tis very true," Lady Teazle admits; but, as she confesses to Sir Peter after the screen has fallen, she had indeed come "at least to listen to his pretended passion, if not to sacrifice your honour to his baseness." "Now I believe the truth is coming indeed," says Sir Peter. "The woman's mad," expostulates Joseph (433–36). Lady Teazle has the virtues of a person of sensibility — her blushes disclose it — not a framer of sentiments. While Joseph Surface is only a sentimentalist on the surface — he fails Parnell's test and plays his double game consciously — Lady Teazle appears to be not just an innocent dupe, like her predecessors in *L'Ecole des femmes* and *The Country Wife*, but a case of an internal hypocrite who has learned the cost of self-deceit.

Lady Teazle, of course, is not one of the sober sentimentalists of Steele's drama; nor is she an apostle of Rousseauean antitheatrical antihypocrisy. Sheridan's play is, after all, a "school" play, and she is a student. As "licentiate" she bids farewell to Lady Sneerwell's "scandalous college" and "begs leave to return the diploma they granted her" (5.3.201–5); what she has learned from Charles Surface (for he takes down the screen) is a strategy of indirection, a playfulness that conceals the sincerity of her love for Sir Peter. The members of the scandalous college spoof a vision of society that Bellegarde takes seriously, full of backbiting Tom-Doubles. But Charles and Maria and Lady Teazle represent a generation led by their hearts.

In the epilogue to *School for Scandal* Frances Abington, who created the role of Lady Teazle, echoes Othello and Prospero: "Farewell! Your revels I partake no more," she declaims, evoking a satirical picture of the country life to which she must now retire:

And Lady Teazle's occupation's o'er!
All this I told our bard. He smil'd and said 'twas clear
I ought to play deep tragedy next year.
Meanwhile he drew wise morals from his play
And in these solemn periods stalked away.
"Blessed were the fair, like you her faults who stopped,
And closed her follies when the curtain dropped!
No more in vice or error to engage,
Or play the fool at large on life's great stage."

Coleman's epilogue is richly complex. The high-toned quotations from Shakespeare run from the extended quotation from *Othello* through allusions to *The Tempest* and *Hamlet* ("It is offended," say the guards in the first scene of the ghost; "See, it stalks away"[1.1.54]) and to *Lear*'s great stage of fools. As usual, the conventions of the epilogue blur the distinction between Lady Teazle retreating to the country and Mrs. Abington demonstrating her gift for tragic declamation. A further joke rests in the actress's contention that she should switch to "deep tragedy": "Like many of her profession," John Taylor put it, Mrs. Abington "thought herself capable of characters not within the scope of her powers. I once saw her play Ophelia to Mr. Garrick's Hamlet; and to use the simile of my old friend Dr. Monsey, she appeared like a mackerel on a gravel walk."[27] The dropping of the curtain refers of course to the screen scene as well as to the imminent drop of the curtain after Mrs. Abington's speech. (That Frances Abington herself, prior to her engagement as a player, had been in service to a French milliner in Cockspur Street adds to the screen scene's ironies.) The epilogue reopens the issue of possible problems with the Teazle marriage as Lady Teazle, playing Othello, echoes her husband's jealous worries. The solemn, sentimental periods attributed to "our bard" mock the notion that "wise morals" can be drawn from this play at all. And why? Because leaving the town for the country, as the Teazles plan to do, or the stage for "life's great stage," as Mrs. Abington is about to do, is no guarantee of an end to folly.

When Mrs. Abington played tragedy, she was a fish out of water, ridiculously miscast. Making himself ridiculous by striving to be taken seriously constitutes the fate of Molière's Alceste, both understood as a comic figure and most poignantly as understood by Rousseau. Rousseau's distress at the pervasive bad faith and feminization of culture that he attributes to theater comes from a desire to make theater as unlike real life as possible, linked with a concomitant awareness of the impossibility of that quest. Commentators on Rousseau like Judith Shklar and Arthur M. Melzer argue that this sense of not belonging, of self-alienation, is a key if not *the* key aspect of modernity. G. W. F. Hegel, too, as Shklar points out, describes the world of the modern bourgeois as one in which hypocrisy prevails. And the "bad faith" which Sartre singles out further emphasizes this linkage of self-deception with self-delusive acting. Mrs. Abington thinks she can play tragedy; the result is all the more comic and pathetic because she does not know how ridiculous she is making herself in the effort.

The modern obsession with sincerity, the fact that "above everything else, we loathe hypocrisy, cherish self-disclosure, and long to be ourselves," as Melzer puts it, derives from the self-contradictory roles that society requires of its members. "In sum, the modern commercial republic, generating sociability from selfishness, necessarily creates a society of smiling enemies, where each individual pretends to care about others precisely because he cares only about himself," Melzer argues. What makes the modern bourgeois simultaneously ridiculous (and the object of the moralistic scorn that Parnell visits upon the sentimentalist) and pathetic is that this contradiction cannot be resolved through social performance. Authenticity, as Alceste claims in wooing Célimène to join him in the desert, requires withdrawal from society, rejection of performance: so it never can be demonstrated or displayed. "Rousseau's main argument," Melzer states, "is indeed that modern society builds on a massive contradiction: it is based on individualism, and for this very reason it destroys all sincere individuality. Both sides of this contradiction combine, in Rousseau, to produce an intense and redoubled longing for individuality — an obsession with sincerity." What was countercultural—Alceste's stubborn forthrightness— becomes the dominant culture: "Today, everyone denounces conformity and longs for sincerity."[28] Rousseau, Hegel, and Sartre sought to characterize a new kind of hypocrite who differed from the old-style hypocrite in being false not only to others but to herself.

Scene Three

IBSEN'S SMALL STAGE OF FOOLS

There is no playwright in the drama more notorious for exposing self-delusion than Ibsen, whose assaults upon bourgeois pieties combine a strategy of ruthless comic exposure with a full sense of the human cost exacted when the call of the sincere ideal clashes with the lies that make life possible. And Ibsen most frequently characterizes the dilemma by means of the theatrical tropes of being miscast, of finding oneself in a script or play that is in the wrong genre. Nora's famous decision to leave Torvald at the end of *A Doll's House* stems from her discovery that the rules of well-made drama — in which Torvald would nobly sacrifice himself for her as she has, she imagines, done for him — do not apply in this play's world. *The Wild Duck* introduces itself to its audience, through its first act set and exposition, as a play concerned with the world of the Werles and then goes on, in the remaining four acts set in the Ekdal attic, to show how grotesquely misplaced are Gregers Werle's claims of purgation. "The moment he came, he got his room in beautiful shape," Gina Ekdal points out of Gregers. "He wanted to do everything himself, he said. So he starts building a fire in the stove, and the next thing he's closed down the damper so the whole room is full of smoke. . . . But that's not the best part! So then he wants to put it out, so he empties his whole water pitcher into the stove and now the floor's swimming in the worst muck." [29] Mired in self-contradiction, neither Gregers with his claim of the ideal nor Dr. Relling with his embrace of the life-lies that uphold the status quo understands quite what has gone wrong at the end of the play. Hedvig's literal misreading of the metaphor of the duck brings into the Ekdal attic the "muck" and weeds of entrapment in both social and theatrical intrigue.

The mixture of social and theatrical entrapment is most intensely dialectical in *Hedda Gabler*. Hedda is like Hamlet in being a character imprisoned in a world of hypocritical double-talk and corruption; she is like Tartuffe in the skill with which she manipulates her dupes and in the way she is brought up short in her audacity. Like Molière's Alceste, she misanthropically despises the social set in which she finds herself; and like Rousseau's Alceste, she holds society to a higher standard of authenticity and insists upon fidelity to the claims of her own self. Protean, changeable, theatrical in the extreme, she is like Rousseau's vision of his feminized self in *Le persifleur*. In the character of Hedda, Ibsen dramatizes the modern, self-alienating claims of sincerity.

Metatheatrically, in the play that bears Hedda's name, Ibsen dramatizes the way the normal conventions of nineteenth-century drama betray the self-contradictory nature of these claims. *Hedda Gabler* looks like, and has frequently been mistaken for, a problem-play typical of its period — an exploration of a social problem troubling and disturbing to the complacency of its bourgeois audience. Its mode is realistic; its action takes place within a drawing room; costumes — like Auntie Julie's hat — perform the necessary function of providing us with social distinctions. A woman of aristocratic background has married into the distinctly middle-class, middle-brow family of a pedantic professor. Her resistance to assimilation is reflected in her refusal to take the name of Mrs. Tesman, in her decision to ridicule her aunt-in-law's new hat, and in her violent rejection of the fact of her own pregnancy. Described in these terms, Ibsen's play becomes a specimen of nineteenth-century realistic social drama, a play like his rival Bjørnstjerne Bjørnson's *The Newlyweds* (1865), in which such resistance to marriage arises from the woman's awareness of a double standard and awakening to feminist consciousness. As Joan Templeton has pointed out, critics from the earliest to the most recent have had trouble reconciling the character of Hedda with this formula.[30]

But there is no proposal in Ibsen's play of a way to solve the problem, no obligatory discussion-scene (unless we count the curious discussion of the railway carriage between Hedda and Judge Brack). Hedda simply assumes that the audience understands her grievance. Like Hamlet, she attacks the notion of theatrical mimesis by demanding that we judge her not by what she does but by what she is. What she resists is not so much the ludicrous sentimentality of Auntie Julie and the horrid possessiveness of Tesman as the whole shape of the play in which she finds herself.

On Hedda's first entrance, she criticizes the open window (which

Aunt Julie has just opened), disparages the flowers brought by Aunt Julie, plays the famous joke with Aunt Julie's hat, and is well on her way to total victory when Tesman brings her up short by pointing out how much she has "filled out" (704). To Brian Johnston, this entrance is like the beginning of a military campaign, in which "frustrated minor skirmishes" like this one lead to Hedda's recruitment, in Løvborg, of an "army by means of which to mount a major attack." Johnston carries the military metaphor further, seeing Hedda as a virtual prisoner of war: the accouterments of the Tesmans' "small, stifling, benevolently mediocre world . . . have taken possession of her as a plebian [*sic*] mob in Rome might have acquired a defeated empress."[31] Johnston is known for his radical reading of Ibsen's prose plays as literally depicting the phases of spiritual development in Hegel's *Phenomenology*; but an obvious echo of Hegel here is the incorporation of Hegel's characterization of the modern world as beset by a new kind of hypocrisy. "Hegel thought there had been a change in the quality of hypocrisy that made it peculiarly repulsive," Judith Shklar comments. "The new hypocrite simply adjusts his conscience by ascribing noble, disinterested, and altruistic intentions to his behavior," she notes in her summary of Hegel's argument about hypocrisy. "He is the sole instructor of his own conscience." The new hypocrites idolize sincerity, prizing truth to self above all. "At most," Shklar concludes, "these sincere folk might from time to time confess to their only possible moral failure: the betrayal of their real inner self. . . . Hegel apparently expected these habits to become universal, and he saw before him an unchecked anarchy of puffed-up hypocrites."[32]

In his earlier plays Ibsen presents just such an anarchy: *Pillars of Society* and *Enemy of the People* are crowded with puffed-up hypocrites proclaiming their selfless pursuit of duty. But after *Wild Duck* even those who point out the complacencies and falsehoods of the bourgeois world are not free from Ibsen's scrutiny: Gregers Werle's claim of the ideal is exposed as a life-lie of the same order as Hjalmar Ekdal's fantasies. Hedda not only wages war against the forces of self-deceiving self-righteousness in Tesman, his aunts, and Berte the aged retainer but will herself be exposed as self-deceived. The action of the first small scene is paradigmatic of the action of the play as a whole: Hedda's vigorous resistance to being assimilated into the Tesman family reflects her larger resistance to any kind of human relationship. Aunt Julie's sudden change of heart — "(*with quiet feeling*). I won't let a day go by without looking in on you two" (705) — foreshadows ironically the utter futility of Hedda's aloofness. Whether Hedda chooses to be a Tesman or not doesn't matter: Auntie Julie's shrewd guess that she is carrying a little Tesman undercuts Hedda's play of freedom.

Left alone, "raising her arms and clenching her fists as if in a frenzy," Hedda "flings back the curtains from the glass door and stands there, looking out" (705). We see an actor trapped in a box-set, in a drawing-room world of colliding intrigues and social imperatives, yearning for a release that the form of the play itself forbids. "The cobra strikes, and misses," memorably says Muriel Bradbrook. Raymond Williams borrows T. S. Eliot's famous description of *The Jew of Malta* to dub the genre of *Hedda Gabler* "savage farce."[33] Jens Arup, who translated the play for *The Oxford Ibsen*, describes it as a mixture of melodrama and farce, "theatrical in the extreme": "*Hedda Gabler* includes melodrama and farce, elements that against the delicately balanced background of allusion seem outrageous." "The unity of the play," he concludes, "seems rather to depend upon a most elusive balance of elements often apparently discordant, than to arise from any unity of theme."[34] In Arup's translation Hedda herself seems aware that she is locked into a generic incongruity: coming as close as she ever will to informing Tesman of her pregnancy, she cries out: "Oh, it'll kill me, it'll kill me, all this!" "All what, Hedda? Eh?" asks the doltish professor. "All this . . . farce . . . Jorgen."[35] Tesman, of course, is oblivious to her despair, although she is once again clenching her fists, and rejoices that she at last has condescended to use his first name.

Describing the moment at the end in which Thea produces from her pockets the notes for Ejlert Løvborg's book, Ibsen almost chortles in his notes: "Then comes the burlesque touch: both T. and Mrs. E. devote their lives to solving the riddle." Tesman and Mrs. Elvsted seem to be made for each other as they sit down to work on the book in the last act. All of Hedda's manipulations of amorous triangles have come to this, a reunion between her husband and his old flame, whom he cannot keep from calling by her maiden name. "Life is not tragic — Life is ridiculous — And that cannot be borne," runs Ibsen's note on Hedda's suicide.[36]

If Ibsen permits Hedda the luxury of an own self at all, it is by means of a metaphor of the stage. As the play unfolds, items of special importance to Hedda — her piano, her dueling pistols, her father's portrait — come to be visible in the inner room. This alcove becomes

Hedda's private chamber, and it is to this room that she retreats at the play's end. She mocks her husband's speech tic, passes her hand lightly through Thea's hair, and exchanges a final glance with Judge Brack. She closes the curtains and plays a wild dance tune. As the music sounds from within her alcove, we see a bizarre family tableau: Thea and Tesman peacefully at work, the Judge serenely seated in the armchair, contemplating a future full of adulterous opportunities with Mrs. Tesman. Hedda's intransigence, however, animates the music itself, and Tesman is forced to invoke the decorum of mourning to get her to stop. Impishly, Hedda puts her head out between the drawn curtains of her inner room; her last appearance is as a head peeping from the inner stage, occupying the same space in the center of the upstage wall as the General's portrait. For Thomas Whitaker, Hedda's position here "mirrors our own: behind the curtains opposite our fourth wall."[37] Through the fourth wall, in other words, we look upon a drawing-room that itself looks upon (or is looked upon by) a stage. The drawn curtain transforms the characters on stage into a bourgeois audience so conventional that the significance of the death will elude them. "Shot herself in the temple! Can you imagine!" shrieks Tesman, drawing back the curtain. "But good God! People don't *do* such things!" gasps Judge Brack, *"prostrated"* in his chair (778). Hedda has left this small stage of fools for an even smaller one of her own making.

To argue that Hedda in her death converts her "defeat into a moment of subversive, militant *beauty*, retreating loftily into her inner room to die," as Brian Johnston has put it, is to sentimentalize this ending. In Johnston's Hegelian master-narrative, Hedda represents the "Hellenic values of beauty and joy-of-life," as they engage in dialectical struggle with the repressive forces of Christianity, so the ending becomes by definition tragic.[38] And the temptation to grant her a kind of integrity, like the temptation to agree with Fortinbras that Hamlet would have made a good king, is powerful. "Ibsen presents Hedda as in the most marginal sense a hero," John Northam has argued. "Marginal because every affirmation by her and about her is contradicted by contrary affirmations. Contradicted but not denied. She is a heroine pared to the bone, stripped of moral force, of forthrightness, of courage in the accepted sense, of positive action; she is muddled, inarticulate, destructive, trivial, and yet. . . . We can respect her hard and late-won integrity for those very reasons. For it is demonstrated in circumstances which seem to make any degree of integrity impossible."[39]

These circumstances, agree the political philosophers and moralists we have invoked (Rousseau, Bishop Butler, Bellegarde), are those of social life. And the paradox acted out in Hedda's embroilment in scandal — that her striving for dominion over others leads her deeper and deeper into subjection — underscores Bellegarde's vision of civil society as a kind of kidnapping. The audience may not "scoff over her corpse," as Hermann Weigand put it, but Johnston's or Northam's hero-worship seems equally unappealing.[40]

Hedda's nascent awareness that she is cast in a "farce" whose rules are antipathetic to her need for autonomous selfhood gives her an added, Rousseauean, antitheatrical dimension. And the final scene itself underscores the point by itself taking the form of the melodrama it satirizes. Indeed, it does so with such success that many commentators such as Ronald Gray have seen it not as a parody of melodrama but as the thing itself: "[T]he scene resembles a Victorian melodrama in which the maiden takes her life rather than suffer a fate worse than death," Gray huffs his "dissenting view" of Ibsen.[41] In refusing to see any difference between Ibsen's ending and, say, the ending of *The Second Mrs. Tanqueray*, Gray inadvertently reveals the full force of Ibsen's satire: the world Hedda is trapped in is utterly indistinguishable from the debased worlds of the popular entertainments of melodrama and farce.

Gay Gibson Cima has recently argued that the actor in the role of Hedda exposes a larger truth about melodrama and popular entertainment. Performing Hedda in the late nineteenth century reveals "the performance of gender as a series of repeated melodramatic acts." According to Cima, early audiences saw such Hedda Gablers as Elizabeth Robins in three ways: "(1) as an actor; (2) as the character; and (3) as the role the character plays. The third layer, the actor's creation of Hedda's awareness of the absurdity of the role she plays, is what constituted, for female actors and audience members, a new subversive lever in the theatre." Robins herself, a successful author of problem-plays with progressive themes — *Votes for Women* has recently been anthologized — found Hedda to be delightfully transgressive: her "UNPARDONABLE SENSE OF HUMOR," Robins claimed, led to her downfall.[42]

Generically, Hedda would of course prefer to be in a tragedy, as her references to Dionysian vine leaves and interest in Løvborg's revels suggest. And some critics, like Northam, would offer her a hero's burial.

But the antitheatrical vein in *Hedda Gabler* runs deeper than this. Ibsen not only imprisons his heroine within the constrictions of popular entertainment but also entraps her in a vision of tragedy that proves elusive. The critics who admire Hedda in her death do so because she demands, through the play, identification with an aristocratic esthetic associated with the General's portrait, the piano, the pistols, and the duel. Her wishful casting of Løvborg in the role of duelist — first as she imagines him in conflict with Tesman for the university post and then as she arms him and sends him out to achieve a beautiful death — leads to her assumption of the role herself: she achieves the mode of death, the Lermontovian bullet in the temple, that he fails to achieve. She arrogates an aristocratic masculinity to herself that leaves Tesman and Brack gasping with incredulity.[43] But the pregnancy undercuts this masculinity just as it does her repudiation of any intimacy with Tesman either in the Tyrol or here, where, according to Hedda, he has "no opportunity for anything" (704). Hedda's enlistment of Løvborg as true companion and proxy tragic hero, who will return at ten o'clock with vine leaves in his hair, ensnares her in a substitution that will ultimately lead to failure and require her to fulfill the role of scapegoat in the sacrificial rite she imagines.

The spectacular degree to which Løvborg fails Hedda makes it impossible to see her taking on of the scapegoat role as triumphant in any way. In fact, the deployment of Løvborg on his final mission is parodically reminiscent of the voyeuristic days, under the General's watchful eye, of Ejlert's confessions and Hedda's absolutions, their "companionship in a thirst for life," as he somewhat unfortunately describes it (739). Løvborg's bohemianism is sordid and degrading, not mythically ennobling, as the Mademoiselle Diana jokes make clear. He is not an Actaeon entering a bower, but a dissatisfied customer returning to a brothel. Hedda's ignorance in these matters leads her to a romanticizing of Løvborg which founders: "searching for Dionysus," quips G. Wilson Knight, "he finds himself in a police-station."[44] The play's network of allusions to heroic self-definition and sacrifice is part of its wider critique of theatrical mimesis. Whatever Hedda's role might be — as linchpin in an adulterous farce, as Brack envisions, as melodramatic villainess, as Løvborg suspects, as tragic heroine, as she would wish — there is no fit with any theatrical model; nor is there a sense that an alternative model can be provided.

This matrix of inadequate and insulting theatrical models that frames Hedda makes it possible for us to see her as Rousseau's modern type or as one of Hegel's self-deceiving hypocrites. Joan Templeton chides her for failing to be true to her own self: "Hedda's notion that she would be less unhappy if Tesman were a cabinet minister is akin to the self-deceiving reasoning of what she termed the 'bargain' of her marriage, her giving her self in return for financial security and social standing." "What Hedda reckons with in neither case," Templeton continues in a Rousseauean vein, "are her feelings."[45] Her claim of aristocracy is everywhere shown to be snobbish, mean, and petty; and the audience is given as much liberty to imagine that Løvborg's second book is as mediocre as his first (after all, Tesman admires it). Hedda's insistence on her own integrity and inviolability, the precious value she places on her own self, derives from a Rousseauean misanthropy — unlike Alceste, she really is surrounded by dolts — that might lead to a retreat into the counterculture or bohemia in Melzer's words. But Ibsen is ahead of her here, too, satirizing even the bohemian, even the notion of escape, in Løvborg's ridiculous death and in Hedda's almost petulant decision to amend it by putting the bullet in the right place. Like Hamlet or Alceste, Hedda claims an authority, a self-knowledge, and a right to self-definition that are heroic and that set her apart from the social world. Ibsen's satiric mode, however, makes it clear that in the highly theatricalized social world she inhabits there is no escape from theatrical self-representation. Alceste keeps leaving the room: the play opens as he is storming out of one irritating social encounter and ends as he storms out of another, and Philinte chases him both times. Molière's misanthrope is caught in a circle of storming out and storming in. Hedda breaks the cycle and, for many, achieves beauty and transcendence. But beauty and transcendence have no place in the world of the play.

Hedda's admirers among critics and audience members participate in a process of creative misreading that is not unlike Rousseau's hero-worship of Alceste and denigration of Philinte. The antitheatrical prizing of the sincere individual, innocently beset by the Tom-Doubles and Wheedles of society, exposes a "massive contradiction," in Melzer's words, that reaches full expression in the manipulative wheedling of Hedda. A conscious performer surrounded by dupes, she attempts to preserve her private integrity by retaining the upper hand, by orchestrating events to her own liking. But she ends up overacting: cackling witchlike over the manuscript as she burns it, playing a wild dance tune to accompany her end. If it is impossible to be a sincere individual and function in society at the same time, as Rousseau and his followers contend, Ibsen presents us with a vision in which theatrical modeling intrudes even into the arena of self-definition. Hedda's romanticizing self-definition relies no less than Tesman's imagination of his "prospects" upon already discredited conventions and genres.

Yet the Rousseauean vigor with which Hedda attacks the conventions that surround her is essential to her appeal. One of the ways that playwrights make characters seem real is to have them condemn the improbable fictions that embroil them. Hedda's dilemma — searching for an authenticity that is not somehow already tainted with the theatrical, the literary, the bogus — leads many to admire her even in her failure. The whole enterprise of subjectivity, as Montaigne pointed out at the very beginning of the early modern period's investigation of the inward, own self, is fraught with danger. "It is no part of a well grounded judgement, simply to judge our selves by our exteriour actions," he ruminates in Florio's Elizabethan translation: "A man must thorowly sound himselfe, and dive into his heart, and there see by what wards or springs the motions stirre. But forsomuch as it is a hazardous and high enterprise, I would not have so many to meddle with it as doe."[46] To see Hedda as an overmatched casualty of a high and hazardous enterprise is not to mock her: Ibsen's delicate balance is to entice us to see her as heroic while showing us the pettiness of her ambitions, the narrowness of her world.

Like Hamlet and like Alceste, vehemently decrying the falsity and theatricality of social performance, Hedda is a character who embodies the paradox of acting. What we should pay attention to, Hamlet insists at the beginning of his play, is what passes show; but theater audiences can only see the actions that the actor before them might play. Michael Goldman sees in Ibsen a terrifying problem for actor and character alike: "In any case, Ibsen's greatest theater texts require that the actor project an inner life that threatens to evacuate, expose, paralyze both performer and character."[47] Diderot in *Paradoxe sur le comédien* offers an early example of the thinking that recognizes this threat to an actor's own self in theater, and the solution from Diderot's point of view is the vision of the actor who is unmoved, self-possessed, emotionally remote from the passions being played. "[O]ne of the paradoxes of the dialogue," says David Marshall, "is that the self-possessed actor advocated by the first interlocutor seems to lack a self to begin with."[48] What

Diderot accepts with a certain amount of aplomb is for Goldman fraught with existential terror. The possibility that Hedda might lack a self, that an actor might lack a self — that social performance might so structure it that we all lack selves — is a fear which draws much of its energy from antitheatricalism. Antitheatricalism holds up against theater the idea of an unperformable selfhood and projects a vision of inviolability. Cluttering his stage world with clunky melodramatic and farce plot structures and tormenting his characters with "a terrifying whirl of unwieldy, mishandled objects (pianos, pistols, photograph albums),"[49] Ibsen puts this idea of inwardnesss to the full dramatic test. One might "lack a self to begin with": Ibsen presents that possibility in its full horror.

Scene Four

PRINCELY HYPOCRITE

Introducing the modern politician to the world stage, Niccolò Machiavelli debunked the traditional — classical and Christian — idea that the good ruler should first be a good man. He catalogs the virtues and then steps back: "A prince, therefore, need not have all of the good qualities mentioned above," he declares, "but he should certainly appear to have them."[50] The Machiavels of the Renaissance stage flaunted their theatricality, as Richard of York does, envisioning his bloody way to the throne in *Henry VI, Part Three*:

> Why, I can smile, and murder whiles I smile,
> And cry "Content" to that which grieves my heart,
> And wet my cheeks with artificial tears,
> And frame my face to all occasions.
> I'll drown more sailors than the mermaid shall;
> I'll slay more gazers than the basilisk;
> I'll play the orator as well as Nestor,
> Deceive more slyly than Ulysses could,
> And, like a Sinon, take another Troy.
> I can change colors to the chameleon,
> Change shapes with Proteus for advantages,
> And set the murderous Machiavel to school.
>
> (3.2.182–93)

In his Protean exuberance, Richard is an old-style hypocrite; well aware that he is a villain, he takes advantage of the openness and honesty of others. Mr. Wheedle — like Joseph Surface and Hedda Gabler — practices his chameleon and Protean craft in the domestic sphere. Richard aspires to play the orator on a bigger, public stage.

Rousseau, as we have seen, is the architect of a vision of public life as a kind of violation of the private self. The career of Shakespeare's Prince Hal, in the plays in which we find him (*1 Henry IV, 2 Henry IV,* and *Henry V*), anticipates this shift of focus, as Shakespeare evokes the powerful moral language of antitheatricalism to explore his character's movement toward full commitment to public life. Critics of the plays, too, expose the depth of antitheatricalism's penetration of the modern moral vocabulary as they attempt to classify and judge the actions of Hal — is his reform authentic, sincere, or staged? The two late-twentieth-century film treatments of *Henry V*, finally, throw into relief this post-Rousseauean privileging of the private and distaste for public life.

"Presume not that I am the thing I was," King Henry V, no longer the familiar Prince Hal, tells Falstaff. "For God doth know, so shall the world perceive, / That I have turn'd away my former self" (*2 Henry IV,* 5.5.56–58). Many critics have been vexed about the nature of the "former self" that he tells Falstaff he has turned away. The bald declaration of Hal's agenda in the soliloquy in *Part One,* certainly, makes it clear that Hal has never been *really* in thrall to Falstaff, never really a member of the criminal rout at the tavern. In *Part Two* he wearily wastes his time with them. When he "please[s] again to be himself," he tells us, he will "imitate the sun" (*1 Henry IV,* 1.2.194, 191): but if he has not been himself in the tavern, who has he been? What was he doing?

"Go, you thing, go!" Falstaff dismisses the hostess in *Part One.* "Say, what thing? what thing?" she cries, and when Sir John calls her a beast, she pursues the issue: "Say, what beast, thou knave thou?" "What beast? Why, an otter." "An otter, Sir John," Prince Hal interrupts. "Why an otter?" "Why? She's neither fish nor flesh; a man knows not where to have her" (3.3.116–29). Yet it is not the hostess but Hal who has just shown himself to be the amphibian in the play. Here he has just returned from the scene in which he convinced his father of his loyalty and zeal. He is flourishing in both of his environments, the tavern and the court.

The amphibian has its own complex range of suggestion. "Poor monster," Viola pronounces herself, neither man nor woman; her brother, lost at sea, was last glimpsed "like Arion on the dolphin's back," in amphibious linkage (*Twelfth Night,* 2.2.34; 1.2.15). Ophelia, briefly, floats "mermaidlike" — "Or like a creature native and endued / Unto that element" — until her clothes pull her down (*Hamlet,* 4.7.177, 180). A "mermaid on a dolphin's back" sings the rude sea civil in *A Midsummer Night's Dream* (2.1.150); less pleasantly, Caliban emits a "very ancient and fishlike smell" as he hides — "a man or a fish?" — under his gabardine (*The Tempest* 2.2.26, 25). Nor is this fascination with amphibious beings — dolphins,[51] otters, mermaids, mermen — unique to Shakespeare in this period. Sir Dauphine (pronounced like *dolphin*) Eugenie finds himself among a riot of amphibians in the list of persons in Ben Jonson's *Epicoene*, along with Madame Centaure and Sir Thomas Otter, "a land and sea captain." Mistress Quickly vigorously repudiates the name of otter in *1 Henry IV*, falling into Falstaff's trap: "Thou or any man knows where to have me, thou knave, thou!" (3.3.129–30).

No one knows where to have Viola, who strikes a homiletic note, blaming her attractive outside, her masculine garb: "Disguise, I see, thou art a wickedness / Wherein the pregnant enemy does much" (2.2.27–28). Her sentiment here is in sympathy with the antitheatrical writings of the period, with their rejection of disguise and repudiation of the amphibious boy actors of the public stage. More vigorously aligned with that tradition of antitheatrical thinking is Jonson's representation of Morose's house of babble, a cacophonous theater in which the key revelation turns on the person of the boy actor himself. Hal, however, until he repudiates "the thing I was," seems content to be an otter; like Francis the apprentice shuttling from one room to another, he is continually promising "Anon, anon," while shuttling between his two worlds.

The linkage between the otter, the "thing" that Hal was, and the boy actor points toward an indeterminacy in Hal. Like the boy actor or the apprentice, he is at a liminal phase of his development, neither fish nor flesh. As such, he joins the ranks of dubious creatures that populate the tracts of antitheatrical moralists — Protei, polypi, and chameleons. Hal's repudiation of the "thing" he was, of his festive or amphibious other self, postulates an unknowable real self, a true self, that has been concealed throughout his two plays and that may, indeed, remain unknowable in *Henry V*. The unease we feel about the Protean Hal, like the unease evoked by the unreal Hedda in her realistic play, is an unease about theatrical mimesis, written into the plays themselves. To the extent that Hal is a kind of otter, a cipher like Viola into whom significances can all too easily be read, criticism of Hal and of his reformation has tended rather to reveal the critics' attitudes toward mimesis than to pin down Hal's elusive essence.

While Prince Hamlet rejects utterly the proposition that a true self, an own self, can be publicly known, Prince Hal wants to be known most fully in his public self. "I do; I will," Hal announces in the Boar's Head tavern when Falstaff urges him that to "banish plump Jack" is to "banish all the world" (*1 Henry IV*, 2.4.475–76). There is nothing of Hamlet's riddling uncertainty in the expression of this resolve. Hal has fully prepared the audience in the theater (as opposed to his drunken onstage audience) for his resolution in his famous first-act soliloquy:

> I know you all, and will awhile uphold
> The unyoked humor of your idleness.
> Yet herein will I imitate the sun,
> Who doth permit the base contagious clouds
> To smother up his beauty from the world,
> That when he please again to be himself,
> Being wanted he may be more wondered at,
> By breaking through the foul and ugly mists
> Of vapors that did seem to strangle him.
>
> (1.2.189–97)

Hamlet envisions self-revelation as impossible, but Prince Hal sees it as a cosmic *coup-de-théâtre* in which he will reveal himself to be at one with his iconic image, as the blessed sun of heaven, the son of England, the prodigal son returned — as, in short, the resolution of that impossible paradox, a Christian king. In his first soliloquy he proposes a narrative, a way of seeing his career, that transforms him into the answer to history's desire for fully legitimate authority.

Legitimation, Hayden White has argued, is specifically the task of history in the theory of Hegel. "Only in a State cognizant of laws," Hegel wrote, "can distinct transactions take place, accompanied by such clear consciousness of them as supplies the ability and suggests the necessity of an enduring record." As White paraphrases it, "the reality that lends itself to narrative representation is the conflict between desire and the law." Historical studies, by Hegel's definition, have a specific subject matter: "those momentous collisions between existing, acknowledged duties, laws, and rights, and those contingencies that are adverse to this fixed system." In Hegelian terms, the project of historical narrative is the legitimizing of authority, the self-definition of the state.[52]

But Hal is not Hegel, and historical narrative and popular drama are different genres. His method, we note (and not for the first time, for critics like Anne Righter and James Calderwood have led the way here), is theatrical.[53] Upholding the unyoked humor of idleness is what professional actors do: Hal will present himself as a surprise not only to his erstwhile companions but also to the audience. "I'll so offend to make offense a skill," he promises, "Redeeming time when men think least I will" (1.2.210–11). The skillful acting of offensive behavior is what attracts the audience's eyes to the public stage. When Hal says, "I know you all," the actor speaks through the character directly to us. Hal knows what we want — a fully fledged vision of a triumphant, true prince — and he knows how to give it to us. "By how much better than my word I am, / By so much shall I falsify men's hopes" (204–6): this description of Hal's strategy suggests an element of fraud. The hopes he will falsify, of course, are those of his criminal friends (Falstaff's name echoes in the line itself). But he will also surprise and dazzle his audience, falsifying expectations to the extent that the expectations themselves fall short in imagining their consummation.

Hal achieves his objective of appearing in iconographic or emblematic triumph in a surprising way. It is in the rebel camp that we see his first convert. Hotspur asks Vernon, who has just returned from a parley with the royal forces, where Hal is, "the nimble-footed madcap Prince of Wales, / And his comrades, that daff'd the world aside / And bid it pass." Much to his surprise, what he gets in reply is a mannerist painting, a highly decorated emblem (or *impresa*) of the true prince. "All furnished, all in arms," reports Vernon (although we in the theater know that none of the Eastcheap gang has reformed along with Hal):

> All plumed like estridges, that with the wind
> Bated like eagles having lately bathed,
> Glittering in golden coats, like images,
> As full of spirit as the month of May,
> And gorgeous as the sun at midsummer,
> Wanton as youthful goats, wild as young bulls.
> I saw young Harry, with his beaver on,
> His cuisses on his thighs, gallantly armed,
> Rise from the ground like feathered Mercury,
> And vaulted with such ease into his seat,
> As if an angel dropped down from the clouds

To turn and wind a fiery Pegasus,
And witch the world with noble horsemanship.

(4.1.97–110)

"No more, no more!" Hotspur cries out. The images pile together here, with a range of reference from the heraldic (the estridge, or ostrich, is special to the Prince of Wales) to the mythological (the taming of Pegasus was considered in Renaissance iconography to be an allegory of self-mastery, triumph over the appetites, and statesmanship). That the witness who testifies to the transformation of the madcap Hal into a gallant feathered Mercury is a member of the rebel forces only adds to its potency. Hal is amphibious here, but he now inhabits the elements of air and fire.

Hal presents himself as master of his situation, both as prince and as actor. But there are moments in the play when the richly ambiguous world of seeming appears to confound him. At the end of *1 Henry IV* Prince Hal seems actually to be taken in by Falstaff's sham death. He is baffled upon returning with his brother John to find the fat man up and Hotspur over his shoulder. But he gilds the story with a lie and as a result loses sufficient credibility to make *Part Two* necessary. And in *Part Two*, looking at his sleeping father, the Prince makes the same mistake. Like the funeral orations over Hotspur and Falstaff, Hal's speech as he takes the crown is undercut by his inability to tell false death from real. "This sleep is sound indeed," he pronounces:

> This is a sleep
> That from this golden rigol hath divorced
> So many English kings. Thy due from me
> Is tears and heavy sorrows of the blood,
> Which nature, love, and filial tenderness
> Shall, O dear Father, pay thee plenteously.
> My due from thee is this imperial crown,
> Which, as immediate from thy place and blood,
> Derives itself to me.

(2 Henry IV, 4.5.35–43)

Hal's leaping to a conclusion here is especially revealing of the moral historiography of his agenda. As he staged his victory in *1 Henry IV* to conform to our expectation that the prodigal prince should triumph over both Hotspur and Falstaff in an instant, so Hal scripts his succession here. "Place and blood" and, later on, "lineal honor" (46) are the keynotes here. For Hal's plan to succeed, he must inherit the crown not earn it; the transaction must be as private and mysterious as conception itself. It is not for the legitimate prince to study deserving like the bastard Edmund. By claiming the crown through right of blood alone and by doing so secretly, with none but the dead king by, Hal replaces his father's crime of usurpation with a mystic rite that proclaims the king's two bodies to be one.

In the process he attempts to satisfy the craving for narrative, historiographical coherence that he aroused in the audience with the soliloquy. More to the point, an audience to the play has desired this consummation more devoutly perhaps than he has, especially an audience that has experienced the frustrations of *Richard II* and *1 Henry IV*. For Hal has been England's sweetest hope in two special senses: first, he can resolve the dilemma proposed in *Richard II*, where the blood of Edward III is wasted by both the lineal successor, Richard, and the usurper, Henry. Hal's succession will not be parricidal. Second, Hal figures not simply a dynastic but a historiographical hope. He can move us from a kind of history that is cyclical and (finally) nihilistic in its vision to a kind of history that is linear and leads to a coherent moral ending, the crowning of Henry V and the banishment of Falstaff. But the sense we get in the whole of *2 Henry IV* that we have seen all this before threatens a linear narrative line, and Hal's secret rite, to his revived father's eyes, seems an utterly Bolingbrokian maneuver. (Hotspur remembers his first encounter with "this vile politician, Bolingbroke" vividly: "Why what a candy deal of courtesy / This fawning greyhound then did proffer me!" [*1 Henry IV*, 1.3.240, 249–50].)

Just as Falstaff refuses to be dead and permit the prince's reformation to glitter untarnished, so too the deathbed scene in *2 Henry IV* does not fit the prince's plan. Not only are we reminded of Falstaff's revival as King Henry awakes, but we notice that somehow the play has coerced Hal into reenacting his father's highly significant gesture in the abdication scene in *Richard II*. "Here, cousin, seize the crown," Richard prompts there, and Bolingbroke, unhappily, must theatrically act out his crime (*Richard II*, 4.1.182). "Where is the crown?" cries Henry when he awakes. "The Prince hath ta'en it hence" (*2 Henry IV*, 4.5.57, 59). Like father, like son, the third play in the sequence suggests.

An inheritance has changed hands, legitimized not by blood but by the family gesture of seizing and taking.

Hal has set himself a task of legitimation, and Vernon, at least, cannot see the young man without seeing the true prince. Yet the moments in which he most triumphantly enacts his legitimation, as he transcends the vanity of Falstaff and Hotspur at the end of *Part One* and as he succeeds to his father's crown in *Part Two*, take place without witnesses and in error. Hal promises a transformation that will be sudden, devastating, miraculous. But what is most surprising about his triumph in *Part One* is his reversion to idleness. Falstaff's claim to have fought Percy and vanquished him (also without witnesses) both points to the weakness of Hal's tale that he in fact killed Percy (with, he now discovers, a witness who won't back him up) and serves as a brilliant counter to Hal's exposure of Falstaff's false story of the men in buckram suits in the tavern scene. Falstaff may not know what time it is, but he knows when it is a good time to get even.

A common answer to Hal's disappointing performance — why can't he expose Falstaff on the battlefield as he did in the tavern? — has been to side with Warwick's assessment in *Part Two*, that Hal was maturing, growing up, going to school:

> The Prince but studies his companions
> Like a strange tongue, wherein, to gain the language,
> 'Tis needful that the most immodest word
> Be looked upon and learned, which once attained
> Your Highness knows, comes to no further use,
> But to be known and hated. So, like gross terms,
> The Prince will in the perfectness of time
> Cast off his followers, and their memory
> Shall as a pattern or a measure live,
> By which His Grace must mete the lives of other,
> Turning past evils to advantages.
>
> (4.4.68–78)

Warwick's interpretation of Hal's conduct is reminiscent of Renaissance defenses of theater, which tend to be similarly reductive and homiletic. By this token, Hal is like an actor, studying baser types of human being in order to be fluent in the role should he be called upon to play it. He is not infected by the "gross terms" he learns, in the same way that actors are assumed to be protected by their professionalism from the badness of the characters they play.

One key Renaissance defense of theater, Thomas Heywood's *Apology for Actors*, explicitly analogizes the theater to the university. Heywood ambitiously argues that rhetorical competition in universities is good training for life: it "teacheth audacity to the bashfull Grammarian, being newly admitted into the private Colledge, and after matriculated and entred as a member of the University, and makes him a bold Sophister, to argue *pro et contra*, to compose him Sillogismes, Cathegorike, or Hypotheticke (simple or compound) to reason and frame a sufficient argument to prove his questions, or to defend any *axioma*, to distinguish of any Dilemma, & be able to moderate in any Argumentation whatsoever." This assertion of the utility of performance drew quick and fierce response from "I. G." [John Greene?], whose *Refutation of the Apologie for Actors* appeared shortly after Heywood's volume. "For Plaies as saith the *Apologyst* makes a bold *Sophister*, that is plainely, a too cunning, or false reasoner, to knit preposterous and intertangled syllogismes, obscure Sorites, Aenigmaticall Crocodilities, and forkehorned *Dilemmas* to ensnare and obnubilate the truth as now M. Actor himselfe faine would doe."[54] Heywood may give some comfort to those in the academy currently involved in the rehabilitation of the sophists and their Renaissance admirers, like Susan Jarratt, but I. G.'s position is that clever social performance is not a desirable end for education.[55] Educational practice in the early modern period and the emphasis on rhetorical education in the discussions of theater in Plato and Aristotle lead both Heywood and I. G. to see acting as a kind of education and the theater as a place to rehearse necessary (as Heywood would have it) or pernicious (as I. G. would have it) social skills.

To the antitheatrical moralists, playing vicious characters accustoms actors to vice, hardens them, and their dissolute lives confirm this. The problem of Hal's studying and practicing cuts both ways. As Canterbury points out in *Henry V*, Hal's reformation is little short of miraculous, for we "never noted in him any study." To Ely, however, this points to secret study: "the Prince obscured his contemplation / Under the veil of wildness," an explanation Canterbury must accept because "miracles are ceased" and the alternative is therefore impiously unthinkable (*Henry V*, 1.1.58, 64–65, 68). Hamlet, too, puzzles audiences by announcing to Horatio, as the duel with Laertes approaches, that he has been "in continual practice" (5.2.209): when? The problem in theatrical terms here is rehearsal, which audiences of course do not see and are urged to forget about so that the actor's feats can appear miraculous. The problem is a moral one, too: is rehearsal a kind of education by immersion, a habituation to vice or to virtue? When an audience watches Hal perform in the tavern, rehearsing his meeting with his father before it takes place by playing both himself and his father, how does that affect our perception of his promises before the real king?

The issue of Hal's rehearsing is complicated because the rehearsed gesture is commonly associated with the notion of the dishonest, the disingenuous, the insincere. Joseph Surface is a practiced hypocrite, Charles spontaneous in his self-exposure. Upholding the mutual idleness of both his vicious companions and the theater audience, Hal entertains while he practices. Yet somehow all his practicing does not help when Falstaff rises to claim credit for Hotspur's death. If the Francis joke shows Hal to be getting ready to be a popular ruler, it also shows him playing a cruel practical joke. Hal is not, in this view, a true amphibian, but merely a visiting swimmer.

For Thomas Van Laan, for example, only Falstaff can be allowed the fluidity, the liminality, of the actor:

> Falstaff's is a world for playing roles for pleasure, as many as possible, and the more innovative the better; the emphasis falls on the role of the playwright-actor. In the heroic world, however, such role-playing would be unequivocally evil. There the ideal consists of finding one's proper role from an approved list of existing possibilities and striving to fulfill it satisfactorily by obeying its dictates. In Falstaff's world, all roles are possible because none is crucial. In the heroic world, only certain roles can be tolerated, and one of them, that of king, matters more than all the others.[56]

Van Laan's distinction between a "heroic world" and "Falstaff's world" of play is well taken, but what are we to make of "unequivocally evil"? The main tenet of Plato's antitheatricalism is that the proliferation of roles identifiable with the actor is socially destabilizing. Is the antitheatricality here Van Laan's or Hal's? To condemn Hal for merely playing, not being, the true prince is to miss the complex engagement of theatrical and iconic conventions in Hal's playing.

James Calderwood finds a more subtle distinction in dramatic modes: Falstaff is a "rebel" against the "realism" of the play's genre of history play, bringing into it the rules of his own brand of festive comedy, threatening "a secession of the theatrical from the mimetic aspects of the play." The distinction between "theatrical" and "mimetic aspects" of what is after all a play suggests that somehow the theater itself can be reduced to the status of improvisatory clowning and banished in favor of serious business.[57] The strongest exponent of this hard-nosed approach, though, is not Calderwood but Richard Levin, who rejects Falstaff as though his own soul were at risk. Falstaff is dangerously immature, he argues, because "Falstaff does want to make all the year one continuous Saturnalia, this being the ritual corollary of his perennial childishness and obliviousness of time, which is brought out most forcefully in his parallel attempts to extend his misrule into the serious climaxes of both parts of *Henry IV* and in the Prince's parallel rebukes." For Falstaff's "timeless, static world," Hal must learn to substitute a world of real time.[58] Certainly *Hal* has a right to complain about Falstaff's festive irruptions into the serious parts of his plays. Hal's project is making moral sense of himself, staging his reform so that it is maximally surprising. To be fully known, for Hal, is to be known as a true prince, casting off his followers as the sun dissolves the mists "in the perfectness of time." His problems with corpses that refuse to stay dead suggest that Hal is so successful in making others see him iconically, as prodigal son or ideal prince, that he has a tendency to read others iconically as well. They are also, of course, problems with timing: as long as King Henry lives, Hal cannot be allowed to be seen fully as England's sweetest hope. The theater complicates the promulgation of his image, but in the end it is the medium in which his image can be most luminous.

Subscribing wholly to this luminousness is an older tradition, which tends to do so without reference to the worlds of the stage at all. E. M. W. Tillyard, of course, celebrates Hal as a true prince without irony; for Joseph A. Porter, Warwick's analogy to a language-lesson is the key to Henry V's emergence from Hal as a "many-tongued monarch, who, using a wide range of language purposefully and responsibly, initiates a reign of 'high . . . parliament.'" Porter seems to adopt in a quite literal way a "Whig view of history" as Henry becomes a parliamentarian, just as the old Whig view saw in the antitheatrical Puritans of the early seventeenth century later parliamentary forces. By focusing so exclusively on language as speech and eschewing talk of spectacle, Porter reveals a different kind of antitheatrical bias.

"Many-tongued" is not quite the same as Protean: this Hal has an ethical, sincere self, which he can fluently express.[59]

There is division, too, among those critics who believe that Hal has a sincere self and those who believe he does not, especially in the way in which Hal works with readily recognizable iconography. Robert B. Pierce describes the royal interview (*Part One*, 3.2) as richly satisfying in this way: "In the parable, the Prodigal Son restored to his father is man restored to God, and in the Elizabethan system of correspondences the king is to his kingdom as God is to the universe. Hal's reconciliation with his father symbolizes a larger commitment to all that is good and orderly in the world."[60] John Wilders strikes a more cynical pose, arguing that the prince is only acting: "The winner in this game of deception is Hal, who deliberately impersonates the prodigal son and feigns the false impression he knows his subjects have formed of him in order that, eventually, they will be convinced by his equally contrived reformation."[61] More positive in his attitude toward theater (and less eager to appear naively sucked in than Pierce) is John Blanpied, who sees Hal as having the nature of "an 'actor' with all the doubleness the term implies"; his "dramatic genius lies in his coolly playing the prodigal son."[62]

Hal has played more than the parabolic role of the prodigal son. He has also arrogated to himself a large number of exclusively theatrical models, especially as drawn from morality plays. "Hal may be Lusty Juventus, counseled by Vices and Virtues, learning to be the true prince and the savior of the commonwealth," muses Alvin Kernan, "but Vices and Virtues like Falstaff and Hotspur speak with such ambiguous voices that it is difficult to tell which is which, and 'the mirror of all Christian kings' is so complex a character, and the nature of rule so mixed a business, that we are left wondering whether the restoration of the kingdom represents a triumph of morality or of Machiavellian politics."[63] The evocation of old morality patterns in the rejection of Falstaff is, for John Cox, a mimetic enactment of real historical use of those patterns in Elizabethan image-management. "Whatever the truth about the relationship, the most important thing for Hal is that it be defined in the categories of morality drama, because those conventions are such effective conveyors of the broad generalizations about his supposed moral development that Hal wishes his people to believe about him as he proceeds in securing his power." Hal is as scrupulous about his image as Elizabeth or Essex: as he comes to power, "the heroic king is exactly like the chivalric heroes Shakespeare really knew: utterly opaque in his ability to charge his single-minded quest for political dominance with the compelling vision of a social ideal." Here Hal's virtuosity is seen to intersect with real-life Renaissance self-fashioning.[64]

For Frank Whigham, as for Cox, the issue of sincerity is beside the point. Protean virtuosity, Whigham reminds us, was necessary for courtiers; George Puttenham's "numbing catalog of deceits suggests that the smallest daily acts of courtly life have an infinitely varied symbolic weight (and hence are vulnerable to differing interpretations)." In his analysis of Puttenham's *Arte of English Poesie* Whigham points to a theatrical — tragic — dimension: "Who would not pity and fear this our chameleon?"[65] Whigham's attention, like that of the courtesy tracts he studies, is upon the courtier; the courtier's attention is upon the prince, and the adaptability and suppleness that courtiers must cultivate is irrelevant to the prince himself. That is, the more closely Prince Hal can be seen to recall "chivalric heroes" like Essex, the more he appears to be a competitor for power, the less he can lambently appear to be a true prince. The tragic competitor for power in the *Henry IV* plays is Hotspur, and he is less chameleon than parrot, an inflexible but loquacious "paraquito," as his wife puts it (*1 Henry IV*, 2.3.85).

By reminding us of the theatricality of daily life, Cox and Whigham help to collapse the distinctions between theater and life that troubled the earlier critics. But this new historicist claim can become exaggerated. David Kastan asserts that theater itself "enacts, not necessarily on stage, but in its fundamental transaction with the audience, the exact shift in the conception of authority that brings a king to trial and ultimately locates sovereignty in the common will of its subjects."[66] By showing that kings are like actors playing roles, in other words, the seventeenth-century English theater legitimized the seventeenth-century English regicide. Kastan's article is a corrective to the totalizing language of Stephen Greenblatt's famous invisible bullets; he reclaims for the English theater subversion without containment. But in the process he accepts the word of the antitheatrical writers of the age for what theater could do, what theater could make people do. "New historicist and cultural materialist critics of Renaissance drama tend to share with Phillip Stubbes and Thomas Nashe the assumption that the theater mattered to the shape and direction of English society," Paul Yachnin observes.[67] Yachnin's point is the opposite, that theater did not matter very much; for that reason, the authorities were content to leave it alone.

Whigham's sense of the pathos of the courtly climber and Cox's insistence on *Realpolitik* signal a more moderate engagement of the theater's confusion of realms. Blurring of distinctions, confusion of realms, as the antitheatrical argument runs, is endemic to the theater, and Kastan succumbs to its lure as he transforms it into historical narrative. The ambivalence that many critics feel about Hal's acting is similar to the ambivalence they must feel about Shakespeare's institution. The problem is first and foremost historical: the peculiar institution of the early modern English theater is a phenomenon that we cannot grasp phenomenologically. "Between drama and its meaning," Herbert Blau puts it, "particularly an older drama, there is always the distance of history, which moves fast in the space of perception between the desire for meaning and the currency of any play." He imagines "some contribution to scholarship from science fiction" that could actually take us back to seventeenth-century London, so we "could see what 'they' saw." "It should be obvious that to have been there is, in some definitive approach to meaning, a rather dubious privilege."[68] By insisting upon the complexity of plays in performance, and stressing the dubious quality of extracting meaning from performance, Blau is not antitheatrical; rather he is aware of how confusing and complex the theatrical experience can be.

To extract a moral meaning from Hal's glittering reformation, audiences have to endorse Vernon's narration (in the face of their own witnessing of Hal's continued sponsorship of Falstaff); to ratify the eulogy over the panting and obviously undead fat man; to approve of snatching the crown away from the sleeping king. It is the fact of performance itself that blurs the contours of Hal's performances. Hal's agenda, the historical narrative in which he reveals himself like the sun, is in conflict with the theatrical means of its production. Approaching meaning is indeed a dubious activity, when the desire for meaning that Hal provokes and indulges is so often, like Vernon's vision, set up as wishful seeing.

Attempting to make sense out of Hal's acting embroils both scholars and audiences. The plays do not help by identifying acting, through Falstaff, with fraud and deceit. The rejection of Falstaff could be a rejection of bad, fraudulent acting (or excessive, festive overacting); but then we are forced to endorse the Protean skills of Hal. "Always the chameleon player," Jean Howard and Phyllis Rackin note, "Hal, unlike Hotspur, is capable of a variety of roles and voices: plebeian, regal, comic, heroic, Welsh, English, subversive, authoritative — the list is not complete." Rackin and Howard see Hal's virtuosity as a performer as liberating in contrast to Hotspur's singleness of self-definition. And they see it as utterly successful as political propaganda: "his performance projects as a personal achievement early modernist fantasies of extended monarchial power." In this view Hal is clearly of the family of Machiavelli's prince, appearing to have all the virtues. Since to the feminist critics Hal is a projection of male fantasies about royal power, it is pernicious that Hal's kind of acting is so successful on the stage and in the world of early modern Europe. Not only are the other inhabitants of Hal's stage world, like Vernon, fully convinced by Hal's performance, but so too are Elizabethan audiences, dreaming of "extended monarchial power," and those critics who see Hal as a moral person rather than a chameleon. For Howard and Rackin, Hal is as much a fraud as Falstaff, playing out masculine, royalist fantasies.[69]

"Let the end try the man," Prince Hal declares cryptically to Poins, refusing all "ostentation of sorrow" despite the fact his "heart bleeds inwardly" at the fact of his father's illness. "What wouldst thou think of me if I should weep?" "I would think thee a most princely hypocrite," Poins rejoins, and the prince agrees: "It would be every man's thought, and thou art a blessed fellow to think as every man thinks" (*2 Henry IV*, 2.2.47–53). The prince acts the part of indifference to his father's sickness lest his true feelings be interpreted as feigned. "Behold how like a maid she blushes here!" Claudio exclaims against Hero in *Much Ado about Nothing*; "Would you not swear, / All you that see her, that she were a maid, / By these exterior shows?" (4.1.33, 37–39). That Hero looks modest becomes an index of her immodesty; for Hal to appear saddened by his father's sickness would be similar proof of his inward joy. "Every man" would think so — just as every man thinks he knows the truth about Hero.

Theatrical mimesis itself is misleading, the antitheatrical thinkers tell us. Students, laboriously rehearsing the conflict of appearance *versus* reality, seem to agree. The problem, of course, is that sometimes things *are* as they appear. The basic assumption of theater is that appearances somehow do reveal realities, and it corresponds to the assumption in the Anglo-American legal system that the degree of doubt must be reasonable. To consider appearances always misleading is to consider too curiously much of the time. The difficulty is knowing when to trust an appearance and when not to trust it. As Poins confidently declares what he knows "every man" knows, and what the audience knows to be at least simplistic, if not dead wrong, Shakespeare's play generates a vortex of theatrical antitheatricality. The choruses of approval or disapproval about Hal's behavior cannot avoid the language of antitheatricality, for to judge Hal ethically is to judge him as a real person — and as the interlude with Poins points out, "every man" confronts a hall of mirrors here.

This is true even when the attempt is to offer a balanced perspective: "Not quite the paragon some would have him nor the heartless prig others see," Robert Ornstein says, staking out a middle ground. "Like a clever Elizabethan shopkeeper, Hal knows how to display the merchandize of his behavior in such a light that it appears richer than it is." [70] Tarring the theater with the brush of commercialism, Ornstein is able to accept Hal without embracing him. So, too, according to Jean-Christophe Agnew, did the Stuart courtiers dodge the contagious commerciality of professional players by sealing them off in the world of the antimasque. [71]

The new historicist blurring of the boundaries between theater and life allows us to see broad ramifications in the problem of Hal's acting, as it branches away from Falstaff's toward Essex's, Queen Elizabeth's, and our own. Drawing from Erving Goffman, the new historicist can assert that we are always acting, always playing roles, managing our images. This sounds like Hal, imitating the sun behind the base contagious clouds. Acting in everyday life becomes hypocrisy; as we have seen, critics who praise Hal's acting skills, like Blanpied or Wilder or Greenblatt, tend to see him as Machiavellian, although not to agree on the moral weight this should bear.

"Theatre reveals, but does not reveal at all clearly the limits of its ability to reveal," Bruce Wilshire says. "Does theatre reveal what is the case or only what we would like to be the case? The distinction enshrined by the question is grossly misleading. For what could be more actual than the dreams and desires we do have? How can we know ourselves unless we know what these are? Theatre is peculiarly apt to reveal them" (*Role Playing and Identity*, 252). Again we can find Hal, teasing the audience's desire for a true prince, its dream of a prodigal son, lurking in the general statement of the problem. The plays dramatize a powerful ambivalence about what theater can reveal about our dreams

and desires. A further complication is that the dreams and desires re-
volve around the problem of kingship.

The *Henry IV* plays are ambivalent about theater insofar as they are
ambivalent about kingship, and they are ambivalent about kingship insofar as kingship is theatrical. The same goes for the criticism of the
plays, too. Prince Hal presents his transformation from prince to king
as a miraculous change, planned from the outset, carefully rehearsed,
and well worth waiting for. The premature self-coronations (over Falstaff and over the sleeping Henry) merely whet the appetite. As king,
Hal becomes Shakespeare's most successful public man, Henry V. Critics who argue the issue of King Henry V's sincerity or opportunism
miss the point. Kings are ambiguous beings, unavailable to public
knowledge: this is the truth ensconced in the doctrine of the king's two
bodies, one of which is a body physical, visible to the eye, and one of
which is a body politic, visible everywhere but by no means a mortal
body like ours.

In a different sense actors, too, have two bodies, one of which belongs to them personally as ours do, and one of which belongs to the
role. "No, that's certain, I am not a double man," says Falstaff with
Hotspur slung over his shoulder; "but if I be not Jack Falstaff, then am
I a Jack" (*1 Henry IV*, 5.4.137–38). Here the true prince confronts a parody of his own plan to use Percy as a factor, engrossing up glorious
deeds on his behalf. Falstaff has taken the true prince's heroic part (just
as — "Depose me?" — the prince took away Falstaff's royal role in the
tavern scene). He embodies theatrical vitality, the theater's resistance to
the moral scheme of Hal's narrative of legitimation. But he goes further. As in the tavern scene, Falstaff here plays Hal, showing Hal himself reduced to the most ridiculous level, to the "thing" he has become.

At the end Falstaff is a double man: a riddle not unlike the duck/rab-
bit or the Rorschach blot — what you see is more a matter of how you
see than of what is there. Norman Rabkin, in a famous article, describes
Henry V as a duck/rabbit, simultaneously a great war play and a great
antiwar play, pulling audiences in two equal and opposite directions.[72]
Stephen Greenblatt sees a similar pull in two directions, and for him
these are the characteristic strategies of subversion and containment:
"The play deftly registers every nuance of royal hypocrisy, ruthlessness,
and bad faith — testing, in effect, the proposition that successful rule
depends not upon sacredness but upon demonic violence — but it does
so in the context of celebration, a collective panegyric to 'this star of

England,' the charismatic leader who purges the commonwealth of its incorrigibles and forges the martial national state."[73]

Both Rabkin's duck/rabbit and Greenblatt's model permit the critic to have the cake and eat it too: in spite of the moral charge made against the play by Greenblatt — "bad faith," "demonic violence" — the critic stands back and withholds judgment on historical grounds. What appears repugnant conduct to the modern reader or audience member, Greenblatt suggests, is best understood as part of the larger Renaissance project of state- and self-fashioning. *Henry V* negotiates poles that appear to moderns to be opposites but that are inextricably interdependent in the making of Shakespeare's cultural matrix. What seems like shocking cynicism, the condoning of demonic violence, only reveals the gulf between the modern viewer and the early modern context of the play. Once again, Hal is what we make him: but Greenblatt insists that we reshape our consciences to fit an imagined model of the early modern conscience. To do otherwise, to impose our own modern notions of bad faith, is to indulge in anachronism.

The two important twentieth-century film versions of *Henry V* (Laurence Olivier's 1944 version and Kenneth Branagh's 1988 version) have helped to bring questions of anachronism and bad faith to the fore. The two function well in criticism and in the classroom as duck and rabbit, especially since Branagh's film offers an almost frame-by-frame commentary on Olivier's. Where Olivier's film is brightly lit, Branagh's is dark; where Olivier is a poised, self-assured actor (in the Globe scenes at the beginning of the film) and monarch (in the French section), Branagh shows uncertainty and, to most critics, growth to maturity through the film. For Michael Manheim, Olivier's film offers "from beginning to end the perfect embodiment of the new Machiavellian prince — not a figure to be hated, feared, and scorned (that would come later with *Richard III*) — but one who would strengthen and preserve the state, the declared objective of *The Prince*." On the other hand, Manheim contends, Branagh's Henry is "the Henry for our time basically because along with his ingenuousness, sincerity, and apparent decency — he is also a ruthless murderer." While a merging of contraries makes Henry V a typical Renaissance figure in Greenblatt's eyes, such a merging makes Branagh's Henry "*our*" contemporary in Manheim's. To Manheim, Olivier's film highlights the staginess and artificiality of image-making, as king, actor, director, and even Chorus participate in the management of Henry's charisma. Despite the Book-of-Hours backdrops and the painted panoramas of London and France, Olivier's version succeeds in being historical because it fully dramatizes the whole agenda of Machiavelli: the old stage Machiavel is slanderously reductive, and Olivier's Henry, who may even possess the virtues he seems to possess, is "probably the sole instance in drama of what Machiavelli really had in mind."[74]

Insofar as Machiavelli raised for his first readers questions about the necessity of a correspondence between public and private ethics, the two films provide a dramatic instance of a shift in the late twentieth century toward a privileging of the private. Olivier's film insists in its dedication to the "[c]ommandos and airborne troops of Great Britain" upon the public, historic importance of the film's parallel to World War II. Branagh in interviews has resisted the association of his film to the Falkland Islands war. Instead, he claims, "I feel the play is about a journey toward maturity."[75] This shift of emphasis can be best observed by taking note of some of the cuts both directors have made in the playtext as they adapt it for film. Generally, where Olivier cuts, Branagh restores: but what Branagh cuts from his own restorations is equally revealing.

Olivier's highly visible Henry is spared some of the more embarrassing moments provided in the text. For example, as the English army is preparing to set sail for France, Olivier's Henry wastes only a little time before an inspiring departure to pardon a drunken man who "railed against our person. We consider / It was excess of wine that set him on / And on his more advice we pardon him" (2.2.41–43). Against the backdrop of cranes, barrels, and other accouterments of a busy wharf, Henry dismisses the advice of a pair of lords who urge more severity and, with a nod to the archbishop of Canterbury (who opens the scene concluding a blessing of the ships), makes to board his vessel: "Cheerly to sea! The signs of war advance! / No king of England, if not king of France!" (192–93). Olivier's energetic performance is matched by no less energetic cutting on his part as a director. Between Henry's pardon of the drunkard and his departure for France, the text devotes about 130 lines to the king's exposure of a conspiracy against his rule, fomented by descendants and allies of the late Richard II.

Branagh restores this episode. The lords who advise severity against the drunkard are of course the conspirators themselves, and Henry turns aside their pleas for mercy on the grounds that their "own counsel" has "suppressed and killed" his royal clemency (2.2.80). Where

Olivier sets sail from a busy port, Branagh sets the scene on shipboard, in a dark cabin. As the scene begins, a hand shoots the bolt of the cabin door: the audience knows something dangerous is afoot. Branagh exchanges slight nods with his uncle Exeter, who at one point grips his dagger apprehensively, just in case the trick does not work; the lords themselves, once they realize they have been exposed, draw their weapons and have to be subdued. Branagh stresses the personal aspect of the betrayal: he directs his speech to Lord Scroop, his former bedfellow, in relentless close-up. Henry lies atop Scroop on the table, holding his face between his hands, as he chides him. Scroop's betrayal is a lover's betrayal, and Exeter brings the point home by slapping Scroop, and Scroop alone, on the face as he ceremoniously tears the emblems of office from around the necks of the traitors. Where Olivier shies away from the whole scene — from Henry's Machiavellian entrapment of the traitors, from the erotically charged language of the Scroop speech — and simply does not allow it to happen, Branagh revels in the scene's ambiguities. Branagh's Henry may be more vulnerable than Olivier's, but the conspiratorial nods suggest that Branagh's Henry is more self-consciously vulnerable, more aware of the political potential in telegraphing his vulnerability, than Olivier's.

Branagh, too, cuts a number of lines from the Scroop speech that directly characterize Scroop as a false friend and flattering royal favorite:

> Show men dutiful?
> Why, so didst thou. Seem they grave and learnèd?
> Why, so didst thou. Come they of noble family?
> Why, so didst thou. Seem they religious?
> Why, so didst thou. Or are they spare in diet,
> Free from gross passion or of mirth or anger,
> Constant in spirit, not swerving with the blood,
> Garnished and decked in modest compliment,
> Not working with the eye without the ear,
> And but in purgèd judgment trusting neither?
> Such and so finely bolted didst thou seem.
>
> (2.2.127–37)

This catalog of virtues, to the audience well-acquainted with the *Henry IV* plays, casts Scroop in the role of anti-Falstaff. These are the virtues Falstaff enumerates in his own defenses, most poignantly as he pleads with the mock-king Hal against banishment in the tavern scene

of *Part One*. Scroop becomes a viler kind of false flattering friend, for
Falstaff at least appears to be what the catalog shows he is: frivolous,
ignoble, irreligious, fat, subject to gross passions, mirth, or anger, inconstant, immodest, unpurged in judgment as in urine. Neither director takes advantage of the way in which Scroop, a new boon companion to audiences who have become accustomed to seeing Hal either in
unsuitable companionship or alone, becomes something worse than
Falstaff here. Henry pardons the drunk at the beginning of the scene,
and the scene itself is sandwiched between the two scenes of Falstaff's
final illness and death. "The King has killed his heart," the Hostess reports (2.1.88), and Nym and Pistol repeat the diagnosis: "The King
hath run bad humors on the knight, that's the even of it." "Nym, thou
has spoke the right. / His heart is fracted and corroborate" (121–24).
Henry's outrage at betrayal by a man who *seemed* the opposite of the fat
knight he discarded draws much of its energy from the discovery that
he cannot avoid bad companions even once he has turned them away.
In place of Falstaff, who rose from the dead to spoil the iconic close of
Part One, Scroop rises to challenge the iconography of vice in his lean,
religious, sober mien. While both directors take full advantage of the
pathos of Falstaff's death, neither takes pains to note the incursion into
this play of the pious seemer, so much more dangerous because he es-
chews the gross physical display of Falstaff's festive seeming.[76]

The catalog of Scroop's seeming virtues, too, points an audience toward another possibility that Branagh's cut elides. The play abounds in
anti-Falstaffs, not the least conspicuous of whom is of course Henry
himself. His prudence and piety are what the churchmen marvel at in
the opening scene, finding his reform little short of miraculous. As
Fluellen struggles to formulate a parallel in which Henry can be likened
to "Alexander the Pig," the fat man keeps creeping into the discussion.
"Alexander, God knows, and you know," says Fluellen, "in his rages
and his furies, and his wraths, and his cholers, and his moods, and his
displeasures, and his indignations, and also being a little intoxicates in
his prains, did, in his ales and in his angers, look you, kill his best friend
Cleitus." "Our king is not like him in that," Gower counters. "He never
killed any of his friends" (4.7.33–38). The introduction of Alexander as
a kind of anti-Scroop, a drunken, raging friend-killer, puts Fluellen on
the defensive as he tries to praise Henry as a kind of anti-Alexander,
who, "being in his right wits and good judgments, turned away the fat

knight with the great-belly doublet" (46–47). Fluellen forgets his name, and Gower has to remind him: but the dazzling refusal of the fat man to be pinned down in a simple moral parallel is of a piece with the problem of apparent virtue and temperance embodied in the false friend Scroop. "I was not angry since I came to France / Until this instance," Henry declares, interrupting Fluellen's exercise in Plutarchian moral history (54–55). Scroop, who seems to embody all the virtues, is intimately linked with the problem of the dismissal and death of Falstaff and with the problem of the king's own anger.

The two films offer an instance where Branagh restores part of what Olivier has seen fit to cut and where the king's anger is a key issue. In Olivier's film the citizens of Harfleur sound a parley: the governor appears on the walls and declares that the Dauphin has failed to fulfill his promise to raise the siege. Olivier accepts their surrender graciously and urges his uncle to "use mercy to them all" (3.3.54); he gazes out at a painted pastoral landscape as the scene ends. Branagh rides up to the flaming breach in the dark monumental walls of Harfleur and restores the speech, cut by Olivier, in which Henry threatens to massacre the inhabitants if they do not surrender their town. "If I begin the battery once again," he cries, "I will not leave the half-achieved Harfleur / Till in her ashes she lie buried" (8–9). "In a moment look to see," he warns:

The blind and bloody soldier with foul hand
Defile the locks of your shrill-shrieking daughters,
Your fathers taken by their silver beards,
And their most reverend heads dashed to the walls,
Your naked infants spitted upon pikes,
Whiles the mad mothers with their howls confused
Do break the clouds.

(33–40)

Strong stuff — and the governor of Harfleur hears it with some dismay. When he surrenders, Henry, exhausted and (as we in the audience can see but the governor cannot) relieved, slumps away on his horse. It was all a bluff; Henry is especially careful to make sure that Exeter understands it as such and will indeed use mercy. Then he collapses from his ordeal.

Branagh plays the speech outside the walls of Harfleur, in other words, as pure performance. Henry is not in a rage, and his soldiers are not out of his control, rampaging: they are reined in, and it is debatable whether Branagh's weary and dirty men will turn savage and rape and pillage as he threatens. Michael Goldman has pointed out that playing Henry V is strenuous exercise for an actor and that the play emphasizes the effort required of actor and audience. He anticipates Branagh's actorly collapse at Harfleur by stressing the strain involved in the projection of Henry's image: "he must pay the price of his role."[77] Branagh foregrounds the physical fatigue involved in the presentation of Henry here at Harfleur. Being a duck/rabbit is hard work: or, as Montaigne puts it, "the sharpest and most difficile profession of the world is (in mine opinion) worthily to act and play the King."[78]

While Olivier has been faulted for excising the references to massacre and rape from his version of the play, and Branagh praised for reincorporating them in his, the distinction is not easily reducible to a contrast between a simplistic, jingoistic piece and a complex, "darker" one. For Branagh, too, has cut some lines here: lines that might suggest that his film's emphasis on Henry's vulnerability and sensitivity privileges his private pain at the expense of something public — and not public in the sense of Olivier's pageantry and clarity. The lines Branagh omits from the Harfleur speech refer directly to the play's chief moral concerns. "What is it then to me," Shakespeare's Henry says,

> if impious war
> Arrayed in flames like to the prince of fiends,
> Do with his smirched complexion all fell feats
> Enlinked to waste and desolation?

And again:

> What is't to me, when you yourselves are cause
> If your pure maidens fall into the hand
> Of hot and forcing violation?
>
> (3.3.15–23)

The disavowal of responsibility here — the king's apparent willingness to condone atrocities and blame the victims, the cynicism of "what is't to me?" in this context — seems to have frightened away both Branagh and Olivier. Readers of the play, though, recognize in Henry's threats a fulfillment of the Chorus's desire, expressed at the play's very opening, to evoke a presence directly from the past, rather than a feeble reenactment:

Then should the warlike Harry, like himself,
Assume the port of Mars, and at his heels,
Leashed in like hounds, should famine, sword, and fire
Crouch for employment.

(prologue, 5–8)

In the context of the siege of Harfleur, these lines return with an apocalyptic shudder. The language lesson, with its litany of body parts, and the wooing scene, in which Henry identifies Katherine with the cities he has conquered, both link to this vision of war as rape.[79]

While it is possible, then, to portray Olivier's Henry as glorious and public and contrast with him Branagh's Henry as private, vulnerable, and growing up, the films, despite multiple excisions from the text, fail adequately to simplify Shakespeare's figure.[80] Enough of the play's riddling complexity remains as a kind of residue. Donald K. Hedrick calls this "moral and political mud," drawing his image from the ubiquity of that substance on soldiers' faces and in the battlefield in Branagh's film. What Branagh does, Hedrick claims, is to perform a "neutralization of the questionable dealings of the king" by portraying "all the key actions of Henry as spontaneous: spontaneous tears, spontaneous beatings, even spontaneous religious feelings." Moral and political issues are reduced to emotions; Branagh's Henry is true to himself, like Clint Eastwood's Dirty Harry or Sylvester Stallone's Rambo.[81]

Michael Manheim, too, finds the sincerity and spontaneity of Branagh's Henry troubling: "What now strikes home more deeply than the story of the subtle leader making war is that of the sincere leader making war," he comments on the difference between the two films. "The battles that lie ahead in our time are very likely those between sincere, noble, and quite possibly youthful leaders willing to massacre all before them for principles that make about as much sense as resistance to the 'salique law.'"[82] Seen in this light, Branagh's privileging of the private feelings of Henry bespeaks a kind of ruthlessness and self-aggrandizement that Olivier's self-dramatization lacks. Branagh's eschewing of the theatrical in his film — from its anti-Olivier opening on a film soundstage to counter Olivier's opening with the panorama of London and the Globe — marks what he is out to do as realer, grittier, tougher. "If Olivier's film is a cutification of the play, Branagh's is a brutification," says Susanne Fabricius.[83] Brutally honest, the film shows us a Henry who has fears, sheds tears, and really falls in love with the French princess.

The staginess of Olivier's film, on the other hand, roots *Henry V* in the world of performance. "Olivier's film is about the stage itself, about illusion, about history and myth, heroes and dreams," Pilkington concludes. "It presents (but does not offer simplistic explanations for) love, evil, courage, isolation, and the unity of shared imaginings."[84] There is a pointed irony here, as the two director/stars engage in a task that the playwright has already called impossible, striving to bring forth the "warlike Harry, like himself." The tautology enforces an iconic insistence on theatricality even on the part of the original, "assum[ing] the port of Mars." Branagh's Henry, true to his own feelings, created with an actor's assumption of inwardness, and Olivier's Henry, a magnificent artifact, created by an actor utterly at home in his body and uncomfortable with inwardness, both struggle toward this notion of unplayable selfhood that can only find expression in fictive theatricality. Where does Harry end and Mars begin? How can we tell the player from the king?

Act Three

THEY DRINK

They're hard to miss — Charles Surface, Ejlert Løvborg, Jack Falstaff. These three drunks play their roles in the second act with extravagance and theatricality, if not with vine leaves in their hair. Ever since its association with Dionysus, acting has always been seen as a kind of intoxication, and the preachers and moralists who despised theater in the early modern period also railed against alehouses and against drink. As might be expected, the most vehement attacks upon actors as drinkers come from William Prynne. In act 6, scene 7, of part one of *Histriomastix*, Prynne declares: "The 7. consequent or effect of Stage-Playes, is luxury, drunkennesse, and excesse." The argument is made from proximity, as Prynne notes the ubiquity of taverns in the neighborhoods of theaters: "For who more luxurious, ebrious, riotous or deboist, then our assiduous Actors and Play-Haunters? Who greater Taverne, Ale-house, Tobacco-shop, Hot-water-house haunters, &c? who greater stouter drinkers, health-quaffers, Epicures, or good-fellowes then they? What walke more usuall then from a Play-house to a Taverne, to an Ale-house, a Tobacco-shop, or Hot-water Brothel-house; or from these unto the Play-house? where the Pot, the Can, the Tobacco-pipe are alwayes walking till the Play be ended; from whence they return to these their former haunts." Prynne depicts a vigorous two-way traffic of prodigality, as audience members and consumers walk back and forth. "Youngsters," Prynne warns, are here lured to destruction, "to their owne undoing, their friends and Parents griefe." [1]

As Prynne's fevered list suggests, drinking, gambling, whoring, smoking, and wearing perfume are all dangerous social activities which can be associated with playing. A similar list is drawn out by Thomas Adams, in "The White Devil, or, the Hypocrite Uncased," a 1612 sermon. What is "waste," the preacher asks:

Shall I say our upholding of theatres, to the contempt of religion; our maintaining ordinaries, to play away our patrimonies; our four-wheeled porters; our antic fashions; our smoky consumptions; our perfumed putrefactions: *Ad quid perditio haec?* — Why are these wastes? Experience will testify that these are wastes indeed; for they waste the body, the blood, the estate, the freedom, the soul itself, and all is lost thus laid out; but what is given (with Mary) to Christ is lost like sown grain, that shall be found again at the harvest of joy.[2]

Adams turns the parables of the prodigal and the sower against the institutional sponsors of vice. Taverns — "ordinaries" — transform dutiful sons into wastrels, gambling away their patrimonies, and are part of a whole structure of vain enticements that begin with theater and move through sedan-chairs, foppish dress, tobacco, and perfume.

For the antitheatrical divines of the seventeenth century, theater is associated with waste and prodigality. Drink provides a metaphoric umbrella that covers all the ways in which theater dissipates and diverts useful social energy and indeed commerce. In the eighteenth century Rousseau, too, sees the vice of prodigality spreading from the theater into society at large through the mechanism of the actor:

I observe in general that the condition of the actor is a condition of license and bad morals; the men there are delivered up to chaos; the women there lead scandalous lives; one and the other, stingy and prodigal at once, always burdened with debts and always throwing money away by handfuls, are as little restrained in their dissipations as they are scrupulous in the methods by which they gain access to them.[3]

For both Rousseau and Adams, profligacy and waste are signs of the actor's life offstage that threaten to spread into society at large. Actors fail to preserve or secure or save themselves, and their extravagances can leach out not just in the theaters but in the taverns they frequent and the brothels in which, according to Stephen Gosson, "these wormes" live "when they dare not nestle in the pescod at home . . . and are hidden in the eares of other mens corne." Waste and loss lurk, too, in other resorts of recreation: "Common bowling alleyes are privy mothes," warns Gosson, "that eate up the credite of many idle citizens."[4] Richard Head's Mr. Wheedle frequents spas as well as theaters: "His greatest *Mart*, and largest of contrivance, is *Epsom*, or *Tunbridge Wells*, where (blind-fold) he cannot miss of *Misses* enough to mislead, and of *Males* to unman for his profit."[5] This conflation of actors' lives with wasteful recreations—and the concomitant attack upon recreation as wasteful because theatrical — is closely related to the long tradition that identifies actors with prostitutes.

Prynne was not exaggerating in his description of the close proximity of the theaters to the "Hot-water Brothel-house." The theatrical entrepreneur Philip Henslowe took over the site of the Little Rose, a brothel, and built his theater, the Rose, on its grounds. New historicist critics like Steven Mullaney have responded strongly to these juxtapositions and have in some ways endorsed Prynne and his cohort by putting theater in its proper place at the margins of society. "The theater could not change its image because it could not change its nature," writes Joseph Lenz of the early modern English theater, for example: "by definition the professional theater is a fabricator of pleasurable illusions for profit, in a culture that conceives the act of seeing as copulation and the transaction of trade as base. The more it succeeded at attracting, pleasing, and profiting from audiences by making a spectacle of itself, the more it resembled a prostitute," he concludes. For Lenz, the public playhouse offered not only a "sight" of prostitution that stimulated the viewers with sumptuous costume and "effeminate, cross-dressed actors" but also a "site" where quite literal assignations could take place, hard by the brothels themselves.[6]

By literalizing the antitheatrical complaints against the theater, the new historicist misses a larger point. The kind of waste complained of is not just commercial, although plainly the language of commerce enters into it. "As I am woman — now, alas the day! — / What thriftless sighs shall poor Olivia breathe," exclaims Viola in *Twelfth Night* (2.2.38–39). Olivia wastes her sighs on the boy-actress: as Northbrooke puts it, "an effeminate player, while he faineth love, imprinteth wounds of love."[7] The actor is feigning, but the response is genuinely "thriftless" or, in the terms of Gosson's abuse, gratified adulterously and sodomitically in "conclaves," convened in nearby taverns. The exchange of money for the illusion of love (in either case) infuriates the moralist. Theaters and taverns, places where entertainment and drink are bought and sold, are marts of flesh. Now that cash has entered the equation, so does the possibility of the swindle. Theaters and taverns are not only wastes of time, they are places where money is wasted: good money spent on falsehood, illusion, and disease.

For Rousseau, too, theater diverts money from the poor by permitting audience members to sympathize with the distresses of fictional characters rather than real poor people. And shamming leaches into civil society. Early modern moralists found it difficult to separate the deserving poor from the sturdy beggars who impersonated them. Imposture and waste threaten even acts of charity. "It is so easy to personate Misery, and feign Distress," complained John Alcock in his *Observations on the Defects of the Poor Laws* (1752),

> that you are oftentimes at a loss to know, whether a Man's Wants be real or pretended, and whether you ought to relieve him as a Pauper, or punish him as an Impostor. No Law can define who are or who are not properly Paupers. The Idle, the Bold, the Impudent are always most forward to offer themselves and most clamorous for Relief: while the bashful Poor, the really distressed, keep aloof, and almost starve in Silence, and are ashamed and afraid to open their Mouths for Charity, and come a begging.

Throughout his critique of the poor law, Alcock adverts again and again to the problem of imposture. Poor relief, in his view, leads to waste: "The Sluggard, upon this Presumption, is tempted to continue in Sloth; the Glutton, as he receives his Gains, eats them, and the Drunkard, drinks them. In short, they labour less and spend more; and the very Law that provides for the Poor, makes Poor." The poor law should be suppressed, Alcock argues, because it gives "a Pretence for Strolling, and an Opportunity to a Number of Impostors to obtrude themselves upon the Public, and deceive or rob the Unwary." Alcock's arguments against the poor laws are filled with terms — *strolling, imposture, impudence, clamor, pretense,* obtruding upon the *public, deceit —* drawn from the vocabulary of theater. The vices of the poor share an illusory nature. For Alcock, tobacco, like "Dram drinking" and "Tea-Drinking," substitutes illusory for real nourishment. The ill effects of tea are in fact heightened by the diet of poverty: "in Concurrence with a low, coarse, vegetable Diet, the chief Food of poor People, its effects are mischiveous" and wasteful — "considerable Time attends this silly Habit, in preparing and sipping their Tea."[8] The dissipations of the poor lead them into acting and imposture, where they are both victims of the "silly Habit" and victimizers of the virtuous. The charitable cannot tell the impostors from the deserving poor, so completely is imposture entwined with poverty.

As the repeated emphasis on impostures suggests, behind the problem of wasting money or wasting emotion lurks a larger problem of entrapment in illusion. Even as the theater in the seventeenth and eighteenth centuries came to a more fully illusionistic aesthetic, the very notion of illusion foundered in the moralist's deploring of illusion. The English public playhouses of the late sixteenth century were professional commercial ventures with deep roots in the sacred rhythms of the old, amateur, liturgical drama. In them, *how* to see was a primary thematic concern: the old chestnut of "appearance versus reality" has its source in a problem for the early modern audience of whether to see events as secular or providential in their unfolding. For the moralists, this uncertainty of perception was anathema: the theater's world of mere appearances, of sham passions and misleading and arousing costume, had to be shamed by comparison with a higher order of reality.

And while early modern England is certainly a place where this problem found acute and extreme expression in both theatrical and antitheatrical literature, Herbert Blau points to it as central to all discussion of theater: "Yet, if it is only appearances we are talking about, then we must ask, as the theater does over and over — out of the unnerving implication that appearances are a deceit — why does reality, whatever it is, choose to play false? which is, in its interrogative substance, as close as we may get to a definition of theater. This may also be, through the camera obscura, as close as we may come to the appearance of ideology."[9] New historicist critics, noting the terror of illusion and illusory pleasures in the early modern theater, locate this in a historical moment. Blau, gnomically, suggests that theater everywhere in space and time is ontologically unsettling.

For the moralists and throughout this third act *drinking* stands in for a whole range of wasteful activities and illusory pleasures. The act begins, as it should, in the tavern, with some scrutiny of how deeply the vocabulary of the theater infuses the language of drinking in Shakespeare. Then the scene shifts to two other locations: Mr. Hardcastle's old house Liberty Hall in *She Stoops to Conquer* and Harry Hope's down-at-heel Raines-Law hotel. In both of these places a therapeutic, restorative agenda, prizing sincerity and truth to self, struggles with the languages of theater. Finally, in a last scene, acting itself seems to become a kind of compulsive, addictive behavior, like gambling. The modern actor, like the modern drunk, is more to be pitied than censured, less a monster of Protean excess than a regressive narcissist in need of help.

Scene One

THE TAVERN

"O God, that men should put an enemy in their mouths to steal away their brains!" Cassio exclaims after his drunken brawl. "That we should, with joy, pleasure, revel, and applause transform ourselves into beasts!" (*Othello*, 2.3.283–86). The language of transformation, revel, and applause that seeps into his complaint provides an echo of the antitheatrical writers of the early modern period. Throughout Shakespeare the connections between acting and drinking draw much of their energy from antitheatrical rhetoric. For antitheatrical writers, the beastly shameless transformations of actors mimic a kind of diabolic possession; and Cassio, too, calls out "O thou invisible spirit of wine, if thou has no name to be known by, let us call thee devil!" (275–77). Cassio's drunkenness splits him in two: "I have lost the immortal part of myself, and what remains is bestial" (258–60).

If actors, according to the writings of the divines, thwart God's will by laying claim to selves that are not those that God gave them, drinkers become grotesque players. William Vaughan, in *The Golden Fleece* (1626), a tract discovering "the Errours of *Religion*, the *Vices* and *Decayes* of the *Kingdome*, and lastly the *Wayes* to get *Wealth*," portrays the drunk as Protean in his playing: "if he enters after his bibbing into any unseemly passion or borrowes the gestures of a raging Lion, of the toyish Ape, of the sensuall Hog, or of the lascivious Goat, pratling or acting any feates more than are decent, or more than he used at any other times, he may be branded with the note of Drunkard, then which nothing is more odious in the sight of our vertuous Societie."[10] Embodying elements of possession, transformation, shame, and bestiality and threatening the common weal, drunkards and actors are figures that stretch the limits of social performance.

In *Pierce Penniless His Supplication to the Devil*, Thomas Nashe also runs through a bestiary of drunkards, from "ape drunk" through "lion drunk" to "swine drunk," "maudlin drunk," "martin drunk," and "goat drunk, when, in his drunkenness, he hath no mind but on lechery." Nashe warns his readers not to be victimized by the hardened drinker who can reach the level of "fox drunk, as many of these Dutchmen be, that will never bargain but when they are drunk."[11] These complaints and warnings are not so far from the description of the Protean player in Robert Burton's *Anatomy of Melancholy*; where the catalog of beasts runs "to rage like a lion, bark like a cur, fight like a dragon, as meek as a lamb and yet again grin like a tiger, weep like a crocodile, insult over some & yet others domineer over him, here command, there crouch, tyrannize in one place, be baffled in another, a wise man at home, a fool abroad to make others merry!"[12] In their wild prodigality, these figures point to a paradox. "In the Renaissance revival of paganism," writes Anya Taylor, "Bacchus liberates: he encourages an explosive nature, multiplying personal being, an intense quest (because secular) for artistic expression. But even then, Dionysus posed dangers for the human being seeking freedom. Although Dionysus himself is sinuous and slippery, creative and destructive by turns, the human being who takes on his drunkenness can become fixed as a caricature."[13]

Iago seems to have some familiarity with these Protean bestiaries as he embarks upon his scheme to disgrace Cassio:

> If I can fasten but one cup upon him,
> With that which he hath drunk tonight already,
> He'll be as full of quarrel and offense
> As my young mistress' dog.
>
> (2.3.45–48)

Cassio's sudden recovery, his prompt sobering up, likewise reflects the quick changes of the Protean performer: it is, he moralizes, simply another kind of demonic possession: "It hath pleased the devil drunkenness to give place to the devil wrath" (290–91). Cassio's drunken scene plays out in little Othello's eventual descent into bestiality and anticipates the language of diabolic possession that will accompany it.[14] Finding no other name for the "invisible spirit of wine," Cassio calls it "devil," just as Othello demands to see Iago's feet. They share a common sense of bafflement: what has diabolically undone them eludes easy naming and identification.

The grimaces of drunken excess mar Othello's visage. Desdemona recognizes a kind of frenzy in her husband as he threatens her in the bed: "And yet I fear you," she declares; "for you're fatal then / When your eyes roll so." "Alas, why gnaw you so your nether lip?" she cries a bit later (5.2.38, 45). The play's final scene is rich with associations among drink, acting, and diabolic possession. "Blow me about in winds! Roast me in sulfur!" Othello beseeches the devils who will torment him after his death. "Wash me in steep-down gulfs of liquid fire! / O Desdemon! Dead, Desdemon! Dead! O! O!" (5.2.288–90). Othello's speech breaks down into bestial howls.

Both Cassio and Othello live on an edge, a delicate balance: drink threatens Cassio's "reputation," and what remains is bestial; with Othello's "occupation" gone, he embarks upon his "cause" — "It is the cause, it is the cause, my soul" (5.2.1). Othello seems to know about Cassio's problem, as he warns him: "Good Michael, look you to the guard tonight. / Let's teach ourselves that honorable step / Not to outsport discretion" (2.3.1–3), on the very night of Cassio's indiscretion. *Outsporting* moves in two directions: both toward the notion of wild partying (which Othello is cautioning Cassio against) and toward a sense drawn from gardening, of wild fecundity and excessive growth. Iago, of course, puts this sense in our minds when he instructs Roderigo:

> Our bodies are our gardens, to the which our wills are gardeners: so that if we plant nettles or sow lettuce, set hyssop and weep up thyme, supply it with one gender of herbs or distract it with many, either to have it sterile with idleness or manured with industry — why the power and corrigible authority of this lies in our wills. If the beam of our lives had not one scale of reason to poise another of sensuality, the blood and baseness of our natures would conduct us to most preposterous conclusions. But we have reason to cool our raging motions, our carnal stings, our unbitted lusts, whereof I take this that you call love to be a sect or scion. (1.3.323–36)

"It cannot be," whines Roderigo. He finds this analysis reductive: yet drink upsets with ease the beam of Cassio's balance, and Othello is easily led by the nose to the most preposterous conclusions by Iago. Like Iago, the antitheatrical moralists say that reason should counterpoise the weight of carnality in our souls, yet they know that a taste of drink or a glimpse of the playhouse will immediately whirl us out of balance. And at least in *Othello* Iago is right: one drink more destroys Cassio's reputation, and one word of warning — "Ha? I like not that" (3.1.35) — hurls Othello toward perdition.[15]

That Iago is a stage-manager, a playwright, and a director in this enterprise, making unwitting actors of Cassio, Roderigo, and Othello, is a commonplace at least as old as A. C. Bradley.[16] Iago's trick is to transform Othello from all-in-all sufficient general to "murderous coxcomb," a homicidal gull, an armed Malvolio. At the peak of his humiliation and pain, Othello cries out: "Are there no stones in heaven / But what serves for thunder?" (5.2.240, 242–43). Does he intuit above him the heaven of the playhouse in which what Ben Jonson called "the roll'd bullet" — a rolling stone — served for thunder? [17] Cassio's fragile grip on himself is revealed when drink transforms him into something bestial, Othello's in his grotesque performance as Iago's puppet.

"That which hath made them drunk hath made me bold," Lady Macbeth reports of the power of drink. "What hath quenched them hath given me fire" (2.2.1–2). *Macbeth* presents the murder of Duncan as an imposture, a theatrical hoodwinking of its witnesses that is explicitly facilitated by drink. The play relates drinking to theater throughout in its images: "Was the hope drunk / Wherein you dressed yourself? Hath it slept since?" Lady Macbeth charges her husband. "And wakes it now, to look so green and pale / At what it did so freely?" (1.7.36–39). The night before the morning after is recalled here as an episode of costuming and revelry, free doing and dressing that is regretted in the morning. The metaphor of the hangover hangs over the whole play. Macbeth's disappointments are described in terms that are reminiscent of Falstaff's problems. "He cannot buckle his distempered cause / Within the belt of rule," Caithness offers as a diagnosis; but Angus sees him not as bloated but as emaciated: "Now does he feel his title / Hang loose about him, like a giant's robe / Upon a dwarfish thief." The association between ill-fitting clothing and the "green and pale" sickness of the morning after is enforced by Mentieth's recognition of Macbeth's disease as the jangling nerves of a self-loathing drunk: "Who then shall blame / His pestered senses to recoil and start," he muses, "When all that is within him does condemn / Itself for being there?" (5.2.15–16, 20–25). The rebels present themselves as a purge, and Macbeth himself asks the Doctor to "cast / The water of my land": "What rhubarb, senna, or what purgative drug / Would scour these English hence" (5.3.52–53, 57–58). Just before the cry of women that marks his wife's death, Macbeth pronounces himself surfeited: "I have supped full with horrors" (5.5.13), and then the news leads him to imagine the "poor player" (5.5.25) strutting and fretting, miscast and despised.

For James Calderwood, the whole play's dynamic is one of provoking a kind of thirst in audiences: "The dramatic future is planted prophetically in the present and brought to fruition and harvest in good season. The announcement of a want in the present generates a wanting in both Macbeth and us and at the same time assures us that this lack/desire will be filled/satisfied in the future. For us, if not for Macbeth, this is repeatedly the case." The weary repetition of "Tomorrow, and tomorrow, and tomorrow" (5.5.19) coupled with the image of the poor player suggests a cycle of rehearsal and performance that entraps all players, poor and expert alike. "Time will have its way with good ones, too," Calderwood says, "and indeed with all playing and plays to boot. It is in the nature of theater that what is performed on stage is as mortal as Lady Macbeth herself, who died not 'hereafter' but now." "In the irreversible flow of enactment" plays end: but they also keep coming back, like Banquo's line of kings, stretching out to the crack of doom. "Our play is done, but that's all one," sings Feste at the end of *Twelfth Night*; "And we'll strive to please you every day" (5.1.407–8). "[E]ach representation" of *Macbeth*, Calderwood stresses, "will only make the play more wanted" — and "being wanted," Prince Hal says, is to "be more wondered at" (*1 Henry IV*, 1.3.195).[18] Not just *Macbeth* but drama in general repeats the repetitive action of drinking alcohol, where drinking prompts thirst and thirst more drinking.

The Macbeths host parties where the host behaves inappropriately, sneaking away during the feast or frightening the guests. Duncan apparently questions Macbeth's absence from the party in his honor, and Lady Macbeth has to go find him with a testy reminder: "Hath he asked for me?" "Know you not he has?" (1.7.31). The whole banquet scene in the middle of the play is a revelry, a party whose guest of honor attends in ironic response to Macbeth's repeated invitations:

> I drink to the general joy o'th'whole table,
> And to our friend Banquo, whom we miss.
> Would he were here! To all, and him, we thirst,
> And all to all.
>
> (3.4.90–93)

Banquo's unfailing attendance comically unseats Macbeth ("The table's full" [46]), and Lady Macbeth sees his fits and starts as poor performance, "Impostors to true fear": "Why do you make such faces? When all's done / You look but on a stool" (64, 67–68). A language of drink closely weaves itself into Macbeth's association with poor playing, ill-fitting costume, and clumsy imposture. "The wine of life is drawn, and the mere lees / Is left this vault to brag of," he groans, struggling to mask his complicity in the murder of Duncan (2.3.97–98). The grooms, gilded with blood, are stage props, "but as pictures," Lady Macbeth assures him earlier. "Get on your nightgown," she urges as the knocking at the gate begins, taking him off to the tiring house (58, 74).

What the grooms mean as "pictures" is sketched out earlier by Lady Macbeth in 1.7, a scene imbued with the language of drinking. "When in swinish sleep / Their drenched natures lie as in death, / What cannot you and I perform upon / Th'unguarded Duncan?" she prompts (68–71). Here the image of the swinish drunk is reminiscent of the opening of *Taming of the Shrew*. Thrown out of the tavern by the Landlady, Christopher Sly collapses unconscious in the play's induction. "O monstrous beast, how like a swine he lies!" exclaims the Lord in the induction. "Grim death, how foul and loathsome is thine image!" The Lord moralizes the spectacle as one of dehumanization and deanimation; and then he proposes a theatrical imposture: "Sirs, I will practice on this drunken man" (33–35). Sly's vision is both a drunkard's dream and an unsettling hangover: he wakes calling for a hair of the dog ("a pot of small ale" [induction 2.1]) and is forced not only to endure his casting as a Lord and play a part he is unperfect in but also to submit to the discipline of performing as audience to a play he does not understand. "Would 'twere done!" he says of his ordeal (1.1.254) the last time he appears in the folio text; in *Taming of the Shrew*, of course, his unconscious form is dropped unceremoniously back where it came from to close out the frame. In both instances, the movement is from swinishness to imaged death to theatrical imposture and practice. The drunk is not only a carcass, but a carcass animated by unwitting and humiliating performance.

Falstaff, whose water, like Macbeth's, betokens a national disease, also identifies swinishness with being the victim of a theatrical scheme: he suspects that the Prince has given him a small servant in order to make him look ridiculous. "I am not only witty in myself, but the cause that wit is in other men. I do here walk before thee like a sow that hath overwhelmed all her litter but one. If the Prince put thee into my service for any other reason than to set me off, why then I have no judgment," he tells his tiny page (*2 Henry IV* 1.2.9–14). The association between Falstaff's tavern and the theater is proverbial. Less proverbial is Falstaff's own association of sack with the energies of performance. The first of sack's operations, as he puts it, is to stimulate imagination and project it into speech. "It ascends me into the brain, dries me there all the foolish and dull and crudy vapors which environ it, makes it apprehensive, quick, forgetive, full of nimble, fiery, and delectable shapes, which, delivered o'er to the voice, the tongue, which is the birth, becomes excellent wit" (4.3.96–101). Improvisation, with which Falstaff is associated throughout the plays, is a projection or voicing of the delectable shapes of the imagination. Performance is the tongue giving birth to wit.

The "wooden O" itself in the *Henry* plays is not just the open-air public playhouse in which "flat, unraised spirits" (a problem of fermentation?) have trouble staging the battle of Agincourt. In the two parts of *Henry IV* the tavern constitutes a kind of alternative interior environment, set aside from the worlds of the court and the battlefield; hollowness and woodenness evoke not just playhouses but barrels — and barrels, of course, evoke Sir John. Falstaff's playing and his mock death are mocked in *Henry V* by the narrative of his real death (real because narrated, real because unstaged), but the play's epilogue closes off Henry's performance, too, with a narrated death and a reminder of theater's constantly self-renewing repetitions of rehearsal and performance, "which oft our stage hath shown" (epilogue, 13).

Where Falstaff is a staunch advocate of both sack and performance, Hamlet remains hostile to both. He refuses to admit that his dark clothes and tears betoken mourning; he resents clowns who improvise. And, characteristically, he associates drink with swinish performance. "They clepe us drunkards, and with swinish phrase / Soil our addition" (1.4.19–20), he tells the watch in the famous scene on the battlements: the Danes' reputation for drinking has made them Europe's Christopher Slys. The proverbial elaboration upon this observation reaches out to "particular men" who have faults that mar their performance of their virtues and leave them censured. As C. L. Barber has pointed out, this speech "specifies a character defect that is sociable; the description would fit a sociable drinker who becomes an alcoholic. . . . Too much yeast, too much ferment, is suggested by 'o'er-leavens,' a suggestion picked up in the final summary drink image: 'the dram of eale / Doth all the noble substance of a doubt / To his own scandal' (lines 36–38)." "The small 'dram' contrasts with the 'draughts of Rhenish' Claudius 'drains,' even while it develops the theme," says Barber as he imagines Hamlet's reverie to be autobiographical on Shakespeare's part, invoking "one belated anecdote of a merry-cheeked, Falstaffian old man."[19]

Whether Shakespeare's father was an alcoholic or not, the Ghost's very entrances explicitly make a connection between drink and theater. He shows up in the first scene of the play resolutely on cue: markedly on cue, for the clock that chimes when he appears is coincident with Bernardo's narrative: "The bell then beating one — [*Enter Ghost*]." The Ghost's appearance here is pat, almost comical, as it fulfills the guards' promises and discomfits the scholar, Horatio. It is perhaps menacing, too, for those who believe that speaking of the devil will make him appear. Similarly, in Hamlet's scene on the battlements the Ghost appears at the mention of "eale": his cue is "a famous crux," as David Bevington puts it in his edition.[20] Since his third appearance in the play, in the closet scene, is equally marked as on cue, the cue must conjure him up here, too. But is it "evil"? — is it "ease," "esil," or "ale"? Donald Foster, who has pioneered computer applications in the humanities, has recently addressed the editorial problem of the "dram of eale": a search of contemporary printed texts reveals, after "two centuries of leisurely and ultimately fruitless speculation," he reports, that "eale was once a familiar north-country word for heather ale" of legendary potency.[21]

Failed fermentation lurks in Hamlet's suicidal first soliloquy: home brewers know how "weary, stale, flat, and unprofitable" a botched batch can be.[22] The Ghost's link with theater is as strong as its link with beer, for it functions through the first part of the play as its first riddle of ambiguous performance. Ophelia's "garments, heavy with their drink," pull her down as she is unable to sustain "mermaidlike" flotation in the element: this is not *Twelfth Night* and she is no Sebastian, despite Hamlet's own Sebastian-like emergence "naked" from the sea after his adventure with the pirates (4.7.182, 177, 45). Hamlet's return almost parodies the comic shipwrecks of *Twelfth Night* and *Comedy of Errors*, just as the Ghost's entrances almost parody the convention of the "pat" entrance — "and pat he comes like the catastrophe of the old comedy," as Edmund might put it (*King Lear* 1.2.137).

Ophelia, however, does not make a miraculous return like Hamlet's.

She falls into the water:

> Her clothes spread wide,
> And mermaid-like a while they bore her up
> Which time she chanted snatches of old lauds,
> As one incapable of her distress,
> Or like a creature native and indued
> Unto that element,

as Gertrude recounts. Ophelia's madness makes of her a performer, singing old songs, unaware of the danger in which she finds herself. Mermaids, dolphins, and otters are all creatures "native and indued" to the water ("that element") who reminded Renaissance thinkers of humans. Richard of Gloucester expounds upon his own mermaidlike ability to drown sailors. Dolphins were fish that drowned; otters "neither fish nor fowl": like humans, who found themselves somewhere on a sliding scale between beasts and angels and aspired to ascend into the heavens, these watery creatures yearned to live on land. Closely associated with mermaids, the dolphin, too, was also a kind of performer: the dolphin-fish could change its color, like a chameleon, to match its surroundings. Not so Ophelia: not really "native to the element," she only floats "till her garments, heavy with their drink, / Pull'd the poor wretch from her melodious lay / To muddy death" (4.7.175–82). Ophelia's inadvertent and incapable foray into performance ends with the heavy downward pull of her sodden, drunken clothes.

All it takes, as Hamlet says on the battlements, is a "dram of eale" to take you down, and Ophelia's death plays out this persistent threat. Hamlet's concern is not only for "particular men" but also for nations, and like him the polemicists of early modern England felt that a reputation for drinking could lead to national disgrace and ruin. "A storm of criticism erupted against alehouses in the late sixteenth century which continued until the English Revolution," writes Peter Clark. The opponents of the alehouses, not surprisingly, correspond to the opponents of the theater. Clark notes how the alehouses, during the controversy over Sunday games and sports, became places where drinkers resorted during church hours. "Often no doubt the cramped premises forced many of the entertainments to spill outside into the yard, street, or adjacent green: here one finds games of football between the parish youth, bear-baiting, and morris dancing. On other occasions, the whole building was taken over as when a group of Warrington men performed a 'play called Henry the Eight' in the loft of Gregory Harrison's alehouse during Sunday service in May 1632."[23] Alehouses were stigmatized as brothels, attacked for diverting apprentices from their training, reviled for interfering with church: all these charges were leveled against the theater as well. If the enemy of my enemy is my friend, then alehouse and theater find themselves friends in the early seventeenth century. "I may complaine of Ale-houses," wrote King James I, "for receipt of Stealers of my Deere; but the countrey may complaine for stealing their horses, oxen, and sheepe; for murder, cutting of purses, and such like offences; for those are their haunts. Devouring beasts, as Lyons and Beares, will not bee where they have no dennes nor couert; So there would be no theeues, if they had not their receipts, and these Ale-houses as their dennes."[24]

"Drunkards are worse than beasts," writes "R. Iunius," "in that beasts remaine the same they were created; whereas Drunkards subvert natures institution, cease to bee what God made them, reasonable creatures, and suffer themselves to be transformed by drinke into swine, as *Elpenor*, one of *Ulysses* companions was turned by *Circe* into a Hog. . . ."[25] Elpenor is more explicitly under the influence in Homer's poem: he falls off Circe's roof, where he has passed out as a result of the long partying after Odysseus has moved in with Circe. In *Richard III* Gloucester woos Lady Anne, shamelessly invoking the sliding scale in which humans can sink to the bestial or rise to the angelic. "No beast so fierce but knows some touch of pity," Lady Anne reproaches Richard, whose emblem is the boar. "But I know none, and therefore am no beast," counters the dissembler (1.2.71–72). Richard's joke is a good one: while the moralists would claim that actors and drunkards subvert nature's institution and cease to be what God made them, Richard claims to be exactly what God made him — "no beast." "Rise, dissembler," says Lady Anne, won, or at least defeated, by his wooing. She knows what he is, too. And his den, hard by the bear-baiting arenas and the taverns, is the theater. Here he enjoys the full free play of his performance, applauding his shadow, reveling in his courtship of Lady Anne. Clarence anticipates his own ignominious end in the butt of malmsey with a dream in which Richard, having "tempted" him "to walk upon the hatches," "stumble[s]" like a clumsy drunk and pitches Clarence overboard (1.4.11, 18).

Clarence and Lady Anne become Richard's victims because they believe him: such is his power as a performer. "Not a beast" is a self-definition that works because the play demonstrates that Richard does things animals can't do, but it is a test of courage and self-knowledge to go where the definition goes. Beasts feel pity; he doesn't: and that, paradoxically, is what makes him fully human. Linking drink with acting, and drunkenness with swinish death, grotesque or bestial performance, and ill-fitting costume, Shakespeare partakes in the moralists' language of opprobrium and portrays human beings as sinful, terribly flawed actors in the theater of God's judgment. "Shakespeare's villains are all actors: discuss" goes the old exam question. Shakespeare's villains have mastered the world of performance; they are at home there, native to the element. Their mastery, however, marks them as performers who deceive other humans but will not deceive the deity.

This is paradoxical, and so are government policies toward not just theater but also other kinds of public festive practices in Shakespeare's England. The government looked for ways to license and control church ales, which often whirled out of control, and Sunday sports.[26] Policies governing public recreation were often as contradictory as the policies that sponsored the theater while harshly limiting the players' freedom of movement. The Stuart government, particularly, had problems with drunkenness at court and with tobacco.

"Shakespeare said no word of tobacco or smoking; 'the presence of that absence is everywhere,'" writes Sarah Augusta Dickson, a historian of tobacco.[27] But there is no question that tobacco joined drinking and acting in the reproaches of the moralists and in the era's attempts at social reform. "Tobacco and ale are now made inseparable in the base vulgar sort," complained Sir Peter Fretchwill in the House of Commons in 1621; to Barnaby Riche, "there is not so base a groom that comes into an alehouse but he must have his pipe of tobacco."[28] Drinking tobacco, as the custom was called, led to thirst which led to drink: topers used tobacco as a palate teaser, "such as Caveare and salt meates were used among the *Sibarites*," Vaughan declares in *The Golden Fleece*.[29] "'Twas caviar to the general," Hamlet remarks about the play, "never acted, or if it was, not above once," which he wants the Player to quote from. But this play, which he admires, lacked "sallets in the lines to make the matter savory": failing to provoke thirst, the play failed in the theater. Yet after a taste of it Hamlet concludes that "the play's the thing / Wherein I'll catch the conscience of the king" (2.2.436, 441–42, 605–6). Like caviar or salad, performance is addictive.

"Keepers of brothels used tobacco pipes as signs to indicate the nature of their houses," reports George Louis Beer. Tobacco was identified (through imagery of smoke, of course) with waste and self-destructively addictive pleasures. In 1627 Charles I complained that the economy of Virginia was "wholly built upon smoke, tobacco being the only means it hath produced." [30] Charles struggled with his people's dedication to wasteful and illusory pleasures, promulgating laws against those who "live to spend all they have at Alehouses," and de-cried the destabilizing effects of the tobacco trade in a Royal Proclama-tion of March 14, 1638: "The foreigne Plantations of Our Subjects re-main unfortified, the Colonies of other Nations do flourish, the wealth of our Kingdoms is exhausted, in immoderate use of a vain and need-lesse weed is continued, the health of Our Subjects is much impaired, and their Manners in danger to be depraved." [31] Charles found himself in a dilemma that looks familiar: while he prohibited the growing of the "needlesse weed" domestically, he relied upon revenues from its im-portation from Virginia to sustain his rule. Cardinal Richelieu, too, "did not prohibit tobacco," reports Jacques Bonneau, a historian of the French involvement in tobacco; "he did better: he taxed it." [32]

William Vaughan's *The Golden Fleece* specifically sought to remedy the nation's dependency upon the tobacco trade by championing an al-ternative, the Golden Fleece itself, by which Vaughn meant "*the* Plan-tation *and* Fishing *in the* Newfoundland" (3 : 2; Aaar). Rather than ex-pending its resources in the vaporous trade with Virginia, Vaughn saw trade in fish and agriculture with the northern colonies as morally su-perior. Through the spirit of Sir Thomas Smith, invoked by Apollo, Vaughan singles out three "superfluities" that waste the substance of the kingdom: the spirit rails "1. Upon the extraordinary vice of *Tobacco*. 2. upon forraigne stuffes and silks, which wrought the Decay of Eng-lish cloth and consequently of many poore Households which lived by spinning, weaving, fulling, and dressing of Cloth. 3. He enveighed against the multitudes of *wine tavernes* and *Alehouses,* saying that a great part of our *Treasure* were yearly wasted in these fiery houses" (3 : 78, Kkk3v). Nor does the theater escape Vaughan's attack: a mock litany of St. George in his first volume couples the playhouses with another of Vaughan's *bêtes noirs*, lawyers and lawsuits:

From fond Maskes, *and idle mumming:*
From fain'd Playes *and causeless drumming,*

. . . .

From disbursing needful treasure
To maintayne phantastike pleasure,
From greasing Lawyers *hands with Gold,*
Which better serves to keepe a hold,
From fostring Suites *(O poys'nous Toad)*
For Money, *which ends* Warres *abroad,*

. . . .

Great Brittaines *Genius*
Guard and restore us.

(1:91, Mm2)

Vaughan's lumping together of lawsuits, taverns, and imports of cloth and tobacco with playhouses, all under the mantle of waste, characterizes a whole range of activities as threats to useful industry.

As such it participates in a larger social dialogue about the usefulness of any kind of recreation, a conflict in the Stuart period that Leah Marcus has called "the politics of mirth."[33] As Marcus points out, authors of court masques in this period like Ben Jonson struggled to reconcile often contradictory policies toward public festive practices. Drunkenness and excessive feasting among the courtiers often conflicted with the moral messages of the masques that entertained visiting royalty and celebrated King James. Contemporary commentators frequently noted the collapse of these performances, too, into debauchery.

Such a dynamic is enacted in Shakespeare's *Tempest*. Prospero's wedding masque "heavily vanishes" as the magician remembers Caliban's drunken conspiracy against his life. Ariel describes the trio of Caliban, Stephano, and Trinculo — in whose name the word echoes — as "red-hot with drinking," inflamed to violence by the insolence of the air and the ground, bestial, "like unbacked colts," led "calflike" through the gorse to Prospero's "filthy-mantled pool" (4.1.171, 176, 178, 181). There can be no better victims than these for Prospero's "stale" trick of decking the line with "trumpery" and "glistering apparel" (187, 186, 193 [stage direction]).

Shakespeare in this scene links Prospero's grandest theatrical stunt, the masque, with his next theatrical stunt, the decking of the line. For the first, Miranda and Ferdinand are an admiring audience; in the second, Trinculo and Stephano are gross dupes, and Caliban is appalled by their doting on luggage: "Let it alone, thou fool, it is but trash" (4.1.225). Caliban has sobered up and can see the difference; but the play's juxtaposition of the two scenes allows an audience to see the wedding masque, too, as a kind of trumpery, "baseless" and "insubstantial" (151, 154). Prospero presents his revels to Ferdinand as trifles that will vanish into thin air, being made, like them, like the "cloud-capped towers," and like the "great globe itself" of "such stuff as dreams are made on." The globe and all that inherit it shall "dissolve," Prospero intones to Ferdinand: "Enter Caliban, Stephano, Trinculo, all wet," runs the stage direction just a few lines later (154, 193 [stage direction]). Here Shakespeare deploys the motifs of his complex engagement of theater as a kind of entrapment in illusion that reflects entrapment in the illusions of real life — as in Blau's provocative question, "Why does reality, whatever it is, choose to play false?" For both the antitheatricalist, for whom reality does not play false and the suggestion that it does is an outrageous lie, and the new historicist, for whom playing false and reality are the same, Blau's question does not resonate, but *The Tempest*'s island is full of noises.

Feste's song at the end of *Twelfth Night* weaves together Shakespeare's language of drink with his language of theater:

When that I was and a little tiny boy
    With hey, ho, the wind and the rain
A foolish thing was but a toy,
    For the rain it raineth every day.

But when I came to man's estate
    With hey, ho, the wind and the rain,
'Gainst knaves and fools men shut their gate,
    For the rain it raineth every day.

But when I came, alas, to wive,
    With hey, ho, the wind and the rain,
By swaggering could I never thrive,
    And the rain it raineth every day.

But when I came unto my beds,
    With hey, ho, the wind and the rain,
With tosspots still had drunken heads,
    For the rain it raineth every day.

A great while ago the world begun,
    With hey, ho, the wind and the rain,

But that's all one, our play is done,
    And we'll strive to please you every day.

Leslie Hotson, the famous stage historian, felt this song invoked a grim "Drunkard's Progress" from playing with toys to waking up with "drunken heads," a kind of cautionary tale for Sir Toby Belch. But the song reaches out in at least two other directions as well. As the fool's song it comes from the most actorly of actors and invokes a profession that is somehow not "man's estate": coming to adulthood, the fool is locked out, mistaken for a knave or a thief.[34] This may be the actor's fate, but in Illyria everyone is in some way an actor: everyone, Feste suggests, is a Fool.

The song's sphere of reference, however, is cosmic as well as theatrical: "the rain it raineth every day." When that happens occasionally, the performance in Shakespeare's outdoor, open air theater is canceled. But every day? "A great while ago the world begun, with hey, ho, the wind and the rain," sings Feste. "In the beginning God created the heauen and the earth," says the Geneva Bible (1587 — probably the version best known to Shakespeare). The marginal commentaries in this version insist that it is a very watery beginning: on the second day God made a "firmament in the middes of the waters: and let it separate the waters from the waters" (Genesis 1:6). The Geneva commentators adumbrate: "(As the sea and riuers, from those waters that are in the cloudes, which are vpholden by Gods power, lest they should ouerwhelme the worlde.)" Shakespeare's vision of apocalypse as a collapse of the firmament and a dissolving into watery primeval chaos is both traditional and uniquely his own. Tied up in Feste's song with the rhythms of drinking, acting, and regularly scheduled entertainment — "we'll strive to please you every day" — a watery end is just barely held at bay. The actor's ethic of performance struggles to fight off an ever-encroaching rainy darkness. "What's a drunken man like, Fool?" asks Olivia early in the play. "Like a drowned man, a fool, and a madman," Feste replies. "One drink above heat makes him a fool, the second mads him, the third drowns him" (1.5.127–30).

Portraying drinking as a kind of possession or intoxication that leads to beastly transformation of the self, Shakespeare links drinking with acting: both are Protean diversions of the self into misleading and humiliating exposure and performance. In expressing these attitudes, he adopts and echoes in his plays the language of antitheatrical and anti-alehouse pamphleteering. But the theater's reliance upon the illusions of acting leads to wealth and prosperity for its shareholders. Despite the evanescence of performance, audiences come back and pay good money for more. Nothing can be more certain than the uncertainty and transitory nature of this arrangement: the dissolution of the Globe theater by act of Parliament in 1642 makes that clear. With the closing of the theaters, the wooden Os of the Bankside and Shoreditch, the institution that Shakespeare perfected and critiqued in his plays ceased to exist. All that awaits now, as Prospero and Feste prophesy, is the dissolving of the Great Globe itself.

Scene Two

LIBERTY HALL

In the *British Magazine* (February, March, and April 1760) Oliver Goldsmith published an essay that placed him in Shakespeare's most famous site of drinking, "the Boar's-head tavern, still kept at Eastcheap":

> Here, by a pleasant fire, in the very room where old Sir John Falstaff cracked his jokes, in the very chair which was sometimes honoured by prince Henry, and sometimes polluted by his immoral merry companion, I sat, and ruminated on the follies of youth; wished to be young again; but was resolved to make the best of life while it lasted, and now and then compared past and present times together. I considered myself as the only living representative of the old Knight, and transported my imagination back to the times when the Prince and he gave life to the revel, and made even debauchery not disgusting.

As Goldsmith drinks and talks to the landlord, something strange happens: "His cravat seemed quilled into a ruff, and his breeches swelled out into a fardingale. I now fancied him changing sexes; and, as my eyes began to close in slumber, I imagined my fat landlord actually converted into as fat a landlady." The essayist recognizes this figure to be "Dame Quickly, mistress of the tavern in the days of Sir John"; likewise, "the liquor we were drinking . . . seemed converted into sack and sugar."[35] She regales him with the history of the building, as it runs through various incarnations: a convent, a brothel (the two are of course virtually indistinguishable), and a fashionable or less fashionable gathering place for Whigs or for Tories. And she counters his claim that "those were merry times when you drew sack for prince Henry: men were twice as strong, and twice as wise, and much braver, and ten times more charitable, than now" with a narrative of vanity, folly, and vice.

In a passage which Goldsmith did not include when revising the essay for its appearance in his collected essays, she regales her listener with a description of the age of Henry V: "King Henry V. who was one of the best princes that ever sat on the throne, was fond of burning those Wickliffites. There were few feasts or entertainments, in which the people were not delighted with two or three roasted Wickliffites. 'Tis certain, if what was alledged against them be true, they deserved no mercy; they were magicians or witches every one of them; they were sometimes seen eating dead bodies torn from the grave. Sir John Oldcastle, one of the chief of the sect, was particularly fond of human flesh" (3 : 100n34, 104 – 5). This passage goes far in challenging the simple nostalgia of the narrator of the essay: and it partakes of the irony with which the whole essay debunks the notion of a glorious and less vicious past. But more strikingly, it conflates the fictional death of Falstaff ("Sir John's death afflicted me to such a degree, that I sincerely believe, I drank more liquor for myself than I drew for my customers" [3 : 101]) with the martyrdom of Sir John Oldcastle, the character's original name in the earliest versions of the *Henry IV* plays. Oldcastle's appearance in the *British Magazine* version of the essay provides a collision between the sentimental treatment of Falstaff's rejection and death and the barbarous treatment accorded his historical original. The Boar's Head Tavern becomes, in the "Reverie," a place where the essayist must confront a past dominated by superstition, intolerance, and persecution.

"Would it were bed time and all were well," says Kate Hardcastle at the end of the first scene of *She Stoops to Conquer*. She is quoting Falstaff on the eve of the battle at Shrewsbury as she and Miss Neville prepare for their own campaign.[36] As she exits on this allusion to Falstaff, the scene changes: "SCENE, *An Alehouse Room. Several shabby fellows, with Punch and Tobacco*." The scenic transformation of Mr. Hardcastle's *"old-fashioned House"* into the Three Pigeons alehouse, where Tony Lumpkin holds forth, is seemingly conjured by Kate's invocation of Falstaff. The Three Pigeons merges with the Boar's Head as a site of self-consciously theatrical confusion and displacement. Lumpkin's joke is predicated on the likeness between Hardcastle's house and a tavern like the Boar's Head, where, the essayist remarks, "the room also conspired to throw my reflections back into antiquity: the oak-floor, the Gothic windows, and the ponderous chimney-piece, had long withstood the tooth of time" ("A Reverie," 3 : 99). Such a reflection on the passage of time comes to Marlow when he arrives at what he thinks is the Buck's Head and muses on "[t]he usual fate of a large mansion. Having first ruined the master by good housekeeping, it at last comes to levy contributions as an inn" (5:128). Marlow is deceived by Tony's trick because the house really does look like an inn; and Hastings, who at this point in the play is not in on the joke, finds that the "antique" character of the place is likely to inflate the bill: "I have often seen a good sideboard, or a marble chimney-piece, tho' not actually put in the bill, enflame a reckoning confoundedly" (5:128). Marlow and Hastings imagine the Hardcastle house to be an inn like the Boar's Head in Eastcheap, trading on its reputation for antiquity, capitalizing upon nostalgia: a practice which the fantastic Mrs. Quickly in the essay debunks while the real landlord drones on, "giving [the listener] an account of the repairs he had made in the house" (3:111–12).

The suggestion that Hardcastle's house has in common with Old-castle's Boar's Head a kind of theatrical antiquity enhances the sense that this country house is a site of role-playing. Kate, taking on the role of barmaid, insists upon a theatrical model: "Don't you think I look something like Cherry in the Beaux Stratagem?" she asks Pimple, the maid, before presenting herself in this guise to Marlow in act 3 (5:168). The play's title pushes the allusion toward another Shakespearean model, Petruchio's country house in *The Taming of the Shrew*. Shakespeare's Kate is somehow brought from Padua by a nightmare journey (like Mrs. Hardcastle's in act 5) through a boggy, foggy countryside to a place where inept servants with names like Nathaniel, Gregory, Curtis, Philip, Walter, Adam, and Ralph join Grumio (with its pun on "groom") to torment her. And that country house is of course reminiscent of the country house to which Sly is carried in the induction, where again a scheme of imposture and dislocation is under way. Goldsmith echoes the comedy of Petruchio's servants in the opening scene of act 2, where Hardcastle attempts to instruct his servants in "table exercise" (5:125). Petruchio's strategy in *The Taming of the Shrew* relies upon a language of falconry in which the falcon (or "haggard") is deprived of food "and till she stoop she must not be full-gorged" (4.1.179). Goldsmith reverses the dynamic of Shakespeare's play: here it is she who stoops who ventures on a kind of educational exercise with Marlow. "If I could teach him a little confidence, it would be doing somebody that I know of a piece of service," she comments after the sober sentimental interview of their first encounter (5:148). Where Petruchio assaults Kate at their first meeting, denying her name, crudely asserting possession of her person, and (unfairly) insisting that her marriage to him is a done deal, Marlow is tongue-tied in the presence of Kate Hardcastle.

Bernard Harris comments that Goldsmith's strategy of allusion in the play's title "brings with it overtones which we would be stupid to ignore"; the references to *The Taming of the Shrew* must be among those he finds "too familiar to mention," for he does not do so. The play's subtitle, *The Mistakes of a Night*, Harris points out, "is an obvious and provocative allusion to *A Midsummer Night's Dream*." The terrible trip that Tony Lumpkin takes Mrs. Hardcastle on (while pretending to be obeying her orders and transporting her and Constance Neville to Aunt Pedigree's) is reminiscent of Puck's tormenting of the rude mechanicals as he chases them through the woods and his enchantment of Demetrius and Lysander, who chase each other in search of an open place to fight. But Kate is more Rosalind than Puck, taking on the role of bar-maid in part "to take my gentleman off his guard, and like an invisible champion of romance examine the giant's force before I offer to combat" (5:169).[37] Emerging drenched from the horse-pond, the bedraggled Mrs. Hardcastle also evokes the scene of Trinculo and Stephano beguiled and misled by Ariel in *The Tempest*.

This rich context of Shakespearean and other dramatic echoes furnishes *She Stoops to Conquer* with the armament it needs to present itself, as Frank Donoghue has argued, as a particularly English kind of play. Donoghue points out, along with a number of critics, that the opposition Goldsmith draws in his essay "A Comparison between Laughing and Sentimental Comedy" is a false one; Arthur Sherbo and Robert D. Hume have demolished the myth of the "contemporary theater as a sentimental morass."[38] Goldsmith insists upon the continuity of his play with the comedies of the Restoration and with Shakespeare. Regardless of the strictures of Hume and Sherbo, Goldsmith himself presented his work as offering a challenge to a prevailing fashion for "genteel," French-style comedy that was not funny, not English, but, more importantly, not authentic. The genre is also, Goldsmith avers in his essay,

> of all others, the most easily written. Those abilities that can hammer out a Novel, are fully sufficient for the production of a Sentimental Comedy. It is only sufficient to raise the Characters a little, to deck out the Hero with a Ribband, or to give the Heroine a title;

then to put an Insipid Dialogue, without Character or Humour, into their mouths, give them mighty good hearts, very fine cloaths, furnish a new sett of Scenes, make a Pathetic Scene or two, with a sprinkling of tender melancholy Conversation through the whole, and there is no doubt but all the Ladies will cry, and all the Gentlemen applaud. (3:213)

The agenda here is nationalistic, refuting the French style in favor of a native English vigor, but also moral: the sentimental comedy, as Goldsmith describes it, is bogus, not just a French hybrid but a grotesque threat to the survival of comedy at all. And it is popular: with this stigma, Goldsmith marks his target as a kind of fake tragedy that "aims at touching our Passions without the power of being truly pathetic." Paradoxically, by returning to a classical division of genres, and by persistent allusion to Shakespeare, Goldsmith purports to be restoring generic integrity and national dignity to a theater he portrays as debased by greedy writers who measure their "fame by [their] profits" (3:212).

Turning the tables, of course, and proving the values in Goldsmith's play to have been "not untouched by the cult of sentiment" has had its attractions for a number of critics.[39] Certainly the test that Marlow passes in this play's screen scene (where Kate hides the fathers to witness the depth of Marlow's sincere attachment to her) is a sentimental one, in that he demonstrates the good nature and "mighty good heart" of Goldsmith's satirical summary of the genre. Kate herself, as she proposes the screen scene to her father and Sir Charles Marlow, satirizes young Marlow's addresses as those of a sentimental poseur:

SIR CHARLES: And how did he behave, madam?
MISS HARDCASTLE: As most profest admirers do. Said some civil
    things of my face, talked much of his want of merit, and the
    greatness of mine; mentioned his heart, gave a short tragedy
    speech, and ended with pretended rapture.

(5:201)

Sir Charles finds this portrait of his son utterly unconvincing: "This forward canting ranting manner by no means describes him, and I am confident, he never sate for the picture" (201). In the screen scene itself, Kate prompts Marlow to all the excesses of the genre Goldsmith purports to satirize. He extols what he now claims to see as her "refin'd simplicity" and her "conscious virtue." As she plays the role of poor relation and resists his proposal, Marlow promises to make his "respectful assiduities atone for the levity of my past conduct." Finally he quite literally stoops before her:

> MARLOW (*Kneeling*): Does this look like security. Does this look
> like confidence. No, Madam, every moment that shews me your
> merit, only serves to encrease my diffidence and confusion.
> Here let me continue —
>
> (5 : 210, 211–212)

This "short tragedy speech" is mercifully broken off as the two fathers emerge from behind the screen, and Marlow is mortified.

It is of course doubly ironic that Marlow is eloquently discoursing on his diffidence and confusion at this moment and that he is in no way tongue-tied in his expression of his lack of security and confidence. In the sober sentimental interview of the second act, he stutters lamely and struggles with the balanced style in which he proves himself adept at the end. Kate, indeed, takes it upon herself not only to finish his sentences but to mock his attempt to play the man of sentiment:

> MISS HARDCASTLE: You were going to observe, Sir —
> MARLOW I was going to observe, madam — I protest, madam,
> I forget what I was going to observe.
> MISS HARDCASTLE (*Aside*): I vow and so do I. (*To him*) You were
> observing, Sir, that in this age of hypocrisy — something about
> hypocrisy, Sir.
> MARLOW: Yes, madam. In this age of hypocrisy there are few who
> upon strict enquiry do not a — a — a — a —
> MISS HARDCASTLE: I understand you perfectly, Sir.
> MARLOW (*Aside*): Egad! And that's more than I do myself.
> MISS HARDCASTLE: You mean that in this hypocritical age there
> are few that do not condemn in public what they practise in
> private, and think they pay every debt to virtue when they
> praise it.
>
> (5 : 147)

Kate here takes the initiative and (cruelly) pretends that Marlow has introduced the theme of hypocrisy. He struggles to frame a moral apothegm on this theme, but she, in a sense, springs it on him ready made, pretending to extract it whole from his incoherent stammer. Just as Theseus, in *A Midsummer Night's Dream*, has "picked a welcome" out of "fearful duty" and read as much in bashful silence as from the "rattling tongue / Of saucy and audacious eloquence" (5.1.100–104), Kate magnanimously pieces out Marlow's imperfect speech. But by forcing him to discourse on hypocrisy, she brings into play her knowledge of his "very singular character," as explained to her by Constance Neville in the first act: "Among women of reputation and virtue, he is the modestest man alive; but his acquaintance give him a very different character among creatures of another stamp: you understand me." "An odd character, indeed," responds Kate; "I shall never be able to manage him" (5:114–15). Kate begins her management in the sober sentimental interview by forcing Marlow to speak of hypocrisy and then by generously (?) filling out his sentiment by focusing on the discrepancy between private and public conduct that mars "this hypocritical age."

Of course a gross disjunction between private and public behavior is precisely Marlow's problem. In society, with women of the sort he should marry, he is inept and shy; he utterly fails to perform as required. But it is a problem of genre as well. Marlow, in the sober interview, fails to play the role of, say, Bevil Junior in *The Conscious Lovers* or the role which Joseph Surface will parody some years later in *The School for Scandal*. When Kate approaches him, however, in the guise of the rural barmaid, "Cherry from the Beaux Stratagem" (5:168), he has no trouble slipping into the role of Restoration rake. As he does so, he shifts identities, portraying himself as a chatty familiar of the Ladies' Club, "their agreeable Rattle," and then abruptly introducing himself as "Mr. Solomons, my dear, at your service" (5:172). Marlow is not just fluent when in the company of women he imagines to be his social inferiors: he wildly improvises for himself a whole series of roles. When Kate laughs at the image of him as the agreeable Rattle among the "old women," he experiences a momentary pang of embarrassment: "She looks knowing, methinks. You laugh, child?" When Kate deflects his discomfort, Marlow consoles himself: "All's well, she don't laugh at me" (5:173).

"Lechery, sir, it provokes and unprovokes; it provokes the desire, but it takes away the performance," the porter memorably says of drink in *Macbeth* (2.3.28–29). Marlow's stammering with his social equals and his swaggering before barmaids make it clear that the empowerment that overtakes him in the third act is sexual. And it is connected with his conviction that the Hardcastle home is an inn. Upon arrival at what he thinks is the Buck's Head, Marlow calls for "warm punch," pointedly reminding Mr. Hardcastle: "This is Liberty-Hall, you know." He gets "cup" instead and grumbles that "this fellow, in his Liberty-hall, will only let us have just what he pleases" (5:133). Yet the Hardcastle home functions as just such a liberating environment as a tavern or inn for him and provides an atmosphere of free play in which he can express his attraction to Kate (and she can flirt with him). The sentimental interview is notoriously "sober"; when he fancies himself alone with a barmaid, Marlow calls for another kind of drink: "Suppose I should call for a taste, just by way of trial, of the nectar of your lips; perhaps I might be disappointed of that, too." "Nectar! nectar! that's a liquor there's no call for in these parts," responds Kate; "French, I suppose. We keep no French wines here, Sir" (5:171). Marlow's empowerment is a kind of intoxication — "Such beauty fires beyond the power of resistance," he growls, seizing her — and is frustrated in the performance — "Pshaw! The father here!" he cries as Hardcastle's entrance forces him to disengage (5:174).

The duping of Marlow begins with Tony Lumpkin's improvised joke, which is stimulated by the disgust Marlow and Hastings show for his favorite tavern, the Three Pigeons. Hastings, again improvising, decides to keep his friend in the dark in order to pursue his own intrigue. So drinking, acting, and wooing are all inextricably tied in the atmosphere of Mr. Hardcastle's Liberty Hall. Marlow's problems with women have of course received their Freudian and feminist diagnoses, but what happens to Marlow seems more like what happens to characters in the middle of Shakespearean comedies.[40] As C. L. Barber famously pointed out, "the fundamental method" of Shakespeare's comedy "is to shape the loose narrative so that 'events' put persons in the position of festive celebrants: if they do not seek holiday, it happens to them." "Much of the poetry and wit, however it may be occasioned by events, works in the economy of the whole play to promote the effect of a merry occasion where Nature reigns," he continues.[41] Northrop Frye explicitly describes the Shakespearean comic structure in terms of a ritual movement from "preparation . . . a somber and gloomy period where there is an attempt to recognize and get rid of the principle of sterility, later identified with sin and evil," through "the period of license and confusion of values represented by the carnival, the

Saturnalia and the festivals of promiscuous sexual union that appear in early religions" to, finally, "the period of festivity itself, the revel or *komos* which is said to have given its name to comedy." For Frye, this tripartite structure is characteristic of all comedy. "These three aspects of ritual do not always appear in the order, but this order happens to be a very effective one dramatically, and it is this order that we find reproduced in the typical Shakespearean comic structure."[42] Kate stages for Marlow a comic ritual in which the sterility and impotence of his first encounter with her is cured through the license and confusion of her carnivalesque performance as Cherry the barmaid and then redirected toward an appropriate object of desire through her performance as the poor but virtuous relation of the Hardcastles.

Because of Marlow's own abstemiousness he endeavors to please the landlord by urging his servants to get drunk, a policy that Mr. Hardcastle finds so offensive that he insists Marlow and his "drunken pack leave [the] house directly" (5:181). Thus while Marlow may not drink, as comic scapegoat he undergoes a ritual of festive intoxication from which he must sober up to his new responsibilities. As he enters the Hardcastle house, frozen in time because of Mr. Hardcastle's love of everything old, he enters a time warp much like that experienced by the essayist in the "Reverie at the Boar's-Head-Tavern." But where the essayist is disabused by the ghost of Mrs. Quickly of his naive admiration of Falstaff and Prince Hal, Marlow undergoes the full transformative dynamic of Shakespearean comedy.

Kate's similarity to the enterprising heroines of Shakespearean comedy has often been noted. She creates through her role-playing the kind of free space in which to observe her suitor that Rosalind makes in *As You Like It* and that Viola is forced to occupy in *Twelfth Night*. She even alludes to the process as a change of gender, for she wittily observes that by dressing as a barmaid she will be "*seen*, and that is no small advantage to a girl who brings her face to market," but at the same time she will also "like an invisible champion of romance examine the giant's force before I offer to combat" (5:169). The paradoxes here — of becoming invisible in order to be seen, of disguising in order to "make an acquaintance" (169), of becoming an invisible knight to prepare for combat — are central to the paradoxes of Shakespeare's boy actresses and celibate stage.

But Kate does not play the androgynous Ganymede to Marlow's

Orlando. She moves fluently through a number of roles that are all explicitly gendered as female and keyed to appropriate dramatic genres. As Miss Hardcastle at their first meeting, she embodies a sophisticated society girl whose fluency stifles Marlow and finishes his garbled sentences. As Cherry the barmaid, she embodies the spirit of Liberty Hall, freeing Marlow from his embarrassment and empowering his sexuality — even to the point that he takes revenge upon Miss Hardcastle by criticizing her "squinting" (5:172). As the poor relation, she goads Marlow into his performance as the hero of a sentimental comedy, dispraising himself, praising her virtue, and casting himself at her feet. In all these roles (and this may be why Christopher Brooks offers the only explicitly feminist reading of the play) Kate does not challenge the patriarchal society in which she finds herself and indeed works hard to bring about the marriage that her father had planned but decided against on the basis of Marlow's impossible behavior. Unlike Constance Neville, who resists the union with Tony, struggles against her greedy guardian, and only reluctantly embraces the call of duty, Kate throughout accepts her father's choice of mate — playfully: in the final scene she and Marlow *"retire, she tormenting him, to the back Scene"* as the night's other mistakes are resolved (5:213). But it is Hastings who has the last word: "Come, madam, you are now driven to the very last scene of all your contrivances. I know you like him, I'm sure he loves you, and you must and shall have him." Or is it her father? "And I say so, too," he pronounces, *"Joining their hands"* (216).

Like so many Shakespearean heroines, Kate ends her play in silence — unless the stage direction *"she tormenting him"* and his identification of her as a "little tyrant" (216) suggest a full reversal of the paradigm of *The Taming of the Shrew*.[43] Kate may pursue the man her father has selected for her, but only after she has had a chance to study him and indeed has already enjoyed tormenting him for some time. A popular guide to teasing one's friends and getting one's own way in the eighteenth century was Jane Collier's *An Essay on the Art of Ingeniously Tormenting with proper rules for the use of that pleasant art, humbly addressed in the first part, to the master, husband, &c, in the second part to the wife, friend, &c, with some general instructions for plaguing all your acquaintance.* This mock courtesy-book delineates all the ways in which a cunning tormentor can manipulate others. Collier warns that most sisters, because of their natural affection for each other, might not need her book: "However, should two sisters choose to play at friendship whilst one considers the other as her property or dupe, to such these my rules may be of some service."[44]

In a chapter devoted to the ways in which husbands might best torment wives, Collier goes one better than the techniques of Petruchio in *The Taming of the Shrew*: "Never let the time of dinner pass, without being displeased with everything that comes to the table. You may blame your wife for the fault of the fishmonger, the poulterer, the butcher, and the cook; particularly the latter, as it gives an ill-natured wench (who hears from the footman this your kind and tender practice) an opportunity of wreaking her spleen on her mistress, by the wrong-headed anger of her master" (96–97). Collier encourages wives, too, to adopt a strategy of contrariety. She especially counsels such treatment of their husbands' sisters: "Be sometimes over-civil and formal to them; at other times perfectly rude, insolent, and ill-bred; but never leave, till you have, by some means or other, intirely alienated your husband's affections from them. Then change your views, and consider *them* as new subjects of your own power; practice every art of Teasing and Tormenting toward them; and your husband also (if he is under proper management, and you have a due influence over him) will join with you in the sport: and unless they, by some means of independence, escape your power, you cannot well have better game" (120–21). Here wife and properly managed husband join together in tormenting dependent female relatives.

Kate and Marlow, properly managed though he is, have not reached this point yet. Instead, Kate's tormenting of Marlow seems to fulfill Collier's highest claim for it, that it is an end in itself:

This love of Tormenting may be said to have one thing in common with what, some writers affirm, belongs to the true love of virtue; namely, that it is exercised for its own sake, and no other: For, can there be a clearer proof, that, for its own sake alone, this art of Tormenting is practised, than that it never did, nor ever can, answer any other end. I know that the most expert practitioners deny this; and frequently declare, when they whip, cut, and slash, the body, or when they teaze, vex, and torment the mind, that 'tis done for the good of the person that suffers. Let the vulgar believe this if they will; but I, and my good pupils, understand things better; and, while we can enjoy the high pleasure of Tormenting, it matters not what the objects of our power either feel, think, or believe. (6–7)

As for demonstrations of good heart and benevolence, Collier advises carefully watching your proposed dupe, "till you can catch him doing such actions himself, as far as it is within his power; doing them, also, without ostentation. Then mark him down as your own; and you may make good sport with him, if you rightly understand the game" (137–38). Kate, exposing Marlow's spontaneous act of good heart, indeed makes him her own, and the play's title maps out not just a comic inversion of shrew-taming but a domestic relationship promising her indefinite enjoyment of the "high pleasure of Tormenting."[45]

Scene Three

HARRY HOPE'S SALOON

"The fresh air of out-of-doors sweeps through the windows of the Hardcastle mansion," effuses George Henry Nettleton.[46] Nettleton embraces Goldsmith's claim that his laughing comedy is an attack upon the lifeless sentimental stage. But Raymond Williams, in his astute reading of Goldsmith's essay on sentimental and laughing comedy, cautions his readers: "The identification which some critics seem to make, in fantasy, between themselves and the insouciance of Cavalier rakes and whores, is usually ridiculous, if one goes on to ask to what moral tradition they themselves practically belong. Nor is this the only respect in which, if we are honest, we shall confess ourselves the heirs of the eighteenth-century bourgeois." Noting earlier that Goldsmith's "casual dismissal of the novel should make us pause," Williams warns:

> The wider basis of sentimental comedy, and of a main tradition in the novel, was that particular kind of humanitarian feeling, the strong if inarticulate appeal to a fundamental "goodness of heart"; the sense of every individual's closeness to vice and folly, so that pity for their exemplars is the most relevant emotion, and recovery and rehabilitation must be believed in; the sense, finally, that there are few absolute values, and that tolerance and kindness are major virtues. In rebuking the sentimental comedy, as in both its early examples and its subsequent history it seems necessary to do, we should be prepared to recognize that in the point of moral assumptions, and of a whole consequent feeling about life, most of us are its blood relations.[47]

Thus to point out that Kate's rehabilitative demonstration of Marlow's good nature before the two fathers is sentimental in spirit is to point out the extraordinary degree to which Goldsmith succeeds in convincing audiences that *She Stoops to Conquer* represents something honest, fresh, and new. His attack on the theatrical fashion of the age is of a piece with the contention throughout the antitheatrical tradition that certain conditions of the self cannot be represented through available theatrical means. Shakespeare, Molière, and Ibsen all participate to a degree in the strategy of identifying older theatrical forms with hypocrisy that allows their own theatrical forms to pose as closer to reality.

Something similar happened, according to Louis Sheaffer, when Eugene O'Neill's *Beyond the Horizon* premiered on Broadway: "Here was an author determined to speak his mind and guts without regard for the shibboleths of Broadway," he declares. "James O'Neill's son had already signaled his intent in his one-act plays. In *Beyond the Horizon* he committed the deed: he introduced the American theater to life, the sad realities of everyday life, and began changing that theater into one more genuine, more vital, more sensitive to the human condition." The play's unaccustomed length and its "distinct shortcomings and flaws" in language, for Sheaffer and for many of the original critics, are excused in light of its sincere evocation of the "genuine," the "vital," the "sensitive."[48] "Before O'Neill, the U.S. had theater; after O'Neill, the U.S. had drama," crowed *Time* magazine in 1953; attributed to John Lahr on the back cover of a recent casebook on O'Neill, the quotation pushes antitheatricalism a bit further: "Before O'Neill, America had entertainment; after him, it had drama."[49]

Criticism of O'Neill, making the case for his preeminence among American playwrights and determined to enlist him in the pantheon of dramatists of the first rank, insists upon the extraordinary, heroic nature of his quest for self-knowledge. What distinguishes O'Neill, according to Robert Littell, is a "groping, smoldering, passionate sincerity many times more intense, relentless, and mysterious than that of any other American playwright — and nearly all foreign ones, too." O'Neill burrows "in the depths of human nature," Littell continues: "The endless burrowing is a mole's progress toward salvation — his own salvation far more than that of his characters. . . . And if O'Neill had three grains more of the humor which causes a writer to laugh at his own solemnities, he could not indulge himself so freely in just those inarticulate cries of cosmic pain which make his characters, a great deal of the time, singularly strange and moving creations."[50]

O'Neill, who, as Harold Bloom has memorably put it, "tells his one story and his one story only, and his story turns out to be himself,"[51] offers a clear case of what Henri Peyre has called the "cult of sincerity" in literature. Where Littell celebrates O'Neill for his "smoldering" sincerity, Peyre would recoil: "by itself, sincerity in a writer never sufficed to give merit to a work of art." Placing a high value on personal honesty, Peyre argues, has "led to a large number of works containing no subject matter, referring to nothing (and sincerity should refer to something behind and beyond itself), involving little constraint over a rebellious material or little restraint, banishing even style from many works of literature."[52] Without joining Peyre and insisting that sincerity in and for itself is detrimental to art, it is possible to see sincerity in O'Neill's career as a value treasured because of its antipathy to the particular art form of theater. O'Neill emerged on the scene, in Sheaffer's narrative, as a figure waging war against a host of related opponents: "theater," "entertainment," "Broadway."

In O'Neill, too, drinking and theater are very much intertwined. "Not drunken bull, but 'in vino veritas' stuff," Jamie promises Edmund in *Long Day's Journey*, and this gives a vivid name to a binarism found throughout O'Neill. Drinking functions as a metaphor in O'Neill's plays both for self-indulgent performance ("booze talking," as Jamie puts it) and for self-revelation. Egil Törnqvist emphasizes one half of this equation by seeing drinking in the late plays as the vehicle of an inner truth that destroys the "sober façade" or mask that characters show the world.[53] But drinking, too, is a vice of the theatrical profession, as the hard-drinking Tyrone men in *Long Day's Journey into Night* can testify; there it serves less as a bearer of truth than as a kind of fog in which they can wrap themselves, as Mary Tyrone does in morphine. While O'Neill's biographers and critics have debated the impact of O'Neill's own drinking problems on his health and his productivity, the language of "recovery and rehabilitation" (which, as Raymond Williams points out, derives from eighteenth-century benevolism) runs throughout a critical narrative in which O'Neill's weakness is not for drink but for theater, for melodrama. And the self-loathing that this weakness inspires is coupled with a vehement anti-theatricalism. O'Neill's critics, in asserting the high value of his plays as literature, as drama, in contrast to their faults or flaws, present an image of an author transcending melodrama (in Michael Manheim's memorable phrase) and achieving a hard-won self-mastery.[54] In this polarity, melodrama stands in for a wild self-indulgence and tragedy for clear-sighted truth-telling.

In other words, O'Neill's plays offer a pilgrim's progress from "drunken bull" to "in vino veritas," as the story that O'Neill's critics tell follows a common pattern. First, there is an enumeration of O'Neill's artistic flaws — his "often egregious intentions";[55] his clumsiness with language; his reliance upon fashionable pop-psychology and upon synthesized versions of ancient myth — and his personal failings — his abuse of alcohol; his cruelty to at least two of his three wives, to his own children, and to the children of his second and third wife; his seemingly limitless obsession with himself and his "psychological family" (father, mother, brother) as material for his art.[56] The litany could go on; and in many unexpected places in the adulatory biographies by Arthur Gelb and Barbara Gelb and Louis Sheaffer a certain defensiveness covers what might otherwise appear to be a growing vexation with the difficult subject. Yet at the end there is the summation: by dint of hard work, by dint of a flawless instinct for theater (inherited, some biographers and critics say, from James O'Neill; learned, others suggest, by growing up on tour with *The Count of Monte Cristo* and watching from the wings), by dint of wide and deep reading in modern philosophy and literature (mainly Friedrich Nietzsche and August Strindberg) and courageous exploration of the psyche (facilitated by familiarity with Freudian models but unassisted by professional therapists to any significant degree), O'Neill conquers these flaws. However confused and banal, hysterical and overblown, inadvertently ridiculous and condescending his output may be in its parts, its whole traces a triumphant coming of age and a fruition of talent in the late masterpieces, especially *The Iceman Cometh* and *Long Day's Journey into Night*. The paradigm of self-mastery achieved through self-discipline and self-knowledge is an attractive one; in keeping with O'Neill's own insistence that he be seen large, it makes of O'Neill, looking inward, tormented by but ultimately forgiving if not overcoming the ineluctable dynamics of family dysfunction, a model artist for modern times.

It is a satisfying paradigm because in O'Neill's own terms it offers a kind of transcendence without God. O'Neill's is a story of "a triumph of the will," of "sheer force of character," a recent anthologist proclaims. O'Neill "sees life straight and strong," Kenneth Macgowan wrote after the premiere of *Beyond the Horizon*, "always getting down to the big emotional root of things. . . . His is a genius that seems incorruptible."[57] O'Neill learns to forgive his intolerable family and enshrine the triad of father, mother, and brother in immortal art — not only in *Long Day's Journey*, which features them undisguised, but, as many critics have pointed out, in play after play in various guises leading up to that work. Hard work does pay off; great suffering does lead to great understanding and great art.

The triumph, as *Time* suggests, is a national one as well. O'Neill's struggle to know himself and to know his own family reflects the country's efforts, in the early twentieth century, to know itself and come into its own as a world power. Thomas Postlewait has pointed out the way in which this narrative of melodrama transcended by O'Neill has become encoded in the histories of American drama.[58] Indeed, "suspect" as the narrative is, O'Neill liked to present himself as telling the harsh truth to his American audiences. "I'm going on the theory that the United States, instead of being the most successful country in the world, is the greatest failure," he told a press conference on the occasion of the Broadway production of *The Iceman Cometh* in 1946; he continued: "Its main idea is that everlasting game of trying to possess your own soul by the possession of something outside it, thereby losing your own soul and the thing outside it too."[59] America itself is a kind of drunk, lost in "drunken bull," reaching out vainly to "something outside it" to give it meaning. O'Neill's cycle of plays based upon American history, "A Tale of Possessors Self-Dispossessed," was to trace a single family from the American revolution to the twentieth century; the surviving plays of the cycle show this family to be recognizably configured like O'Neill's. Greatness and failure are intertwined in his sense of America and in his sense of his family.

As Sheaffer makes clear, for the champions of this narrative, the movement from a false, Broadway esthetic to a sincere, true one is generational: "James O'Neill's son" is the hero of both volumes of his narrative. James O'Neill's own oft-quoted response to *Beyond the Horizon* — "'Are you trying to send the audience home to commit suicide?' he asked huskily," according to the Gelbs (*O'Neill*, 408) — is that of a seasoned theater professional. Plays should be entertaining, not depressing. Critics, unlike James O'Neill, have found it hard to resist Eugene O'Neill's privileging of sincerity over falsehood, of truth to the human condition over Broadway. His Oedipal passion has been conceived to be institutional as well as familial. O'Neill's attacks upon actors and upon theater in his plays and interviews, however, reflect hostility not just to the theater of the past but to the whole idea of theater itself.

Eugene O'Neill learned from James O'Neill's theater an intense discomfort with commercial theater and mistrust of actors. Flora Merrill asked O'Neill about the marked difference between his and his father's kinds of theater. "'I suppose,' he replied slowly (he practically always spoke slowly, weighing each word as though words were traps through which he had to pick his way carefully), 'if one accepts the song and dance complete of the psychoanalysts, it is perfectly natural that having been brought up around the old conventional theater, and having identified it with my father, I should rebel and go in a new direction.' Grinning suddenly, he added, 'I think it would be quite amusing, however, to revive *Monte Cristo* sometime, because, as I look back upon all the old romantic melodramas, that was the best'" (Sheaffer, *Son and Artist*, 181). On the occasion of seeing the Abbey Theatre on tour in 1911, O'Neill experienced a kind of epiphany: "'My early experience with the theater through my father . . . really made me revolt against it. As a boy I saw so much of the ranting, artificial, romantic stage stuff that I always had sort of a contempt for the theater. It was seeing the Irish players for the first time that gave me a glimpse of my opportunity . . . I thought then and I still think that they demonstrated the possibilities of naturalistic acting better than any other company'" (Sheaffer, *Son and Playwright*, 205). As Postlewait points out, O'Neill, like other American dramatists before him, "set up melodrama as the Other, the blocking force against which realism had to struggle."[60]

Despite going out of his way to express his contempt for melodrama and his distaste for "ranting," O'Neill often found himself indicted by friends and critics alike for drama that frequently seemed less to be moving in "a new direction" than to run the risk of becoming itself melodramatic, overblown, and artificial. The Abbey Theatre's new style of acting would be inappropriate to *The Great God Brown* or *Dynamo*, and even the naturalistic style of *Long Day's Journey* permits melodramatic ranting on the part of the theatrical family of Tyrones.

In a curious and quirky little book Virgil Geddes, the founder and director of the Brookfield Players (a summer try-out theater), inveighed in 1934 against what he called *The Melodramadness of Eugene O'Neill* and linked it with thoroughgoing antitheatricalism. "In the world of theatre, where acting, production, and all the arts of interpretation give body and life to the author's world and complete the theatre as art," Geddes maintains, "O'Neill is not at home." Tendentious as he is, Geddes makes an important point in singling out O'Neill's famous stage directions for comment. "His plays are written with strong dictations to the actor and stage directions which invite antagonism more than they spur the imagination," he continues. "In his plays, he sometimes writes as though nothing but bad acting was possible on the stage and he fills in the actor's part with clumsy explanation. At other times he writes for the reader, as though acting had nothing to do with his plays and had never existed as an art."[61] Geddes points to an antitheatricalism in O'Neill which is never far from the surface. O'Neill's "sort of a contempt for the theater" generally expresses itself as a mistrust of actors rather than as a systematic attempt to found—as the members of the Group Theatre attempted to do—an alternative to the commercial theatre he claimed to despise.

Geddes's observation that O'Neill can imagine only bad acting leads him to speculate that O'Neill is led to "constantly relying on the methods of the novelist. His plays are full of writing which never shows on the stage, and even if one eliminates the material which is written between brackets, the dialogue is often undramatically descriptive" (*Melodramadness*, 37). The extensive stage directions in O'Neill's published plays, then, speak of his mistrust of the medium in which he has chosen to work. While certainly other modern dramatists, especially Henrik Ibsen and George Bernard Shaw, offered extensive, prescriptive, and often intrusive stage directions to their readers, O'Neill repeatedly chided actors for failing to follow through on his often highly charged instructions. When *Welded* did not win the praise he had hoped for, O'Neill blamed the actors: "What was actually spoken should have served to a great extent just to punctuate the meaningful pauses. The actors didn't get that." But how, Sheaffer wonders, could actors convey "with a look that it 'becomes impossible that they should deny life, through each other, again'" (*Son and Artist*, 132). O'Neill complained to Kenneth Macgowan about the "difference there must always be between the author's idea as he sees what he writes and the horrible puppet show the actors transform it into, willy-nilly, good or bad." The Gelbs, in reporting this remark, appear to share O'Neill's inability to imagine any but bad acting: "It never failed to infuriate him that despite his knowledge of actor craft and the pains he always took to forestall an actor's personal interpretation of a role by spelling out every important gesture, look, and vocal nuance, he could still not get the effect he wanted." "I don't go to the theatre much," he told Bernard Simon. "I don't like it. It's phony" (Gelb and Gelb, *O'Neill*, 590, 559).

What the Gelbs interpret as O'Neill's desire to "forestall an actor's personal interpretation" can lead not just to the novelistic stage directions for which O'Neill is well known; it can also lead, as Geddes maintains, to "undramatically descriptive" dialogue. What actors are trained to think of as subtext frequently finds its way to the surface in O'Neill. Most notoriously, the experimental inclusion of spoken "thoughts" in *Strange Interlude* represents an insistence on his part that the playwright control the subtext as well. The exploratory investigations of extratextual possibilities encouraged by Konstantin Stanislavsky and his American imitators are utterly forestalled. Lynn Fontanne, who played the role of Nina, found herself much confounded by the need to speak her "thoughts" in asides:

> There were a good many lines intended by O'Neill to be taken seriously, that I thought would get belly laughs from the audience. . . . It would have hurt the play. For instance, I would have to say in an aside something like, "Ned has the bluest eyes I ever saw; I must tell him so." Then I would go to Ned and tell him he had the bluest eyes I ever saw. I felt it was unnecessary to say this twice. I told O'Neill I thought it would be better if I looked at Ned's eyes with admiration the first time, silently, instead of saying the line as an aside. I asked him if I could cut the line. He said, "No, you can't. Play it as I wrote it." But the play was so long that I felt O'Neill wouldn't realize if I cut a line here and there, so, with fear and trembling, I cut a few of those horselaugh lines. O'Neill never knew about this sly business of mine.

After recounting this anecdote, the Gelbs offer a response of sorts from O'Neill: "During rehearsals O'Neill told Langner, 'If the actors weren't so dumb, they wouldn't need asides; they'd be able to express the meaning without them'" (*O'Neill*, 649–50).

Identifying acting with his father's theater and identifying his father's theater with star actors out of control, strutting and fretting at the expense of literary texts, O'Neill protects his plays by forestalling interpretation, demanding fidelity to the lines as written and elaborating intention in explicit dialogue and stage directions. From these precautions develops the painful repetitiveness of which Lynn Fontanne is not the only actor to complain. If O'Neill's extensive precautions against the actor's freedom seem reminiscent of Hamlet's strictures against the players, the identification is not an idle one. O'Neill himself alluded to *Hamlet* when he told Barrett Clark that he would not release any of the cycle plays for production until they were all completed. "The play, as written, is the thing, and not the way actors garble it with their almost-always-alien personalities (even when the acting is fine work in itself)" (Sheaffer, *Son and Artist*, 469). The apparent grudging compliment to "fine work" again insists that what the actor does is at least alien to and often hostile to "the play." O'Neill's mistrust of actors may stem from a wholly understandable frustration with a star system and with a commercial theater that undervalued the written word, just as Shakespeare may have put the urging that clowns speak no more than is set down for them into Hamlet's mouth as a direct critique of Will Kemp and just as Ben Jonson railed against the loathed stage. But O'Neill's aversion to performance and refusal to acknowledge the collaborative nature of the theater enterprise affects the "play, as written," as well.

"I don't go to the theatre because I can always do a better production in my mind than the one on the stage," O'Neill once declared (Gelb and Gelb, *O'Neill*, 559). Yet the production in the mind can be tyrannical: not only do actors find themselves unable to convey in glances a play's big themes, but readers, too, can find the stage directions a nuisance. George Jean Nathan, ordinarily one of O'Neill's greatest champions, expressed this frustration when he published, as a kind of free-verse poem, the stage directions from *Dynamo* in the March 1929 *American Mercury*:

Arguing tormentedly within himself
With angry self-contempt
Furiously clenching his fist
His eyes lighting up with savage relish
Suddenly horrified
Protesting petulantly
With indignant anger
With evangelical fervor
With lifelong resentful frustration

With bitter self-contempt
With a resentful side-glance
With a gloomy glance
(quoted by Sheaffer, *Son and Artist*, 323)

The experiment can be repeated with many of the plays with similarly comic results.

"EDMUND— (*moved, stares at his father with understanding — slowly*) I'm glad you've told me this, Papa. I know you a lot better now."[62] Here, in a key moment from *Long Day's Journey*, O'Neill uses a stage direction to force an interpretation which seems to contradict previous action in the play. In the earlier acts Edmund and Jamie are all too aware of their father's story of youthful promise wasted. Thus it is conceivable that Edmund's response could be ironic and dismissive; if not, then he is moved to "*understanding*" not by any new information his father has given him but by his father's performance of oft-repeated material. (Or, perhaps, it is an indication of Edmund's immaturity and susceptibility to booze that he accepts an account which he would otherwise challenge or criticize.) All of these possibilities, however, are forestalled by the playwright's insistence that real understanding has happened. Actor and director are discouraged from exploration. But the options, curiously, remain open. Despite the playwright's endorsement of a therapeutic assent on Edmund's part, the other possibilities proliferate. This is not necessarily bad playwriting: it is simply a fact of playwriting that declaring one option to be the author's intention will not necessarily make it the actor's. Extensive stage directions and surfacing subtexts are both conspicuous elements in O'Neill's reputation for bad writing, and both stem from his mistrust of theater.

Bad writing in another sense dogs O'Neill's career. He was acutely aware of his failings in poetic language and his difficulty with elevated rhetoric. *Long Day's Journey* represents an attempt on his part to solve this problem through extensive quotation from Shakespeare and from the Victorian poets. This is generally considered to be a successful strategy, a way of infusing lyricism and charged language into a naturalistic play. Jamie's recitation of Swinburne's "A Leave-taking" in act 4 at the end of the play moves in effective counterpoint to Mary's obliviousness. He "*does it well*," runs the stage direction (how the "dumb" actor is to do "it well" is not specified). When the stage direction points out that "*She does not seem to hear*," the reader perceives an echo in the recitation: "Let us go hence, my songs; she will not hear. . . . Yea, though we sang as angels in her ear, / She would not hear" (173). George Steiner singles out this kind of citation for special contempt:

> Language seeks vengeance on those who cripple it. A striking example occurs in O'Neill, a dramatist committed, in a somber and rather moving way, to the practice of bad writing. Interspersed in the sodden morass of *A Long Day's Journey into Night*, there are passages from Swinburne. The lines are flamboyant, romantic verbiage. They are meant to show up the adolescent inadequacies of those who recite them. But, in fact, when the play is performed, the contrary occurs. The energy and glitter of Swinburne's language burn a hole in the surrounding fabric. They elevate the action above its paltry level and instead of showing up the characters show up the playwright. Modern authors rarely quote their betters with impunity.

"The 'sodden morass' derided here is widely considered to be the greatest play written by an American," exclaims Richard Moorton, who quotes this passage with disdain.[63] Only performance can resolve the question of whether poetic quotations heighten the pathos or reveal the characters' inadequacy. Steiner's impression that performance contradicts the playwright's intention is in keeping with O'Neill's mistrust of production.

Harold Bloom, editor of another recent anthology of important O'Neill criticism, also struggles with the question of O'Neill's language and its suitability for performance. "They stage remarkably," he says of *The Iceman Cometh* and *Long Day's Journey*, "and hold me in the audience, though they give me neither aesthetic pleasure nor spiritually memorable pain when I reread them in the study." There, on the page, O'Neill's "sheer bad writing" demands attention. But in performance the case is altered, and Bloom argues that the stage directions themselves point toward successful performance. "Certainly a singular dramatic genius is always at work in O'Neill's stage directions," he ventures, "and can be felt also, most fortunately, in the repressed intensities of inarticulateness in all of the Tyrones." The quotations, according to Bloom, rise to the occasion of the "grim ballet of looks" prescribed in the stage directions.[64]

Despite writing against performance, crafting stage directions that prescribe one mental production of the play, O'Neill creates playscripts which demand that the intervention of actors and directors be effective in performance. Steiner, content in the study with the strategy of quotation, finds it ridiculous in the theater; Bloom, grumpy with the bad writing in the study, confesses to being moved on two occasions by productions of the play. O'Neill's problems with bad writing, then, open up some broad areas in the discussion and criticism of drama, with text and performance in a constant dialectic and with meaning constantly contingent and negotiable.

O'Neill "had success," Eric Bentley writes, "in solving the particular problem to which he had addressed himself: rivaling and replacing his father. How better, in any case, can a man outdo an actor than by becoming a playwright? The actor is the playwright's mouthpiece and victim. . . . His father's theatre — the Victorian theatre of Edwin Booth and Henry Irving — was an actor's theatre. The modern theatre would be a playwright's theatre, and Eugene O'Neill was one of the principal playwrights who made it so."[65] Bentley seems to have it precisely backward: O'Neill's constant problem was a fear that the playwright would become the actor's victim, with the meaning of the play transformed in performance, and the mouthpiece the transformer and transmitter of meaning. This is not an uncommon anxiety among playwrights, and Bentley's blithe assurance that a "playwright's theatre" is invulnerable to the interpretive latitude of actors and directors is not convincing. O'Neill was aware enough of the vulnerability of playscripts to the exigencies and negotiations of performance — not to mention the "dreary ordeal of disillusionment and compromise called rehearsal" — to attempt to quash such liberties as best he could.[66]

Despite his contempt for his father's "actor's theatre," O'Neill's heavy reliance on stage directions and his attempts at elevated rhetoric clearly show the influence of nineteenth-century melodrama. According to Robert Benchley, the "royal blood of the 'Count of Monte Cristo'" coursed through O'Neill's veins and led him unerringly to strong theatrical effects.[67] John Henry Raleigh has noted the structural similarities that abound between the early plays of O'Neill and the melodramas of his father's era and has indeed demonstrated the persistence of motifs from *The Count of Monte Cristo* throughout O'Neill's career. "First, *Monte Cristo* is full of asides, soliloquies, and disguises, all of which devices O'Neill was to deploy on a much larger scale and in a much more diversified and sophisticated way. In so doing, he was often thought to be revitalizing Elizabethan techniques, but the real source was much closer to home and much more immediate to memory, namely, the 'Fechter version,' or any of the other melodramas in which his father played." Raleigh demonstrates that the theater esthetic informing O'Neill's early experimental plays was a wholly nineteenth-century esthetic. More importantly, though, Raleigh argues, O'Neill's concept of rhythm as central to dramatic experience comes from this same old source: *Monte Cristo* gave O'Neill a "temporal heritage" that "was twofold and polar: the long-term narrative movement and the brief, explosive, dramatic event." O'Neill's concept of the cycle plays, staging generation after generation of conflict in a panoramic sweep of history, draws much from the old historical dramas of the nineteenth century.[68]

O'Neill thus writes against melodrama in his attempts to rein in the star actor and curtail the liberties of performance while at the same time he has internalized a rhythm of dramatic action and explosive event that shares much with the discredited earlier form. In a recent study Kurt Eisen has pushed the point further, by invoking Peter Brooks's notion of the "melodramatic imagination" as central to the experience of nineteenth-century and modernist novelists. O'Neill's novelistic impulse, in the extensive stage directions and in the taxing of audiences' powers of endurance with long plays (and the plays in the cycle, apparently, kept getting longer and longer), is part of a larger "drive for discovering new ways to use melodrama as a means to express multivalent psychological conflicts." Eisen's argument is that O'Neill's very imagination is melodramatic and that his plays succeed by pitting individual melodramas against one another, in the characters' versions of their own lives. The drama results from the collision of each character's personal, melodramatic version of the past against each other character's version. While this is a likely account of what happens in *Iceman* and *Long Day's Journey*, it is less satisfactory in accounting for the confusion of narratives in *Strange Interlude*. Even in "the best of the early plays," Eisen concedes, "in say, *Desire under the Elms* and *All God's Chillun Got Wings* — the melodrama is not always adequately transformed, especially its stagey rhetoric, frequently crude characterization, and predictable plotting."[69]

Melodrama in the nineteenth century was closely allied to progressive and rehabilitative causes. The dramatic versions of *Uncle Tom's Cabin* fueled widespread support for the abolitionist movement, and plays like *The Drunkard* and the dramatized version of *Ten Nights in a Bar-Room* powerfully aided the temperance movement. In these plays characters like Ejlert Løvborg and Cassio are hurled abruptly into the chaos of drink. "I know his nature well. He has tasted, and will not stop now short of madness or oblivion," exults Lawyer Cribbs in *The Drunkard*.[70] Temperance dramas shored up the social order by enacting rehabilitative narratives in which characters could recover themselves and restore domestic tranquillity by kicking the habit. As Jeffrey Mason argues in his Marxist analysis of American melodrama, "drinking is *not* respectable — not only because it releases inhibitions and confuses one's sense of propriety, but also because it hinders economic developments." The temperance narratives took on the antitheatrical divine's language of waste: "visits to the dramshops," Mason says, "waste the capital the drunkard should be conserving."[71] Hitting rock bottom, in Alcoholics Anonymous narratives and in the melodramas, strips a person of identity, which then must be painfully recovered. The AA formula — "My name is Bill, and I'm an alcoholic" — powerfully evokes the self-annihilation of drink, as all social markers and distinctions are lost.[72]

Mary McCarthy, in her review of the original production of *The Iceman Cometh*, was disappointed in the representation of drunkenness she saw "in the day and a half that elapses on the stage of the Martin Beck":

> none of the characters is visibly drunk, nobody has a hangover, and, with a single exception, nobody has the shakes; there are none of those rancorous, semi-schizoid silences, no obscurity of thought, no dark innuendoes, no flashes of hatred. There is, in short, none of the terror of drink, which, after all, in the stage that Harry Hope's customers have presumably reached, is a form of insanity. What is missing is precisely the thing that is most immediately striking and most horrifying in any human drunkard, the sense of the destruction of personality.

"And for this McCarthy condemns the dramatist," fumes Steven F. Bloom in a rebuttal to this critique; "she condemns *O'Neill* himself — as an 'incompetent reporter' regarding 'drinking *moeurs*,' and she dismisses the play as the work of a playwright who cannot write." Bloom painstakingly goes about to rebut McCarthy point by point and to assure his readers that O'Neill certainly did know whereof he spoke when it came to alcoholic excess. To do so, he relies to a high degree on the stage directions in the play's text and shifts the blame to the play's performers: "surely she confuses the play with the performance," he huffs.[73]

But McCarthy, whose own personal expertise with hard drinking was as unassailable as O'Neill's, makes a more serious point than Bloom is willing to concede. While O'Neill's stage directions do in fact make it clear that many of the characters are "rancorous, semi-schizoid" and all the rest of it, McCarthy points to a flaw that is a playwright's, not an actor's. "[E]ach of O'Neill's people is in perfect possession of the little bit of character that the author has given him": "the Boer is boerish, the Englishman english, and the sentimental grouch who runs the establishment grouches and sentimentalizes in orderly alternation." What McCarthy is talking about is the "little bit of character" that distinguishes the characters of melodrama from one another, the stereotypical tics of theatrical shorthand.

O'Neill's idol, August Strindberg, lashed out at this kind of representation in the famous preface to *Miss Julie*:

The word *character* has come to mean many things over the course of time. Originally, it must have meant the dominant trait in the soul-complex and was confused with temperament. Later it became the middle-class expression for the automaton, one whose disposition was fixed once and for all or had adapted himself to a particular role in life. In a word, someone who had stopped growing was called a character. In contrast, the person who continued to develop, the skillful navigator on the river of life, sailing not with sheets belayed, but veering before the wind to luff again, was called characterless — in a derogatory sense, of course — because he was so difficult to understand, to classify, and keep track of. This bourgeois concept of the immobility of the soul was transferred to the stage, which the bourgeoisie always dominated. There a character became a man who was ready-made: whenever he appeared, he was drunk or comical or sad. The only thing necessary to characterize him was to give him a physical defect — a clubfoot, a wooden leg, a red nose — or have him repeat an expression, such as "that was splendid" or "Barkis is willin'." . . . Therefore, I do not believe in simple theatrical characters. And an author's summary judgments of people — this one is stupid, that one brutal, this one jealous, that one stingy — should be challenged by naturalists, who know how rich the soul-complex is and realize that "vice" has a reverse side closely resembling virtue.

Strindberg attacks melodrama by devising the notion of the "charac-terless characters," "more vacillating and disintegrating than their pred-ecessors," as befits "modern characters living in an age of transition more compulsively hysterical than the last."[74] What stings in Mc-Carthy's critique is that she confronts O'Neill with his own willingness to allow his characters to be identified by catch phrases, accents, and cu-rious quirks of behavior. They are, in Ben Jonson's term, "humors" characters, each dominated by a single personality trait. A further sting here is that O'Neill much admired Strindberg: especially what he per-ceived as Strindberg's courage and honesty in plumbing the depths of the soul.

The question of flux and fixity that drives Strindberg's discussion of character in the preface is of a piece with the problem that the Protean player and the Protean drunk pose in early modern moral thought.[75] In Harry Hope's bar, both McCarthy and Steven Bloom would agree, the effect of drink has been reductive; the characters themselves have be-come reduced to fragments, parodic of Protean plenitude. What they disagree about is whether such fragmentation is realistic, whether O'Neill's drinkers reveal the insidious "destruction of personality" through drink or not.

While there is a continuity in the Dionysian discourse of drink from the early modern through the romantic period, differences in the tech-nology of distilling and distribution of spirits made a huge difference in the way in which drink came to be seen in the eighteenth century. Fernand Braudel portrays this change as taking place through the whole early modern period: "The great innovation, the revolution in Europe, was the appearance of brandy and spirits made from grain — in a word, alcohol. The sixteenth century created it; the seventeenth consolidated it; the eighteenth popularized it."[76] At the same time drunkenness, as a kind of behavior, moved from being something fes-tive, idle, outside the "community of labor," says Thomas Brennan, us-ing Michel Foucault's terms, to becoming an illness, a kind of madness, "a medical problem, though unlike madness, it never sheds the indict-ment of moral debauchery."[77] Repetitious, self-caricaturing, bloviat-ing, the bit characters in O'Neill's *Iceman Cometh* mark the modern power of strong drink, and Hickey's therapeutic agenda in the play marks them as having arrived at AA's rock bottom. Yet, as McCarthy points out, to achieve this realistic portrayal of a group of hopeless sots the playwright is limited to the means offered by melodrama. To each is apportioned his own "little bit of character"; Harry Hope's bar is Protean only in that it is a stage set that contains lots of different type characters, each sounding in counterpoint to each.

"Bejees, what did you do to the booze, Hickey?" grumbles Harry Hope, as he *"tosses down his drink with a lifeless, automatic movement — complainingly"*: "There's no damned life left in it."[78] Hickey's campaign against the "pipe dreams" of the drunks in the tavern bundles booze and tobacco together as images of their self-deception. It follows the narrative shape of an AA story, a tripartite movement: "Our stories disclose in a general way what we used to be like, what happened, and what we are like now."[79] Hickey presents his enterprise as a continuing narrative, in which he is working to a decisive climax. In act 2 he promises his audience that he is a new Hickey and that the manipulation he puts them through will all be worth it:

> But here's the point to get. I swear I'd never act like I have if I wasn't absolutely sure it will be worth it to you in the end, after you're rid of the damned guilt that makes you lie to yourselves you're something you're not, and the remorse that nags at you and makes you hide behind lousy pipe dreams about tomorrow. You'll be in a today where there is no yesterday or tomorrow to worry you. You won't give a damn what you are any more. I wouldn't say this unless I knew, Brothers and Sisters. This peace is real! It's a fact! I know! Because I've got it! Here! Right in front of you! You see the difference in me! You remember how I used to be! Even when I had two quarts of rotgut under my belt and joked and sang "Sweet Adeline," I still felt like a guilty skunk. But you can all see that I don't give a damn about anything now. And I promise you, by the time this day is over, I'll have every one of you feeling the same way!
>
> (148)

Taking on the role of a temperance preacher, Hickey tells "what it was like" and what he is like now. The tease is that he refuses the middle term: "I think it would help us poor pipe-dreaming sinners along the sawdust trail to salvation if you told us now what it was happened to you that converted you to this great peace you've found," interjects Larry, *"[i]nsistently — with a sneer."* As O'Reilly sketches out the dynamics of a typical AA narrative, Hickey touches all the important themes of "what we used to be like": "the sense of isolation, and the amelioration of loneliness initially provided by drink; the recognition of false conviviality; the material and spiritual privations of addictive drinking; the development of despair and the fear of madness based on the inability to reverse what has become an obviously suicidal progression."[80] But, as O'Reilly and Larry point out, the missing term in Hickey's act 2 presentation "must emphatically if not dramatically represent the mental changes that led the speaker to discover A. A." Instead, Hickey withholds the story: in his ostentatious management of his confession and his parodying of the genre of recovery and rehabilitation, Hickey stages an attack on pipe dreams that is itself fantastic and self-deceptive.[81] O'Neill salts the play with clues: in Hickey's act 2 speech his "what we are like now" phase — "The peace is real!" — suffers from his repeated use of the phrase "you won't / I don't give a damn" to describe what ought to be an experience of "spiritual enrichment" and discovery of "real conviviality." When Hickey finally arrives at his narrative's climax, the revelation of his hatred for Evelyn takes him and his audience by surprise. Hickey's sudden claim of insanity — "You know I must have been insane, don't you, Governor," he *"appeals"* to Harry Hope — before an audience that includes the detectives he has summoned mocks the confessional structure that he has imposed on the moment of his disclosure. Indeed, his use of the affectionate nickname "Governor" at this point is heavily ironic, given the looming imminence of "the Chair." "Crap," says Moran the detective; to him, Hickey appears to be trying out an insanity plea (245).

The screen scenes in *School for Scandal* and *She Stoops to Conquer* feature the inadvertent exposure of good heart by Sir Peter Teazle and Charles Marlow, and Lady Teazle's eyes are opened to her own self-deception. Hickey stages his confession, he claims, as a therapeutic exercise for the patrons of the bar, but his claim to be insane at the end makes the whole business look like a hoax. And of course the patrons of the bar slide back into their pipe-dreams — into their melodramatic, one-tic characters — again as soon as Hickey is taken away. Most critics see this as an especially bleak ending. Michael Manheim, however, finds the return of good spirits, the intoxication of the bar patrons, at the end of the play to be exhilarating: to him, Hickey is "at peace with himself" at the end of the play. "He has grown in a moment of deep, sudden recognition, and his growth adds to his already mythic stature. The 'lord of misrule' has become tragic hero," he argues. The ending of the play becomes "the saturnalia in which all take part but the benumbed Larry," Manheim says of the celebration that ensues. The failure of

Hickey's temperance lecture and confessional self-exposure leads to a celebration of "the essential Hickey."[82]

But the "essential Hickey" is not an uncontested phenomenon. He can also be seen as a con-man, a charlatan, whose torment of the alcoholics in the tavern merely functions as a backdrop to his copping an insanity plea. Unlike the eighteenth-century plays, O'Neill's play presents the audience with an enigma. Hickey is a performer, a salesman, a "bughouse preacher," as Harry Hope puts it (244), peddling the language of recovery and rehabilitation. And his performance at the tavern is presented throughout as performance: he comments on his timing, promises great effects, worries that his therapeutic hectoring is not working. "I've had enough of your act. Save it for the jury," says Moran (244). Whether Hickey's act is a performance, a rehearsal that does not quite work, a rehearsal for a presentation to a jury that just might work, or an authentic journey of self-discovery is finally uncertain. O'Neill's mistrust of actors, his famous explicitness in curtailing their options by circumscribing performance with stage direction, fails here at the end of *Iceman*. The audience does not know, any more than the drunks do, what Hickey thought he was doing. Manheim's sense of Hickey's performance as Falstaffian ("lord of misrule") and festive responds to this sense in the play of Hickey as performer, of his "act" as pure performance. But in the context of O'Neill's distaste for performers who hog the stage the way Hickey does, the cacophonous festivity at the end rings hollow. It functions instead as an ironic counterpoint to the sound effect, *"the muffled, crunching thud"* (257) of Parritt's suicide, which follows Hickey's exit, just as Parritt's assault upon Larry continues in counterpoint during Hickey's confession. "You know her, Larry!" says Parritt, *"with a final implacable jeer,"* "Always a ham!" (248). Larry's exposure as an empty fake with a "coward's heart" (258) strikes many critics as an authentic self-discovery that counters Hickey's stagy story. Here, at least, the stage direction points the way: "Life is too much for me! I'll be a weak fool looking with pity at two sides of everything till the day I die! (*With an intense bitter sincerity*) May that day come soon!" (258). Where Hickey's revelation is timed, planned, staged, acted, Larry's sincerity comes to him by surprise, startles him and shocks him.

It appears from the biographical criticism of O'Neill that 1912, the year in which both *The Iceman Cometh* and *Long Day's Journey into Night* are set, was indeed a special turning point in his own life. These two 1912 plays are complemented by *Moon for the Misbegotten*, set in 1923, after the death of Ella O'Neill and just before Jamie's death. The movement is into autobiography and away from a date that has public historical significance. In this movement O'Neill demands comparison with Strindberg, who likewise obsessively returned to dates of intense private significance in his autobiographical writings. Strindberg's entire canon, as Michael Robinson has pointed out, is autobiographical in nature, whether the specific genre he is working in is historical drama, naturalistic family drama, short story, anthropological research, or even chemical experimentation. Strindberg liked to boast, directly and through the characters who stand in for him in his fictions and dramas, that he was objective and scientific in his self-observations and that his special study of himself could become part of a "natural history of the human heart." One of his alter egos states: "It has in fact seemed to me from an early age that my life was staged before me so that I would be able to observe all its facets. This reconciled me to my misfortunes, and taught me to perceive myself as an object."[83] Strindberg simultaneously reads and writes the text of his life in fifty-five volumes of published works and fourteen volumes of letters; O'Neill's output looks skimpy by comparison.

More importantly, Strindberg, immersed like Sigmund Freud in the intellectual milieu of the 1880s, found himself intrigued by the mechanisms of repression and denial through which people resist knowing the truth about themselves. According to Gunnar Brandell, Strindberg's self-styled Inferno period was a kind of "self-analysis," carried out at "virtually the same moment as Freud was embarking upon the self-analysis which forms the basis of *The Interpretation of Dreams*."[84] While Strindberg anticipated psychoanalytical thought even as Freud was developing its terms, O'Neill reacted to a popularized American version throughout his career, denying that he was a Freudian, emphasizing that all playwrights need to be psychologists, and insisting that the Oedipus and Electra complexes associated with Freud showed by their names alone that they had first been examined by playwrights.

There is an element of rivalry here, as Joel Pfister points out: O'Neill's "principal brief against psychoanalysis was that the dramatist — his profession — got there first." O'Neill had to resist the notion that playwrights were merely amateurs, "unaccredited psychologists," and did so by insisting upon Freud's and Jung's reliance upon ancient myth. The same strategy is adopted by Moorton, defending O'Neill against Bloom's charge that he "tells his one story and one story only, and his story turns out to be himself": "Aristotle understood well that because the spectacle of those who are closest to one another turning against their own is the most tragic, the family, particularly the family in which such pitiable violence erupts, is the source of the most intense tragedy," Moorton counters. "In doing so he explains two millennia before the fact why O'Neill was drawn by artistic as well as psychological reasons to a compulsive retelling of the story of his own house. . . . O'Neill, the genius both gifted and cursed with the memories of a family in which such calamities befell, came back again and again to retelling 'one story and one story only' not merely because his soul compelled him, but because great plays resulted, for reasons that Aristotle grasped with perfect clarity in the fourth century B.C."[85]

This analysis is less than satisfying because it jumbles up O'Neill's "compulsion" to tell his story with its result, "great plays," as though in succumbing to his "soul" O'Neill also bore in mind Aristotle's dicta about family members. But while O'Neill was certainly free with his discussion of the ancient Greeks, Nietzsche, and tragedy and myth in his middle period, in the years of *The Great God Brown* and *Mourning Becomes Electra*, it is he who presents *Long Day's Journey* as a therapeutic exercise. The dedication for Carlotta famously inscribes the play as *"written in tears and blood"* and thanks Carlotta for the gift of *"the faith in love that enabled me to face my dead at last and write this play — write it with deep pity and understanding and forgiveness for* all *the four haunted Tyrones"* ([7]). This sounds closer to Sheaffer's description of O'Neill as an "emotional hemophiliac" than to Moorton's version of an O'Neill consciously pursuing, for "artistic" reasons, Aristotle's observation that great tragedies are often set in the same famous families of myth.[86]

The claim of "deep pity and understanding and forgiveness" is grandiose; but biographers and critics who like to see O'Neill's whole career as a kind of "talking cure" for his problems with his family have been reluctant to take issue with it. Instead, melodrama and theatricality stand in for the falsehood of a family dynamic which O'Neill comes late in his career to be able to depict with forgiveness as well as with something like Larry's "intense bitter sincerity." O'Neill's biographers have provided the background that makes his triumph of self-understanding and forgiveness less total than the dedication suggests. While the three other Tyrones correspond rather closely in biographical detail to O'Neill's father, brother, and mother, Edmund Tyrone is markedly different from his model. In 1912 Eugene O'Neill was married, going through a divorce, and the father of a son; these facts are left unmentioned in the play. As a result, the younger son seems much younger in the play, or at least much less mature, and Edmund is in a manner unfinished: he has the "makings of a poet," but whether he will become one or not is left in the air. The play's insistence upon a repetitive pattern of aggression and regression in the family members' assaults upon each other (and in their *rapprochements*, which only lead to further assaults) paints a grim picture for the future.[87] But in 1913 Ella O'Neill checked into a convent and kicked her habit; Jamie, dissolute as he was, stopped drinking for the last two years of his mother's life; and James O'Neill unbuttoned his wallet enough to allow Eugene, after two days at the state sanitarium, to go to the private institution where his tuberculosis was cured and he made the determination to become a playwright.

This is not to fault the seamlessness of the play's design or its ruthless portrayal of a guilt-ridden family trapped, in psychoanalytical terms, in a network of "*frozen introjects*," as Bennett Simon, a psychoanalyst and literary scholar, has put it. Rather it is to question the art-as-therapy linkage so prevalent in criticism of O'Neill. "If the play and the act of writing it served to help him work through his conflicts with his parents and his brother (all of whom were dead at the time of the writing), it did not help him with his conflicts with his children and stepchildren," Simon points out. Simon takes the play's rhetoric (and the rhetoric in the criticism of the play) of rehabilitation and recovery seriously. And as a therapist, he is more concerned with the living than the dead, and the play's presentation of "parents who are murderously destructive toward children," juxtaposed with the sufferings of O'Neill's own children, gives him pause.[88]

Documenting the discrepancies with the biographical record and the shifts of perspective that place the autobiographical writer in a better light is an acceptable critical strategy when the writer claims, as Strindberg does, objectivity about himself, or claims, as O'Neill does, to have forgiven and understood his domestic trauma. The claim of sincerity can invite the charge of disingenuousness. Neither Bennett Simon as a therapist nor Walter Davis as a theorist who is concerned with the limitations of psychoanalysis can endorse O'Neill's account of his self-transcendence. O'Neill's strength, in Davis's eyes, is to document strongly and ferociously the entrapment of the psyche within a family dynamic that can never be transcended, understood, or forgiven. O'Neill's strategy is to "get the guests"; his drama amounts to a virtual assault upon the audience. "As the frameworks of explanation we use to prevent facing the reality of interfamilial cruelty collapse, we are forced to regress, along with the characters, toward psychodynamic explorations that we can scarcely comprehend, since the psychological theory that would articulate them has not yet been developed," Davis argues in an extended analysis of *Long Day's Journey*. "Much has been made of O'Neill's supposed dependence on psychoanalytic theory; the secret thereby concealed is the deep challenge his work poses to psychoanalysis by exploring the dimensions of the psyche that it has chosen to repress." Davis's point is that drama as a form can go deeper than psychoanalysis into the "crypt" of the human psyche, finding at its bottom a murderous hatred that only drama can express.[89]

O'Neill's failure to recognize his last works as acts of aggression and revenge rather than of forgiveness and understanding is less disturbing than the endorsement by the majority of his critics of his own self-delusion about these works. To present O'Neill as an artist who is wholly sincere and who has worked out his compulsions in great art is to mingle esthetic and ethical concerns irresponsibly. The attractive, benevolist model of art as rehabilitative and recuperative blurs these categories, as both Peyre and Williams suggest in their different ways. O'Neill's late plays are not better than his middle plays because they are more honest: they are better because they are structurally more economical, because their characters interact more believably, and because they trumpet their great themes less loudly. But they are not humane, not generous, not humble. One reason the vision of the family in *Long Day's Journey* is so compelling is the author's own embroilment in that family's mutual self-destruction.

O'Neill's cruelty is, to put it another way, an Artaudian cruelty; his assaults upon the audience are acts of aggression as well as representations of aggression. His mistrust of actors, his contempt for theater, his reliance on crude effects and stereotypical characterizations: all these excesses may be said to flow from this one source. O'Neill's work is not a testimonial to self-knowledge and forgiveness. It is a testament of rage.

Scene Four

CONTESTED SITES

"It is frequently suggested by psychoanalysts and critics that performers are neurotics engaged in a programme of self-treatment," writes Glenn D. Wilson in a study of the psychology of performing artists. He cites a 1972 psychoanalytical study of professional actors, which found they had "poorly integrated, largely hysteric and schizoid personalities. They were exhibitionistic and narcissistic, having much pent-up aggression. They were passive, vulnerable to stress, tended to be overly anxious and had impaired body images. Their major defences were regression, projection, denial, isolation and reaction formation. Last, homosexuality was a major area of pathology." Wilson counsels some caution in interpreting this report for two reasons: "One is that the methods used (depth interviews and projective tests) are notoriously low in reliability and validity. The other is that psychoanalysts tend to see immaturity and pathology wherever they look."[90]

In an influential book on Shakespeare, Meredith Anne Skura sees the psychoanalytic view of the actor as essential to understanding Shakespeare's plays and uses the personal testimonies of modern performers to elucidate their mysteries: "Despite obvious differences," Skura maintains,

the more we learn about Elizabethan culture and playing conditions — about the audience, the social construction of the actor, the social and economic pressures affecting theater companies, and the day-to-day details of rehearsal and performance — the more it seems that their stage, even more than ours, would foster the ambivalence and regressive concerns typical of modern actors and that it would make the player even more vulnerable to the fantasies modern actors report regarding the fickle mob. The popular image of the

Elizabethan player — seen over and over as a "proud beggar" — embodied a paradox intriguingly similar to the one we describe today as the insecurity of narcissism.[91]

Just as the language of alcohol abuse comes to comprise an uneasy mix of medical and religious terminology, so it happens that as actors gain in respectability and social status their narcissistic regressions rather than their morals become cause for concern. "Alcoholism theory is a contested site," says Jane Lilienfeld, with the problem of whether alcoholism is a disease — "and if so, what kind — a disease of the psyche, of the body?" — at its center.[92] O'Neill's use of drinking as a metaphor for self-deception and self-exposure in his plays, coupled with his portrayal of drinkers as grandiose, melodramatic, fragmented, and inauthentic, forges a strong link between drinking and acting. The narratives of O'Neill's critics, seeing a transcendence over melodramatic grandiosity and a forgiveness of the familial wound in the later plays, offer a vision of theater as therapeutic, as a site where truth can be told and psychic damage exposed and explored. But it is a "contested site," too, as the accusations of bad faith, bad writing, and self-indulgence levied by Eric Bentley, Mary McCarthy, George Steiner, and Virgil Geddes reveal.

The linkage between acting and addiction that O'Neill epitomizes opens up a whole series of questions. If actors are not vicious, but merely ill, what uniquely characterizes their illness? "I am struck by the resiliency of the actor to pressures that in others might lead to psychotic episodes," concludes Stephen Aaron, a psychologist who has studied stage fright. Stage fright is the key, Aaron continues, for actors must regularly find themselves confronted with the "gap between the actor as person and the actor as performer." Bridging that gap causes anxiety — but it is an anxiety that has the effect of preserving sanity: "The actor, pretending to be Julius Caesar, feels traumatic anxiety while the delusional schizophrenic, believing himself to be Caesar, does not."[93] While Aaron admires actors for braving the trauma of stage fright and converting it into performances, Skura portrays actors as literally reliving the "developmental history" of childhood "every night on stage": "In particular, just as the actor's exhibitionism draws on the ecstatic and grandiose narcissism of a child, he is liable to reexperience, with a child's intensity, narcissistic wounds from a time when the ego was even more fragile and the audience more powerful" — that is, from the period when the child performed for the audience of the mother

(*Shakespeare*, 18). Acting is a kind of arrested development; the audience both a nourishing and devouring "stage mother," who reenacts the feeding and demanding behavior of the actor's own mother. The autobiographies of individual actors furnish Skura with the details she needs to see narcissistic regression as essential to the actor's psychic makeup.

Skura's use of the modern actors' revelations about their childhood traumas evokes a needy, exhibitionistic personality type as prerequisite to an acting career. As she admits, the lack of personal reminiscences from Elizabethan actors makes categorical declaration difficult: "There can be no proof about what the actors felt, but the circumstantial evidence suggests enough resemblances between Elizabethan and contemporary actors' lives to justify some analogies" (*Shakespeare*, 42). Skura suggests that Elizabethan moralists' complaints about actors' conduct may reveal more about the moralists than about the actors: indeed, maybe the moralists require psychoanalytic treatment, too. "Today's reader will detect ulterior motives behind the antitheatricalists' moral outrage," Skura contends, "and will sort through the accusations with care before accepting such an image of players" (36). Assenting to Barish's view of the antitheatricalism as an unreasoning, compulsive prejudice, she concludes: "The Elizabethan player, even more than our actors, was marked as the Other whose strangeness fascinates and repels, the charismatic transgressor who all too easily becomes a screen for the projection of the audience's disowned impulses" (37–38). The moral outrage of antitheatrical writers is itself a psychic reflex, a wincing at the player's exposure of the audience's wound.

Acting and playgoing are compulsive, mutually dependent behaviors; actors and audiences, in the language of addiction, are each other's enablers. But the case is not as clear-cut as other kinds of substance abuse. "Consider the addiction to gambling," urges Gregg Franzwa: "To what is the gambler addicted? Surely the answer does not include such behavioral categories as pulling handles or watching horses run in circles. Rather it involves the feelings that attend these behaviors in certain contexts; it is the particular form of excitement that the gambler seeks. Or to put it physiologically, the organism acts to reproduce particular kinds of brain states."[94] Actors, too, seem addicted less to particular kinds of behavior or to particular chemical substances than to recreating a particular form of excitement. Two plays about gamblers evoke more precisely the nature of this exhilaration.

"Who is happier than a Gamester, who more respected, I mean among those that make any Figure in the World?" exclaims Valere in Susanna Centlivre's comedy, *The Gamester* (1705):

Who more carest by Lords and Dukes? or whose Conversation more agreeable — whose Coach finer in the Ring — or Finger in the side Box produce more Lustre — who has more Attendance from the Drawers, — or better Wine from the Master? — Or Nicer serv'd by the Cook. In short, there is an Air of Magnificence in't, — a Gamester's hand is the Philosophers Stone that turns all it touches into Gold.

"And Gold into nothing," interrupts Hector, his valet. But Valere is in full spate and cannot be stopped:

A Gentleman that plays is admitted every where — Women of strictest Vertue will Converse with him, — for Gaming is as much in fashion here as 'tis in *France*, and our Ladies look upon it, as the height of ill Breeding, not to have a Passion for play; Oh! the Charming Company of half a dozen Ladies, with each a Dish of Tea, — to behold their languishing Ogles with their Eyes, their Ravishing White Hand, to hear the delicious Scandal which they vent between each Sip, just piping hot from invention's Mint, wherein they spare none from the States-Man to the Cit — and damn Plays before they are acted, especially if the Author be unknown, — this ended, the Cards are call'd for.

Like Marlow in the persona of the agreeable Rattle, Valere boasts that his gaming makes him an intimate of the ladies; like Lord Foppington at Lady Betty Modish's, he is a welcome, not a ridiculous, diversion. "Where is the immorality of Gaming," cries Valere:

Now I think there can be nothing more Moral — It unites Men of all Ranks, — the Lord and the Peasant — the Haughty Dutchess and the City Dame — the Marquis and the Footman, all without distinction play together.

> *And sure that Life can ne'er offensive prove,*
> *That teacheth Men such peaceful ways of Love.*[95]

Valere's effusive apology for gaming is undercut when, at the end of the play, the French marquis is revealed to be a footman. Of a piece with the apology is a treatise that mockingly praises gaming as a uniquely English form of recreation, *A Modest Defence of Gaming* (1754): "the Situation of our Country inclines us to Commerce," proclaims the anonymous author, "and the Genius of our People determines them to Play. The Merchant often risks his whole Effects in one Bottom, and the Gentleman often hazards all his Estate upon one Rubber: 'Tis true they are both liable to the Strokes of Fortune; for one cannot command the Winds and the Wave, any more than the other can the Aces and Honours, but their Designs are the same, equally tending to advance their Family, and to serve their Country."[96] The morality of gaming, as proclaimed by Valere, and its social utility, as delineated by the anonymous apologist, consist in the fact that it erases class distinctions and barriers. All are equal in the eyes of fortune; aristocrat and merchant equally participate in the fluidity of commerce.

"Something seems to be going on in the stubbornly contradictory image of the wealthy penny-grubbing player," says Meredith Skura of puritan and playwrights' attacks upon players for selling themselves cheap and for flaunting their wealth, "as if writers felt that the player was getting away with something he had no right to, whether it was money, sexual license, or social climbing. Or, perhaps more than any particular transgression, it was a matter of what we would now call 'attitude.'"[97] Valere's cocky boasting makes of the gamester a similarly transgressive figure, who can penetrate at will the lady's tea tables and mingle with all classes: "all without distinction play together." Such erasures of distinction, however, make actors dangerous, as Rousseau and the divines repeat. "A sumptuary Law would be of service to the Poor themselves," argues Alcock, for they would then stop spending their meager substance upon lavish dress and upon other wasteful ways of aping their betters, such as *"Dram drinking."*[98]

Centlivre adapted *The Gamester* from a French original, and in her dedication of the published play to the earl of Huntingdon she makes clear her major departure from *Le joueur*: Valere is *"intirely ruin'd in the* French: *whereas I, in Complaisance to the many fine Gentlemen that Play in England, have reclaim'd him, after I have discover'd the ill Consequence of Gaming, that very often happen to those who are too passionately fond of it. . . ."* "I heartily wish," Centlivre continues, *"all Men of Rank and Quality as indifferent to this bewitching Diversion of Gameing as Your Lordship; then wou'd the Distress'd be reliev'd, the Poor supported, and the Virtuous encourag'd, which would distinguish our Nobility as much above our Neighbours, as their Heroick Deeds have done"* ([B3v]). Though playful,

Centlivre's dedication has a serious, patriotic purpose: in reclaiming Valere, she reveals the moral superiority of the English gamester.

What is rewarded at the play's end is Valere's basic goodness of heart. In both versions of the play, Angelica (Angélique) gives her portrait to Valere as a token of her love. In the French version Valère, in the intoxication of play, pawns the portrait to Mme. Ressource, and the betrayal is discovered when the pawnbroker calls on Angélique with jewelry to sell. Centlivre provides instead an exhilarating scene of diceplay, in which Angelica, disguised *"in Mans Cloaths"* (53), bankrupts Valere, wins the portrait, and barely escapes with her life when Valere draws upon her and demands the picture back. "Then to conceal your treachery, you wou'd have committed Murder — excellent Moralist," chides Angelica as he attempts to extenuate his fault in act 5 (64). It seems that Valere, disgraced and disinherited, will indeed have to join the army — "I'll to the Camp, there in the service of my Country, expiate my Follies," he impetuously vows earlier in act 5 (59) — when Angelica, appalled by the cruelty of Valere's father, calls him back and forgives him. "Shall I see him ruin'd — no — that wou'd be barbarous beyond Example — *Valere* come back, shou'd I forgive you all — Would my Generosity oblige you to a sober Life." "Oh let me fold thee in my Repenting Arms," Valere responds, "and whisper to thy Soul that I am intirely Chang'd" (67).

Such scenes of sudden reform and change, of generosity and benevolence, are common in the eighteenth-century drama. Angelica's example inspires Sir Thomas, Valere's father, to reinstate him, and after a country dance Valere urges the audience to join him in pursuing *"Vertue's Pleasing Prospect"* and *"each with me the Libertine reclaim / And shun what sinks his Fortune, and his Fame"* (70). It is, of course, this kind of overt moralizing that Goldsmith chides in his "Comparison between Laughing and Sentimental Comedy," but the therapeutic agenda of the heroine is remarkably similar to Kate Hardcastle's. Like Kate, Angelica humiliates her lover by disguising herself, and subsequently she redeems him and restores him to his father's favor.

In the exposure of the French count as a footman, Centlivre makes use of the device of the pawnbroker's visit from *Le joueur*: Mrs. Security recognizes him as her cousin, and Valere gets to give him a kick and send him off. The play closes with a reinforcement of the class distinctions that Valere mocked in his enthusiasm as a gamester. As in *She Stoops to Conquer*, the social order is restored. The hero's threat to turn

Protean — to become really the agreeable Rattle, to resort ever again to the gaming-house — is deflected into advantageous marriage.

Centlivre's play is the kind that begs for the charge of bad faith to be leveled at it. O'Neill as well as Goldsmith would find much to deplore in it. The arbitrary suddenness of Valere's repentance and conversion, the equally sudden and arbitrary generosity of Angelica, the father's rapid changes of heart — all of these point to the sham at the bottom of the play. The play trivializes its serious issue — gaming — by staging a breeches comedy scene as the crisis in which Valere betrays his mistress. Valere's compulsion to gamble is on the order of a joke, like the mock praise of gaming as an encouragement to stoicism and a counterpart to commercial enterprise.

Edward Moore's tragedy *The Gamester* (1753), in contrast, presents gambling as a vice and a disease, uniting the two in the images of medicine and poison. "Physicians to cure Fevers would keep from the Patient's thirsty Lip the Cup that wou'd enflame him; You give it to his hands," the gamester Beverley's sister Charlotte reproaches Stukeley, his false friend. A knocking is heard at the door: "Hark! Sir — These are my Brother's desperate Symptoms — Another Creditor" (1.5.213).[99] Beverley throughout the play is virtually a somnambulist, misled by Stukeley ("The smooth-tongu'd Hypocrite," as Charlotte calls him [4.1.247]). Instead of seeing Beverley's compulsion to play, the audience witnesses his victimization by the Iago-esque Stukeley (liberal borrowings from *Othello* make the connection clear). But as Beverley loses more and more of his fortune to Stukeley, including his reversion to his uncle's estate, he becomes almost catatonic. "How bore he his last Shock?" Stukeley asks Bates, who reports the observations of Dawson, his accomplice:

Like one (so *Dawson* says) whose Senses had been numbed by Misery. When all was lost, he fixt his Eyes upon the Ground, and stood some Time, with folded Arms, stupid and motionless. Then snatching his Sword, that hung against the Wainscot, he sat him down; and with a Look of fixt Attention, drew Figures on the Floor — At last he started up, look's wild, and trembled; and like a Woman, seiz'd with her Sex's Fits, laugh'd out aloud, while the Tears trickled down his Face — so left the Room.

"Why, this was Madness," exclaims Stukeley. "The Madness of Despair," Bates gravely concurs (4.3.248).

At the end, in a catastrophe that Moore contends some of the audience found *"too Horrible"* (preface, 204), Beverley takes poison and dies before the horrified eyes of his family and friends, who bring him good news and solace but far too late. "A Furnace rages in this Heart — I have been too hasty," Beverley complains as the poison begins to work (5.11.269). The "restless Flames" of Hell torment him; he dies crying out for "Mercy! Mercy!" Lewson, his staunch supporter and virtuous friend, explains to the audience: "Save but one Error, and this last fatal Deed, thy Life was lovely. Let frailer Minds take Warning and from Example learn, that Want of Prudence is Want of Virtue" (271).

With its gruesome ending, Moore's *Gamester* counters the charge of bad faith that can be leveled against Centlivre's. But the former play, in which gambling is taken lightly as a game, and the latter, in which gambling is metaphorized as poison, disease, and Hell-fire, both anticipate the strategies of the temperance melodramas of the nineteenth century. Both clearly address antitheatrical charges against the playhouse by foregrounding and emphasizing the moral content and social utility of the enterprise. Moore defends his ending by invoking the horror of the vice he attacks: *"Nor shou'd so prevailing and destructive a Vice as GAMING be attack'd upon the Theatre, without impressing upon the Imagination all the Horrors that may attend it"* (preface, 204). The same charge was made against the *delirium tremens* scene in *The Drunkard*; in that case the answer made was not only that such horrors should be displayed but that the actual performer, William Henry Smith, had himself undergone the experience before drying out.[100] In response to the charge of excessive theatricality comes the defense of authenticity.

Centlivre's *Gamester* was first performed by Vanbrugh's company, with Jack Verbruggen as Valere and Anne Bracegirdle as Angelica. Through Thomas Betterton, who performed the prologue and played the role of Lovewell, this company could trace its acting legacy back to the Elizabethan theaters, at least in anecdotes of varying degrees of reliability. Moore's *Gamester* was performed by David Garrick's company at the Theatre-Royal in Drury Lane, with Garrick as Beverley. In the almost fifty years between the two performances, Colley Cibber, whose anxious social climbing and wise vanity had made him the most satirized of poet laureates, had done much to elevate the social standing of actors. Garrick, of course, was central to the period's experience of "the new image of the actor as genteel and educated," as Shearer West puts it.[101] Garrick's fulfillment of Cibber's agenda to make the actor a welcome figure in the salons of the elite coincides with repeated praise of his acting style as "natural." "Just as Betterton, the premier actor of his day, had mastered the rhetorical mode, Garrick epitomized its successor," points out Joseph Roach. "It was immediately apparent to all factions, pro and con, that the kind of acting he offered up at his debut in 1741 broke decisively with the past."[102]

In this regard, Garrick's career runs parallel to that of Lekain in France, who also was thought to epitomize "le naturel." Jean Duvignaud, author of a sociological study of the figure of the actor, sees the promotion of "natural" acting as part of the shift away from monarchy toward bourgeois polities in both France and England: "The 'natural' which invades the century corresponds to the reduction of influence of the royal courts and the increasing importance of urban audiences." Duvignaud sees the eighteenth-century actor as mediating between an old order and a new one: "Uprooted from his 'bourgeois' compost, transformed into the transmitter of models of culture, nomadic or resident within a troupe, creator of an image of the human personality without which there would be no theater, vassal to a prince or servant to the public, the actor remains on the margin of monarchical society, which, nonetheless, finds its highest expression in the theater." The emergence of star actors after the revolution leads to a new role for actors: "Conduct that was accepted for the prince was now accepted for the famous actor: that he consume more than others; that he spend and waste; that he deliver himself up to a 'potlatch' where he exalts his own existence, just like the sovereign in the past, in order to win prestige and gain an importance that would sustain his credit with the public."[103] Actors become like monarchs: inviolate, sacred, wonderful in their waste. Such a figure, of course, haunted O'Neill in the form of his father, James, who made the Fechter version of *The Count of Monte Cristo* his own and toured in it for decades. Nor is it far from Duvignaud's "potlatch" to the self-indulgence and self-exposure encouraged by the late twentieth century's cult of celebrity.

Duvignaud's version of the rise of the star actor adds a further dimension to understanding Garrick's interruption of the run of *The Gamester* after ten nights. "It is hop'd that Ladies and Gentlemen who have taken Places for this Play for *Monday* or *Tuesday* next, will not take it ill that it is deferr'd for a few Days, it being impossible to continue acting the Principal Character without some Respite," read a note to the last night's playbill.[104] *The Gamester*'s horrors were not only hard on the audience but intolerable for the genteel actor to sustain for long. By calling the public's attention to the ordeal he must undergo each night that he plays Beverley, Garrick heightens interest in both the play and himself: he foregrounds his delicacy of sensibility and reminds his audience of the gulf he must bridge between the pathetic Beverley and himself.

Garrick's concern to distance himself from the role that he plays marks the actor, in Elizabeth Burns's terms, as an "interloper": "He intervenes between the playwright and the audience so as to make the fictive world, *signified* by the first, a set of *signifiers* for the social reality of the latter. . . . He intervenes also between the *authenticity* of his own life, of his own self, and its past as known to himself (and as known or assumed at least in part to the audience) and the *authenticated* life of the character he is playing. So he acts a lie, too, but a lie circumscribed and exposed, or 'earthed,' this time by the relationship of trust established by theatrical tradition between the players and the audience."[105] However tiresome to Moore and inconvenient for audiences, Garrick's declaration of fatigue lays claim to special status for both the play and the performer.

"In the literature on actors and acting in the 18th century," argues Shearer West, "two trends emerge with this wider argument of justification: first, a conflation of the actor's personal life with his or her role, and, second, a mythologizing of the actor's life, an insistence on his or her refinement and social elevation."[106] Verbruggen as Valere carries no such myth with him; Garrick cultivated and enhanced the myth of his own genius. Joseph Roach has shown how clearly Garrick's sense of genius was based in eighteenth-century ideas of sensibility. William Duff, in his *Critical Observations on the Writings of the Most Celebrated Original Geniuses in Poetry* (1770), adds an elitist note: genius required "a delicacy and refinement in its sensibility . . . which is utterly unknown and inconceivable by the vulgar."[107] Garrick's exquisite sensibility becomes almost incapacitating (as it does incapacitate him after ten nights of *The Gamester*). In 1765 Laurence Sterne wrote from Bath urging Garrick to return to the stage after a hiatus: "The moment you set yr foot upon yr Stage — Mark! I tell it You — by some magick, irresisted power, every Fibre abt yr heart will vibrate afresh & strong & feelingly as ever."[108] This infusion of energy that Garrick must expect from the stage is essential, William B. Worthen argues, to his performance: "If the actor cannot seem to infuse his gesture with feeling, he fails to affect his audience, and weakens the sympathetic structure of all social relationships. He becomes Diderot's courtier, or Rousseau's Parisian hypocrite, and confirms Rousseau's pessimistic vision of the moral vacuity of the theater and of the theatrical society." Garrick's task, which so fatigues him, is to shore up the structures of social performance that characterize eighteenth-century society.[109]

Whether the actor is best understood psychoanalytically (as regressing painfully before the audience to an infantile state of narcissistic grandiosity and vulnerability) or sociologically (as exposing before a bourgeois audience a sense of social marginality and sensitivity that mirrors its own), actors remain circumscribed by an antitheatrical vocabulary that sees them as somehow maimed, incomplete people. The beastly, shameless transformations railed against by the moralists are replaced by a kind of pity for these tender beings. Treated as vagabonds and sturdy beggars under the old Elizabethan laws and excommunicated by the French monarch at whose command they played, the early modern actors relied upon the protection — and tyranny — of their patrons for their very survival. With Garrick and the emergence of the modern actor, a new tyrant comes to rule: the audience.

As Herbert Blau puts it, by the eighteenth century the audience had "entered the sphere of representation as something of a political fantasy: the People, *the will of the People*; or the Public, *the desire of the Public* which, looking for meaning in performance, wanted it to be transparent[.] Which is to say, created in its own image." It was to this public that Garrick appealed by bribing reviewers and writing reviews of his own performances. Blau continues: "So long as it pays, it will get what it wants — putting aside whether it knows what it wants — from actors who are only too subservient, for all their access to their own emotions, to the priority of another will: patron, prompter, author, director, audience. For the actor's freedom has always been — given the emarginated record of the profession — the most pathetic illusion, whether he (or she) thinks he has the audience in the palm of his hand or, surrendering the ego, which has no continuity anyhow, she (or he) is freely revealing the soul."[110] Stephen Aaron identifies the actor's desire to submit to another will as essential to the parent-child relationship that develops between actors and directors during the rehearsal period: "The director is experienced by the actor in many different, often conflicting, ways: as boss, tyrant, companion, collaborator, critic, confidant, teacher." "Actors want 'a mommy' or 'a daddy' to show them what to do and, in very difficult scenes, ones in which frightening, unconscious fantasies are aroused, the 'Show me what to do' can even become 'Do it for me!'"[111]

Eugene O'Neill, with his scorn of "dumb" actors and his prescriptive stage directions, epitomizes this kind of infantilization of actors in the modern American theater. As a rebellion against the figure of the old, tyrannical actor-manager — epitomized by James O'Neill — this becomes in the critical biographies of O'Neill a kind of infantile regression on his own part. But the psychoanalytic language of contemporary acting theory, in its invocation of an infantile model, does not really break new ground from the eighteenth-century model of the exquisite sensibility of genius. Rather it finds a particular pathology to explain actors' hypersensitivity, the "Magick, irresisted power" that overcomes them as they set foot on the stage.

Side by side with the contemporary image of the actor as psychically maimed is a body of thought, alluded to by Blau above, that sees the actor as heroic, shamanic, free. Michael Goldman, in *The Actor's Freedom*, and David Cole, in *The Theatrical Event: A Mythos, a Vocabulary, a Perspective*, have both enunciated such a vision. For Goldman the actor's freedom is not, as Blau implies, a political or social condition, but rather is an aspect of the "terrific" energies involved in the act of personation. As Goldman uses the word, "bearing in mind that word's root suggestion of the awesome and fearful, of manifestations both exciting and terrible," the actor performing becomes uncanny, disturbing, threatening. Yet even here, the infantile is not far beneath the surface. Theater involves playing "games we play with fear and loss." "All art does this," Goldman says, "but theater is closest to the root: to the shaman, the maenad, the obsessive child; to the first loomings of our parents; to ghosts and spirits; to the full physicality of the game and the apprehensions the game springs from, to the actual matter and mastery of our fears."[112] For the crippling anxieties of stage fright, Goldman and Cole substitute an exhilarating exploration of the uncanny, a liberating shamanic journey among the ghosts, but the source remains a psychic wound: the "obsessive child," whose parents loom primally, in Goldman's case; the infantile feeder, in David Cole's *Acting as Reading*, who regresses in the act of devouring the text.[113] The ideology of Stanislavskian acting, as Worthen has pointed out, is explicitly antitheatrical: as the actor "pursues his own authenticity through histrionic performance," the stage comes to matter less and less. For Vsevolod

Meyerhold, Worthen continues: "The actor's performance becomes real by being released from its theatrical limitations. The necessary accouterments of the theater — scenery, properties, mechanical effects, perhaps even dramatic roles — are now 'incidental,' peripheral to the theater's relentless attention to the actor himself."[114] Shamanic or regressive, the actor's pursuit of authenticity becomes, like O'Neill's "endless burrowing," a private exploration of self to which the stage is antithetical. Hence the emphasis on the rehearsal process in most discussions of modern acting, in contrast to what is known of early modern actors, who seem to have managed quite well despite what looks to modern eyes like utterly insufficient time to prepare.

For Rousseau and the antitheatrical writers of the two centuries before him, the actor represented not just a powerful threat to society but a powerful threat to individual identity — that of the actor, no doubt, but also that of the individual audience member under the actor's sway. There was the threat that men might lose their amorous bearings, falling in love with boy actors, and that boy actors might themselves be physically transformed into women. Intoxication is a commonplace metaphor for what can happen to both performer and audience at the theater, and the psychoanalytic critics are quick to notice actors' oral fixations as they nervously smoke and drink before performances. Gambling is another metaphor that emphasizes the heightened excitement, the sense of risk and peril, that characterizes modern discourse about acting. An extreme sensitivity to emotions, like Garrick's, enters the vocabulary as both a blessing and a wound; Dionysus, according to Euripides (in William Arrowsmith's famous translation), is the god "most terrible, and yet most gentle to mankind." Dionysus is "the Liberator," E. R. Dodds famously put it, "the god who by simple means, or by other means not so simple, enables you for a short time to *stop being yourself*, and thereby sets you free."[115] Actors, who are able to stop being themselves regularly, on a professional basis, who practice and sustain "Negative Capability,"[116] are among the god's simple or not so simple means. That these *means* find themselves so often accused of being harmful *ends* — wasteful discharges, shameless beasts — testifies to the fearful uncertainty with which Western culture embraces liberation, freedom, sincerity, truth: its highest values.

Epilogue

Icarius was the first mortal to whom Dionysus gave the gift of wine. The god urged him to share the secret with others, so Icarius brought wine to a group of shepherds, who drank hard and fell asleep. As Roberto Calasso tells the story, when they awoke, "The shepherds began to suspect Icarius was up to something." They struck him with different weapons and then, "to finish the job, they ran him through with their cooking spit":

> As he lay dying, Icarius remembered something that had happened not long before. Dionysus had taught him how to plant the vines and look after them. Icarius watched their growth with the same love he had for his trees, waiting for the moment when he would be able to squeeze the grapes with his own hands. One day he caught a goat eating some vine leaves. He was overcome with anger and killed the animal on the spot. Now he realized the goat had been himself.
>
> But something else had happened that had to do with that goat. Icarius had skinned it, and, with some other peasants, improvised a dance around the beast's mangled corpse. Icarius didn't appreciate, as he lay dying, that the gesture had been the origin of tragedy, but he did sense that the death of the goat was connected with what was happening to him, the shepherds circling him, each one hitting him with a different weapon, until he saw the spit that would pierce his heart.[1]

All the problematic elements of Dionysus are already present in this brief incident: intoxication, possession, scapegoating, substitution, impersonation, error, folly, sudden wisdom, a mingling of the sacred and profane. Icarius is the first instance of the panic that Dionysus can induce, and, as he realizes that he has acted out his own death in the death of the goat, he invents tragedy long before Thespis stepped out in front of the satyr chorus.

The shepherds mistake the mock death of drunken sleep for a real murder plot against them, and in this way the fable speaks to the complexities of theatrical representation. How were they to know that the sleeping potion Icarius brought to them was a gift and not a poison? Their mistake is not much different from Romeo's in the Capulet tomb or Hal's as he looks at the sleeping Henry IV or the shamming Falstaff.

"Why are we so anxious about representation?" asks W. J. T. Mitchell. Throughout this study, the actor functions as a figure whose representations of social conditions, emotions, religious sentiments, and ethical dilemmas provoke anxious and often malicious responses, not just from moralists but also in the works of playwrights. Accusations of bad faith against actors and persistent analogizing of bad faith to acting are, I have argued, two sides of the same coin and demonstrate the persistence and ubiquity of antitheatrical sentiment. But the anxiety, as Mitchell suggests, runs beyond theater into the whole arena of representation. For while Socrates would certainly banish the performer from his ideal city, he thinks of the performer as poet, not just as actor, and would banish not just theater but poetry and painting as well. The error of the shepherds, in mistaking and then taking decisive action on the basis of their mistake, is a tragic error, and it arises from a failure to ask the question that Socrates repeatedly asks: what is the relationship between that which is represented and the representation? Mitchell sees the relationship as "an inherently unstable, reversible, and dialectical structure. The relation of the representation to what it represents, for instance, may transfer power/value to what it represents and drain it from the represented, but inherent in such an understanding would be the assumption that the power/value quotient originates with the represented, that it has been (temporarily) alienated, transferred, and may always be given back."[2] For Socrates, an absolute privilege inheres in that which is represented: the temporary alienation, the "gift" as Mitchell calls it, threatens that privilege. Molière, defending *Tartuffe*, and Elizabeth Burns, describing the way the lies that actors play are "earthed" by the circumscriptions of theatrical tradition, insist on the temporality and contingency of the transfer.[3]

Shakespeare plays out a dynamic of presenting and representing, deferring to and undercutting the power of the audience, that emphasizes not the temporality of representation but its instability. And as a result his plays enjoy the kind of special status that Foucault conferred upon *Las meninas* as "a representation, as it were, of classical Representation."[4] Shakespeare's plays are about play-making and about acting; his characters' language is suffused throughout with theatrical and anti-theatrical idiom. In *The Dialectics of Representation* Susan Wells offers a reading of Puck's epilogue to *A Midsummer Night's Dream* that insists on the role the audience must collaboratively play in the making of Shakespearean meaning: "The dramatic spell is dissolved only by invoking the power of the audience. The hermeneutic circle that interprets the play's indeterminacy as an image of all creative and transformative powers dissolves into the circle of spectators and actors, the circle that is the source and boundary of all representation."[5]

Like Wells, Mitchell sees representation as a dialectical process, a process of giving and taking — or, in the language of *A Midsummer Night's Dream*, of taking and mistaking. But Mitchell asks: "Why are we so anxious about representation?" in the context of two other questions: "What lies outside representation?" and "What is our responsibility toward it?" (*Picture Theory*, 418). For the antitheatricalists and moralists I have examined here, everything worthwhile lies outside the arena of representation, and moral responsibility inheres in attacking representations as false. Christopher Prendergast, in contrast, argues that "for those of us who live inescapably in a culture of representation . . . there is no such thing as the unrepresentable." The problem is "not that representation as such is impossible; rather it fails in its task, thus falling under a negative valuation, or, more radically, under prohibition (as in the case of iconoclasm and the interdiction of graven images)."[6] By falling short, representation misrepresents: better the attempt should not be made at all.

Representation has an inescapably theatrical twist to it in French; as Prendergast and numerous commentators on Foucault have pointed out, *représentation* has as one meaning theatrical production or performance. But its first meaning, even in French, is presenting again: which in at least a few ways is theatrical, too. Rehearsal — *répétition* in French — practice, and doing things over and over again until you get them right are all aspects of theatrical activity that become suspect when they leach into social life, and not merely for Rousseau; "the dangers of theatricality," Burns declares, "lie only in rigidity or repetitiveness" (*Theatricality*, 232). When spontaneity and sincerity are perceived as virtues, repetition and rehearsal appear as vices. "Tonight we improvise" might be a sincere statement on one isolated occasion: to schedule *Tonight We Improvise* for regular performances, or even to perform in improvisatory comedy like Second City or *commedia dell'arte* on a regular basis, opens performers to the charge of rehearsal, memorization, reliance upon set "bits" or *lazzi*. From its inception with Plato, antitheatricalism charges that it is in that very pretense of spontaneity, in the ability to engage audiences' emotions as though the rehearsed actions they witness are somehow spontaneous, that theater most perniciously deceives.

Is representation then a sin? Early modern and modern antitheatricalism differ most strongly in their use of or refusal to use the language of religion. Hypocrisy moves from being specifically associated with the feigning of piety (the index to Bellegarde's *Reflections upon Ridicule*, for example, reads "Hypocrites: see Religion") to the more insidious undermining of civic virtue that Rousseau dreaded. Rousseau's critique of theater in the *Letter to D'Alembert* adopts a secular language of republican virtue in place of the earlier vocabulary of patristic and scriptural citation. Hegel, too, delineating the modern type of hypocrites, who simply adjust the categories governing virtue so that their own conduct will always be virtuous, participates in this process. The religious, whether Protestant or recusant, Puritan or Jansenist, nature of the language of conscience and the own self gradually gives way to a secularized cult of sincerity through the seventeenth and eighteenth centuries. But the main thrust of this study has been to point out the ubiquity of notions of vice as performance and of virtue as unperformable. Antitheatricalism is Protean in its own way, becoming secular and therapeutic as the religious vocabulary wanes.

What changes, then, is not the sense of acting as pernicious and dangerous, but rather the sense that what is violated is less a soul than a self. Prynne's asseverations may represent an extreme, but Prynne's side — in 1642 insofar as he was antitheatrical, and in 1660 insofar as he was royalist — won. In spite of the current fashions in criticism of the drama, especially the social constructionism of feminism and new historicism, privileging, cherishing, and believing in an own self remains a central value of Western culture. Despite the fact that even Rousseau noticed disturbing similarities between his spontaneous, Protean, ever-changing self and the falsehoods of social performance he deplored, he continued to engage in the quest for sincerity and truth to self.

This quest is dialectical in nature and at its most extreme can be cast as an oscillation between Bacchic frenzy and abandon on the one hand and puritan repression and suppression on the other. Nietzsche's famous pair Dionysus and Apollo make their appearance in *The Birth of Tragedy*, a book whose whole vision is dialectical, in that what Nietzsche recounts is less the birth of tragedy (as Calasso does) than its death, its crumbling, its subjection to the rationalist, Cyclops eye of Socrates. But the book concludes with an idyll. Nietzsche imagines a dreamer, traveling in time back to classical Athens before the age of Socrates:

> strolling through walkways under high Ionic columns, looking upward to a horizon that is defined by pure and noble lines, looking around at his transfigured reflection mirrored in translucent marble, surrounded by solemn processions or delicately moving people, with harmonious musical sounds and rhythmic gestures — would he not be compelled, amidst this proliferating abundance of beauty, to raise his hand to Apollo and cry out: "Blissful are the people of Greece! How great must Dionysus be amongst you, if the god of Delphi finds such magic necessary to counter your dithyrambic frenzy!" To one so disposed, however, a grizzled Athenian might answer, gazing at him with the noble eyes of an Aeschylus, "But say also this, you wondrous stranger: How much must these people suffer, in order to be able to become so beautiful! Now follow me to the Tragedy, and *sacrifice* with me *at the temple of both gods*." [7]

Nietzsche would of course later shower upon Richard Wagner abuse that rivals Prynne's. But in *The Birth of Tragedy* he suggests a paradoxical give-and-take between the forces of control and the forces of exaltation.

Dressing up, lying, and drinking all reflect aspects of performance that leach into social life and then find their way back into performance: vice on the stage takes the shape of performance in society. Antitheatricalism, with its demand for a sincerity that cannot be performed and its celebration of an unplayable own self, trumpets its slanders against actors, and the stage takes them up and plays them out. Neither can escape its dependence on the other. It is one of the great ironies of history that a key mechanism for the invention or discovery of the secret self should have been the early modern stage. It is equally paradoxical that the stage's enemies should have offered to the theater the vocabulary with which to celebrate the secret self and attack hypocritical social performance. Likewise, the essential self in all its simplicity needs the threat of dissolution and fragmentation into mere performance for its definition, just as the new historicist construct of the performing self only takes full shape in opposition to essentialism. Antitheatricalism is not coincidental to Western culture, a strange "prejudice"; it is a key to the early modern and modern culture's struggle to define and structure the self.

Notes

PROLOGUE. THE ACTOR AS HYPOCRITE

1. All plays of Shakespeare quoted from *The Complete Works of Shakespeare*, 4th ed., ed. David Bevington (New York: HarperCollins, 1992); subsequent citations appear in the text.

2. William Prynne, *Histriomastix* (1633; rpt. New York: Garland Publishing, 1974), pp. 156, 158–59 (italics in original).

3. Gerald Else, *The Origin and Early Form of Greek Tragedy* (New York: Norton, 1972), p. 59.

4. John Northbrooke, *A Treatise against Dicing, Dancing, Plays and Interludes* (1577?); quoted from *Shakespeare Society of London: Publications, Vol. 15 (#14; #2)* (Nendeln, Liechtenstein: Kraus Reprint Ltd., 1966), marginal note to p. 84.

5. For an elaboration of this line of argument, see Bert O. States, *"Hamlet" and the Concept of Character* (Baltimore: Johns Hopkins University Press, 1992). See also the lively exchange in *Connotations* 2 (1992), which begins with John Russell Brown's "Multiplicity of Meaning in the Last Moments of *Hamlet*," pp. 16–33, and includes interpretations of "The rest is silence" from Dieter Mehl (pp. 182–85) and Maurice Charney (pp. 186–89) and a reply by Brown (pp. 275–76).

6. Lionel Trilling, *Sincerity and Authenticity* (Cambridge, Mass.: Harvard University Press, 1972), p. 3.

7. Jonas Barish, *The Antitheatrical Prejudice* (Berkeley and Los Angeles: University of California Press, 1981), pp. 2, 191, 25, 476–77.

8. David Cole, *The Theatrical Event: a Mythos, a Vocabulary, a Perspective* (Middletown, Conn.: Wesleyan University Press, 1975), p. 161.

9. See David Cole, *Acting as Reading: The Place of the Reading Process in the Actor's Work* (Ann Arbor: University of Michigan Press, 1992); and David Wiles, *Shakespeare's Clown: Actor and Text in the Elizabethan Playhouse* (Cambridge: Cambridge University Press, 1987).

10. For full discussion of Ben Jonson's complicated engagement with the popular theater, see John Gordon Sweeney III, *Jonson and the Psychology of Pub-*

lic Theater: "To Coin the Spirit, Spend the Soul" (Princeton: Princeton University Press, 1985).

11. The word *invention* is drawn from Joel Fineman, *Shakespeare's Perjured Eye: The Invention of Poetic Subjectivity in the Sonnets* (Berkeley and Los Angeles: University of California Press, 1985). In a rather different sense, it finds itself in the title of Harold Bloom's *Shakespeare: The Invention of the Human* (New York: Riverhead Books, 1998). Katharine Eisaman Maus, in *Inwardness and Theater in the English Renaissance* (Chicago: University of Chicago Press, 1995), emphasizes the connection between ideas of subjectivity and English Protestant discourses. See also Paul A. Cefalu, "'Damned Custom . . . Habits Devil': Shakespeare's Hamlet, Anti-Dualism, and the Early Modern Philosophy of Mind," *ELH* [*English Literary History*] 67 (2000), 399–431. In "Hamlet's Recusant Stance and Shakespeare's Catholic Nature," a paper delivered at the Ohio Shakespeare Conference 2001, John Freeman argues that "anguished interiority" is a feature of recusant discourse in the period.

12. Michael Goldman, *On Drama: Boundaries of Genre, Borders of Self* (Ann Arbor: University of Michigan Press, 2000), p. 74.

13. Hobbes and commentary quoted from Stephen Greenblatt, *Learning to Curse: Essays on Early Modern Culture* (New York: Routledge, 1990), pp. 142–43 (italics in original). This passage is also quoted as an epigraph to Stephen Orgel, *Impersonations: The Performance of Gender in Shakespeare's England* (Cambridge: Cambridge University Press, 1996), p. viii.

14. Erving Goffman, *The Presentation of Self in Everyday Life* (1973; rpt. Woodstock, N.Y.: Overlook Press); Bruce Wilshire, *Role Playing and Identity: The Limits of Theatre as Metaphor*, Studies in Phenomenology and Existential Philosophy (Bloomington: Indiana University Press, 1982), p. 275. See pp. 274–81 for his critique of Goffman.

15. Jean-Paul Sartre, *Being and Nothingness*, quoted and critiqued by Elizabeth Burns, *Theatricality: A Study of Convention in the Theatre and in Social Life* (London: Longman, 1972), p. 37.

16. Nina Auerbach, *Private Theatricals: The Lives of the Victorians* (Cambridge, Mass.: Harvard University Press, 1990), p. 12. See also Terry Castle, *Masquerade and Civilization in Eighteenth-Century England* (Stanford: Stanford University Press, 1986).

17. Katharine Eisaman Maus, "Playhouse Flesh and Blood: Sexual Ideology and the Restoration Actress," *ELH* 46 (1979), 604–17.

18. Clifford Geertz, *Local Knowledge* (New York: Basic Books, 1983), p. 27. For an interesting discussion of Geertz and an analysis of the way a particular theater fits into a neighborhood, see Alan Reed, *Theatre and Everyday Life: An Ethics of Performance* (London: Routledge, 1993).

19. Elizabeth Burns, *Theatricality: A Study of Convention in the Theatre and in Social Life* (London: Longman, 1972), pp. 165, 232.

20. David Marshall, "Rousseau and the State of Theater" in *Jean-Jacques Rousseau: Modern Critical Views*, ed. Harold Bloom (New York: Chelsea House, 1988), pp. 267, 273.

21. Burns, *Theatricality*, pp. 4, 134–35; Goffman, *The Presentation of Self*, p. 251, quoted by Burns, p. 134.

22. Charles Marowitz, *The Act of Being* (London: Martin Secker and Warburg, 1978), p. 39 (italics in original).

ACT ONE. THEY DRESS UP

1. Theophilus Lucas, *Memoirs of the Lives, Intrigues, and Comical Adventures of the Most Famous Gamesters and Celebrated Sharpers in the Reigns of Charles II, James II, William III, and Queene Anne*, 2nd ed. (London: for Jonas Brown, 1714), pp. 3–4 (B2r–B2v; italics in original).

2. Marjorie Garber, *Vested Interests: Cross Dressing and Cultural Anxiety* (New York: Routledge, 1992), p. 27; sumptuary proclamation of Queen Elizabeth I, August 18, 1597, quoted by Garber (p. 26); Berowne's "self-indicting metaphors of linguistic excess . . . assume a contextual particularity and power when viewed in the context of Renaissance sumptuary laws" (p. 35).

3. Jeremy Collier, *A Short View of the Immorality and Prophaneness of the English Stage*, ed. Benjamin Hellinger, Satire and Sense: Important Texts, for the Most Part Dramatic, from the Restoration and Eighteenth Century, series ed. Stephen Orgel (New York: Garland Publishing, 1987), p. 142.

SCENE ONE. AS SECRET AS MAIDENHEAD

4. Harley Granville-Barker, *Prefaces to Shakespeare* (London: B. T. Batsford, 1972), p. 15. It is hard to know what to call the boys who acted on the Renaissance stage; Granville-Barker's coinage is appropriately disturbing. Michael Shapiro, *Gender in Play on the Shakespearean Stage: Boy Heroines and Female Pages* (Ann Arbor: University of Michigan Press, 1994), often uses the terms "play-boy" and "boy actor" interchangeably; he also categorizes the kinds of cross-dressed characters the boys played: female pages and boy brides, for example.

5. Juliet Dusinberre, *Shakespeare and the Nature of Women*, 2nd ed. (New York: St. Martin's Press, 1996), p. 271.

6. Dusinberre's vision of a feminist Shakespeare in harmony with contemporary puritan and humanist ideas of equality of the sexes has been challenged by Lisa Jardine, in *Still Harping on Daughters: Women and Drama in the Age of Shakespeare* (Totowa, N.J.: Barnes and Noble, 1983), and by Linda Bamber, in *Comic Women, Tragic Men: A Study of Gender and Genre in Shakespeare* (Stanford: Stanford University Press, 1982). Phyllis Rackin has found in the "boy heroine" a figure of romance: see "Androgyny, Mimesis, and the Marriage of the Boy Heroine on the English Renaissance Stage," *PMLA* 102 (1987), 29–41.

7. W. Thomas MacCary, *Friends and Lovers: The Phenomenology of Desire in Shakespearean Comedy* (New York: Columbia University Press, 1985), p. 183; Coppélia Kahn, *Man's Estate: Masculine Identity in Shakespeare* (Berkeley and Los Angeles: University of California Press, 1981), p. 208.

8. Joel Fineman, "Fratricide and Cuckoldry: Shakespeare's Doubles," in

Representing Shakespeare: New Psychoanalytic Essays, ed. Murray M. Schwartz and Coppélia Kahn (Baltimore: Johns Hopkins University Press, 1980), p. 73. See also Helene Moglen, "Disguise and Development: The Self and Society in *Twelfth Night*," *Literature and Psychology* 23 (1973), 13–20.

9. See Marjorie Garber, *Coming of Age in Shakespeare* (London: Methuen, 1981), and Edward Berry, *Shakespeare's Comic Rites* (Cambridge: Cambridge University Press, 1985).

10. Stephen Greenblatt, *Shakespearean Negotiations: The Circulation of Social Energy in Renaissance England* (Berkeley: University of California Press, 1988), p. 92.

11. Stephen Orgel, *Impersonations: The Performance of Gender in Shakespeare's England* (Cambridge: Cambridge University Press, 1996), p. 30; he quotes Stubbes, p. 29; Prynne, p. 30. "The Renaissance construction of women emanates from a variety of contradictory discourses," Orgel declares. "This does not distinguish it from the modern construction of women (or, for that matter, men), which is hardly single or unconflicted; but even within its own terms there is nothing anomalous about it" (p. 123).

12. Bruce R. Smith, *Homosexual Desire in Shakespeare's England: A Cultural Poetics* (Chicago: University of Chicago Press, 1991), p. 153.

13. Garber, *Vested Interests*, p. 90; Smith, *Homosexual Desire*, p. 155.

14. Laurence Senelick, ed., *Gender in Performance: The Presentation of Difference in the Performing Arts* (Hanover, N.H.: University Press of New England, for Tufts University, 1992), "Introduction," p. ix (italics in original); Alisa Solomon, *Redressing the Canon: Essays on Theater and Gender* (London and New York: Routledge, 1997), p. 3; Laura Levine, "Men in Women's Clothing: Anti-theatricality and Effeminization from 1579 to 1642," *Criticism* 28 (1986), 121–37 (quotations on 121, 136). Levine's arguments are developed further in *Men in Women's Clothing: Antitheatricality and Effeminization, 1579–1642*, Cambridge Studies in Renaissance Literature and Culture, 5 (Cambridge: Cambridge University Press, 1994).

15. Garber, *Vested Interests*, pp. 90, 389; Goldman, *On Drama*, p. 119.

16. For discussion of the status of boys in adult companies, see Gerald Eades Bentley, *The Profession of Player in Shakespeare's Time, 1590–1642* (Princeton: Princeton University Press, 1984), pp. 113–46, and Andrew Gurr, *The Shakespearean Stage, 1574–1642* (Cambridge: Cambridge University Press, 1970), pp. 50, 69–70. Highly speculative but of some interest are T. W. Baldwin's ideas of the casting of Shakespeare's plays in *The Organization and Personnel of the Shakespearean Company* (Princeton: Princeton University Press, 1927). An analysis of *Antony and Cleopatra* that scrutinizes the "mimetic strategy" of the boy-actress "boying" Cleopatra can be found in William E. Gruber, "The Actor in the Script: Affective Strategies in Shakespeare's *Antony and Cleopatra*," *Comparative Drama* 19 (1985), esp. 39–46.

17. Jean E. Howard, in "Cross-Dressing, the Theatre, and Gender Struggle in Early Modern England," *Shakespeare Quarterly* 40 (1988), notes the conserva-

tive dynamics of the play: "The play disciplines independent women like Olivia and upstart crows such as Malvolio and rewards the self-abnegation of a Viola. In the process, female cross-dressing is stripped of nearly all its subversive resonances present in the culture at large." Quoted from this essay as reprinted in Lesley Ferris, ed., *Crossing the Stage: Controversies on Cross-Dressing* (London: Routledge, 1993), pp. 34–35.

18. Leslie Hotson's phrase is quoted in E. A. M. Colman, *The Dramatic Use of Bawdy in Shakespeare* (London: Longman, 1974), p. 57. Colman wonders whether Hotson may not be too "moralistic" in his reading of the song as a cautionary tale for Sir Toby Belch.

19. Marilyn French, *Shakespeare's Division of Experience* (New York: Summit Books, 1981), p. 117.

20. Elaine Showalter, "Representing Ophelia: Women, Madness, and the Responsibilities of Feminist Criticism," in *Shakespeare and the Question of Theory*, ed. Patricia Parker and Geoffrey Hartman (New York: Methuen, 1985), p. 80. Showalter refers here to Michael Goldman's *The Actor's Freedom: Toward a Theory of Drama* (New York: Viking, 1975).

21. Robert Burton, *The Anatomy of Melancholy*, ed. Floyd Dell and Paul Jordan-Smith (New York, 1927), quoted by Barish, *The Antitheatrical Prejudice*, p. 102.

22. Barish, *The Antitheatrical Prejudice*, esp. pp. 99–106; Smith, *Homosexual Desire*, chapter 4, "The Shipwrecked Youth," pp. 117–58.

23. Bentley, *The Profession of Player*, pp. 119–22. Andrew Gurr and Mariko Ichikawa note in *Staging in Shakespeare's Theatres* (Oxford: Oxford University Press, 2000) that "[w]hen their [the boy actors'] voices broke, if they proved themselves capable they might stay on to play juvenile leads, eventually buying themselves a 'share' in the company's fortunes" (p. 39).

24. *An Apology for the Life of Colley Cibber, Written by Himself*, ed. Robert W. Lowe, 2 vols. (London: John C. Nimmo, 1889), 1:120.

25. Phillip Stubbes, *The Anatomie of Abuses*, ed. J. P. Collier, Miscellaneous Tracts, 11 (London: n.p., 1870), p. 139. "In the 16th and early 17th centuries men who wanted to act like women must have seen the stage as a kind of natural home," says Marvin Rosenberg ("Elizabethan Actors: Men or Marionettes," in *The Seventeenth Century Stage*, ed. G. E. Bentley [Chicago: University of Chicago Press, 1968]). He continues: "I certainly do not mean to say here that most — or even many — of Shakespeare's 'boy-actors' were homosexual; but there may well have been some grains of truth in Prynne's furious assaults upon the 'Sodomiticall' theatre" (p. 98*n*). "Their teachers must have been aware of the dangers of confusing them at an impressionable age about their own sex-roles," Meg Twycross says of undergraduate boys who played women's roles, "especially if they were exposed to potential solicitation from homosexual members of their audience, or, in the heightened atmosphere of a production, from each other" ("'Transvestitism' in the Mystery Plays," *Medieval English Theatre* 5 [1983], 156; see also Richard Rastall's response to Twycross, "Female

Roles in All-Male Casts," *Medieval English Theatre* 7 [1985], 25–51).

26. Charles Kingsley, *Plays and Puritans: and Other Historical Essays* (London: Macmillan and Co., 1873), pp. 36, 79.

27. *The London Stage, 1660–1800, Part One, 1660–1700*, ed. William van Lennep, intro. by Emmet L. Avery and Arthur H. Scouten (Carbondale: Southern Illinois University Press, 1965), pp. xxiv–xxv.

28. Granville-Barker, *Prefaces to Shakespeare*, pp. 14–16; Showalter, "Representing Ophelia," p. 80. Jonas Barish describes Clifford Williams's Old Vic production of *As You Like It* (1968) as conveying in its all-male casting "a distracting mélange of female impersonation and homoerotic suggestiveness that (whatever its incidental merits) gave no clue to the character of the original production" ("Is There 'Authenticity' in Theatrical Performance?" *Modern Humanities Research* 89 [1994], 830). Critics like Orgel and Lisa Jardine, however, see this "mélange" as indeed characteristic of Renaissance theatrical experience. Michael Shapiro emphasizes the reflexive nature of the play-boy's female impersonation and suggests that it differs "significantly from the practices of our own day and hence produced different meanings when male performers played women who donned male apparel to pass as men or boys" (*Gender in Play*, pp. 202–3).

29. *The Plain Dealer*, in *The Complete Plays of William Wycherley*, ed. Gerald Weales, Anchor Seventeenth-Century Series (Garden City: Doubleday, 1966), act 4, p. 487.

30. John Harold Wilson, *All the King's Ladies: Actresses of the Restoration* (Chicago: University of Chicago Press, 1958), p. 73; cited in J. L. Styan, *Restoration Comedy in Performance* (Cambridge: Cambridge University Press, 1986), p. 13, and in Elizabeth Howe, *The First English Actresses: Women and Drama 1660–1700* (Cambridge: Cambridge University Press, 1992), p. 57.

31. Howe, *The First English Actresses*, p. 57. Curt Zimansky gives a full cast list in his edition of Sir John Vanbrugh, *The Relapse*, Regents Restoration Drama Series (Lincoln: University of Nebraska Press, 1970), p. 8. Bonamy Dobrée, in *The Complete Works of Sir John Vanbrugh*, plays ed. Bonamy Dobrée, letters ed. Geoffrey Webb, 4 vols. (Bloomsbury: Nonesuch Press, 1927), p. 227, notes that "it was not uncommon for women to act the parts of young men" and quotes Mandeville: "If a Woman at a Merry-making dresses in Man's Clothes, it is reckon'd a Frolick amongst Friends. . . . Upon the Stage it is done without Reproach, and the most Virtuous Ladies will dispense with it in an Actress." Styan, *Restoration Comedy in Performance*, p. 134.

32. Garber, *Vested Interests*, p. 86; Katharine Eisaman Maus, "'Playhouse Flesh and Blood': Sexual Ideology and the Restoration Actress," *ELH* 46 (1979), 607, 614.

33. Kristina Straub, *Sexual Suspects: Eighteenth-Century Players and Sexual Ideology* (Princeton: Princeton University Press, 1992), p. 131.

34. Lesley Ferris, *Acting Women: Images of Women in Theatre* (New York: New York University Press, 1989), pp. 72, 73, 74.

35. Maus, "'Playhouse Flesh and Blood,'" p. 606.

66. Sir John Vanbrugh, *The Provoked Wife*, ed. Curt A. Zimansky (Lincoln: University of Nebraska Press, 1969), 4.1.47–48. Subsequent references to this edition are in the text.

67. Michael Cordner, "Anti-Clericalism in Vanbrugh's *The Provoked Wife*," *Notes and Queries* 28/226 (1980), 212–14 (italics in original).

SCENE THREE. HUMANIZING THE FOP

68. Colley Cibber, *Three Sentimental Comedies*, ed. Maureen Sullivan (New Haven: Yale University Press, 1973), 1.1.244–45. Subsequent references to this edition are in the text.

69. Sir George Etherege, *The Man of Mode; or, Sir Fopling Flutter*, in *British Dramatists from Dryden to Sheridan*, ed. George H. Nettleton and Arthur E. Case (Boston: Houghton Mifflin Company, 1939), 1.1.407–8, 411, 419–20. Subsequent references to this edition are in the text.

70. Cibber, *Apology*, 2:35, 36–37. Kristina Straub discusses this anecdote in *Sexual Suspects*: "The ambiguous role that Cibber uses to describe his relation to Brett allows him to negotiate the suspect sexual identity so often attached to actors by using a rhetoric informed by models of spectacle and homoeroticism that are based more on class structure than on binary oppositions of gender and sexuality" (p. 52).

71. Susan Staves, "A Few Kind Words for the Fop," *Studies in English Literature* 22 (1982), 415, 414–15; Laurence Senelick, "Mollies or Men of Mode?: Sodomy and the Eighteenth-Century London Stage," *Journal of the History of Sexuality* 1 (1990), 34–35.

72. Molière, *The Misanthrope and Other Plays*, trans. Donald M. Frame (New York: New American Library Signet Classics, 1968), 2.5., p. 237.

73. Styan, *Restoration Comedy in Performance*, p. 54. The direct debt of Lord Foppington's levée to M. Jourdain's is demonstrated by Frank M. Patterson in "Lord Foppington and *Le Bourgeois Gentilhomme*," *Notes and Queries* n. s. 31/229 (1984), 377–78.

74. Vanbrugh, *The Relapse*, ed. Zimansky, 1.3.85–89. Subsequent references to this edition are in the text.

75. Lincoln Faller, "Between Jest and Earnest: The Comedy of Sir John Vanbrugh," *Modern Philology* 72 (1974), 18.

76. Koon, *Colley Cibber*, p. 31.

77. Zimansky, in Vanbrugh, *The Relapse*, p. xix.

78. Collier, *A Short View*, p. 258.

79. Faller, "Between Jest and Earnest," p. 18.

80. Cibber, *Three Sentimental Comedies*, p. ix.

81. Hume continues: "Later derogation of Cibber undoubtedly has contributed to the myth that Vanbrugh was attacking him. But consider the facts: *The Relapse* was a Drury Lane production, and the company would scarcely have mounted a destructive satire on one of its few popular successes. Furthermore, Cibber himself played the newly ennobled Lord Foppington, and was

SCENE TWO. PUTTING ON THE CLOTH

36. Søren Kierkegaard, *Either/Or: Part II*, ed. and trans. Howard V. Hong and Edna H. Hong (Princeton: Princeton University Press, 1987), p. 165.

37. Collier, *A Short View*, p. 135.

38. C. L. Barber and Richard P. Wheeler, *The Whole Journey: Shakespeare's Power of Development* (Berkeley, Los Angeles, and London: University of California Press, 1986), pp. 22–23.

39. John Jewel, "Masquery," and Rainolds quoted by Barish, *The Antitheatrical Prejudice*, pp. 162–63 (italics in original).

40. John Cairncross, *New Light on Molière: "Tartuffe," "Elomire hypocondre"* (Geneva: Droz, 1956), p. 36.

41. Molière, *Le Tartuffe, Dom Juan, Le misanthrope*, ed. Georges Couton (Paris: Gallimard, 1973), p. 36: "En vain je l'ai produite sous le titre de *L'Imposteur*, et déguisé le personnage sous l'ajustement d'un homme du monde; j'ai eu beau lui donner un petit chapeau, de grands cheveux, un grand collet, une épée, et des dentelles sur tout l'habit, mettre en plusieurs endroits des adoucissements, et retrancher avec soin tout ce que j'ai jugé capable de fournir l'ombre d'un prétexte aux célèbres originaux du portrait que je voulais faire: tout cela n'a de rien servi."

42. Herman Prins Salomon, *"Tartuffe" devant l'opinion française* (Paris: Presses universitaires de France, 1962), p. 55, n. 1: "sombre, austère, et dévot, mais pas d'un prêtre."

43. "Un homme à petit colet, ou simplement un petit colet; ces mots se disent des gens d'Eglise, qui par modestie portent de petits colets, pendant que les gens du monde en portent de grands ornez de points et de dentelles. Ils se disent ensuite d'un homme qui s'est mis dans la dévotion et dans la réforme (disciplinae severioris cultor), et même on le dit en mauvaise part, des hypocrites qui affectent des manières modestes et surtout de porter un petit colet" (quoted by Salomon, *"Tartuffe" devant l'opinion française*, pp. 52–53n). For an extensive discussion of the possibilities and history of Tartuffe's costume, see Stephen Varick Dock, *Costume and Fashion in the Plays of Jean-Baptiste Poquelin Molière: A Seventeenth-Century Perspective* (Geneva: Editions Slatkine, 1992), pp. 141–47.

44. "L'irruption de l'homme noir en ce milieu bariol fit scandale. Le choc apporté par Tartuffe est d'abord visuel" ("The invasion of this multicolored environment by the man in black created a scandal. The shock delivered by Tartuffe was primarily visual"; Jean-Marie Apostolidès, *Le roi-machine: Spectacle et politique au temps de Louis XIV* [Paris: Minuit, 1981], p. 97). See also Georges Couton's comment, in his edition of *Tartuffe*, p. 12: "Son costume suffisait pour que, dès son entrée, le premier Tartuffe se trouvât catalogué: un postulant aux bénéfices ecclésiastiques, un homme d'Eglise ou qui en sera" ("His costume was enough to identify the first Tartuffe according to type at his first entrance: a postulant for church orders, a man of the cloth or one who would become one").

45. Matthew H. Wikander, *Princes to Act: Royal Audience and Royal Performance, 1578–1792* (Baltimore: Johns Hopkins University Press, 1993), pp. 172–83.

46. Burns, *Theatricality*, p. 232.

47. Salomon, *"Tartuffe" devant l'opinion française*, pp. 13–29.

48. Barish, *The Antitheatrical Prejudice*, p. 196.

49. Louis Bourdaloue, "Sermon pour le septième dimanche après la Pente-côte: sur l'hypocrisie," in *Sermons du père Bourdaloue*, 4 vols. (Paris: aux dépenses de la Compagnie [de Jésus], 1759), 3:33–61; p. 52: "C'est un hommage qu'il lui rend, & dont il ne peut défendre."

50. François, duc de La Rochefoucauld, *Maximes*, ed. Jacques Truchet (Paris: Garnier Frères, 1967), maxime 218: "L'hypocrisie est un hommage que le vice rend à la vertu" (p. 56); maxime 62: "La sincerité est une overture du coeur. On le trouve en fort peu de gens; et celle que l'on voit d'ordinaire n'est qu'une fine dissimulation pour attirer la confiance des autres" (p. 20); Barish, *The Antitheatrical Prejudice*, pp. 215, 217.

51. Salomon, *"Tartuffe" devant l'opinion française*, pp. 84–85.

52. Bourdaloue, *Sermons*, 3:39: "Voilà ce qu'ils ont prétendu, exposant sur le théâtre & a la risée publique un hypocrite imaginaire, ou même, si vous voulez, un hypocrite réel; & tournant dans la personne les choses les plus saintes en ridicule, la crainte des jugemens de Dieu, l'horreur du péché, les pratiques les plus louables en elles-mêmes et les plus chrétiennes, Voilà ce qu'ils ont affecté, mettant dans la bouche de cet hypocrite des maximes de Réligion foiblements soûtenues, au même-tems qu'ils les supposoient fortement attaquées; lui faisant blâmer les scandales du siècle d'une manière extravagante; le représantant conscientieux jusqu'à la délicatesse & au scrupule sur les pointes les moins importans, où toute-fois il le faut être, pendant qu'il se portoit d'ailleurs aux crimes les plus énormes; le montrant sous un visage de pénitent, qui ne servoit qu'à couvrir ses infamies; lui donnant, selon leur caprice, un caractère de piété la plus austère. . . ." See also a sermon quoted in Salomon: "Et voilà, Chrétiens, ce qui est arrivé, lorsque des esprits profanes, et bien éloignés de vouloir entrer dans les intérêts de Dieu, ont entrepris de censurer l'hypocrisie, non point pour en réformer l'abus, ce qui n'est point de leur ressort, mais pour en faire une espèce de diversion dont le liberti-nage pût profiter, en concevant et faisant concevoir d'injustes soupçons de la vraie piété, par de malignes représentations de la fausse" (p. 93).

53. Molière, *Placets au roi*, in Couton, *Tartuffe*, p. 34: "pour mieux conserver l'estime et le respect qu'on doit aux vrais dévots. . . . Je n'ai point laissé d'équi-voque, j'ai ôté tout ce qui pouvait confondre le bien avec le mal, et ne me suis servi dans cette peinture, que des couleurs expresses et des traits essentiels qui font reconnaître d'abord un véritable et franc hypocrite."

54. Molière, *Préface*, in *Tartuffe, Dom Juan, Le misanthrope*, ed. Couton, p. 25: "Les marquis, les précieuses, les cocus, et les médecins ont souffert douce-ment qu'on les ait représentés, et ils ont fait semblant de se divertir, avec tout le monde, des peintures que l'on a fait d'eux; mais les hypocrites n'ont point en-tendu raillerie; ils se sont effarouchés d'abord, et ont trouvé étrange que j'eusse la hardiesse de jouer leurs grimaces et de vouloir décrier un métier dont tant d'honnêtes gens se mêlent."

55. Ibid.: "Ils n'ont eu garde de l'attaquer par le côté qui les a blessés: ils sont trop politiques pour cela, et savent trop bien vivre pour découvrir le fond de leur âme. Suivant leur louable coutume, ils ont couvert leurs intérêts de la cause de Dieu; et Le Tartuffe, dans leur bouche, est une pièce qui offense la piété."

56. Ibid., p. 26: "Je me soucierais fort peu de tout ce qu'ils peuvent dire, n'était l'artifice qu'ils ont de me faire des ennemis que je respecte, et de jeter dans leur parti de véritables gens de bien, dont ils préviennent la bonne foi, et qui, par la chaleur qu'ils ont pour les intérêts du ciel, sont faciles à recevoir les impressions qu'on veut leur donner."

57. See Francis Baumal, *Tartuffe et ses avatars: De Montufar à Dom Juan: His-toire des relations de Molière avec la Cabale des Dévots* (Paris: Emile Nourry, 1925), for an account of this group's early organization and resistance to the play.

58. "It's a court in which Misrule is King" is Donald Frame's translation in *Tartuffe and Other Plays* (New York: Signet Classics, 1967); "Your house is Dover Court," says Mme. Pernelle in Matthew Medbourne's version, *Tartuffe, or, The French Puritan* (London: 1670), Biv.

59. Molière, *Le Tartuffe, Dom Juan, Le misanthrope*, ed. Couton: "soudain changement de la vie" (p. 214); "guide, et sous la conduite de qui je puisse marcher sûrement dans le chemin où je m'en vais entrer" (p. 215).

60. Ibid.: "Il n'y a plus de honte maintenant à cela: l'hypocrisie est un vice à la mode, et tous les vices à la mode passent pour vertus. Le personnage d'homme de bien est le meilleur de tous les personnages qu'on puisse jouer au-jourd'hui, et la profession d'hypocrite a de merveilleux avantages. . . . Tous les autres vices des hommes sont exposés à la censure, et chacun a la liberté de les attaquer hautement; mais l'hypocrisie est un vice privilégié, qui, de sa main, ferme la bouche à tout le monde, et jouit en repos d'une impunité sou-veraine. . . . Combien crois-tu que j'en connaisse qui, par ce stratagème, ont rhabillé adroitement les désordres de leur jeunesse, qui se sont fait un bouclier du manteau de la religion, et sous cet habit respecté, ont la permission d'être les plus méchants hommes du monde?" (pp. 215–16); "l'on doit approuver la comédie du *Tartuffe*, ou condamner généralement toutes les comédies" (p. 28).

61. Colley Cibber, *The Non-Juror*, in *The Dramatic Works of Colley Cibber*, 5 vols. (London: for J. Rivington and Sons, 1777), 3:267. Subsequent references are in the text; all italics in quotations in original.

62. Cibber, *Apology*, 2:80 (italics in original).

63. Isaac Bickerstaff, *The Hypocrite*, in *Bell's British Theatre: Selected Plays 1791–1802, 1797*, with a new introduction and preface by Byrne R. S. Fone and with new author and play indexes, 21 vols. (New York: AMS Press, 1977), 1:7 Subsequent references to this edition are in the text.

64. "Mais en un mot, je sais, pour toute ma science, / Du faux avec le vrai faire la différence."

65. Helene Koon, *Colley Cibber: A Biography* (Lexington: University Press Kentucky, 1986), p. 88.

hugely delighted with the part and the play" (Robert D. Hume, *The Develop-ment of English Drama in the Late Seventeenth Century* [Oxford: Clarendon Press, 1976], pp. 412 – 13).

82. Sir John Vanbrugh, *A Short Vindication of "The Relapse" and "The Pro-vok'd Wife," from Immorality and Prophaneness*, in *The Complete Works of Sir John Vanbrugh*, ed. Dobrée and Webb 1 : 195, 212; Faller, "Between Jest and Earnest," p. 25; Richard Steele, preface to *The Conscious Lovers*, in *British Dramatists from Dryden to Sheridan*, ed. George H. Nettleton and Arthur E. Case (Boston: Houghton Mifflin, 1939), p. 439.

83. James S. Malek, "Comic Irony in Vanbrugh's *The Relapse*: Worthy's Re-pentance," *College Language Association Journal* 26 (1983), 357.

84. Frank McCormick, "Vanbrugh's *The Relapse* Reconsidered," *Studia Neophilologica* 57 (1985), 53, 57.

85. J. Douglas Canfield, "Religious Language and Religious Meaning in Restoration Comedy," *Studies in English Literature* 20 (1980), 397. Canfield quotes an even darker reading of the play than his: Peter Jan Van Niel, "*The Re-lapse* — Into Death and Damnation," *Educational Theatre Journal* 21 (1969), in which "Christian hope is extinguished" (p. 327). "The play is dark but not that dark," Canfield declares (p. 397).

86. Styan, *Restoration Comedy in Performance*, pp. 51, 54.

87. For discussion of Cibber's manipulation of his own image as a fop, see Lois Potter, "Colley Cibber: The Fop as Hero," in *Augustan Worlds*, ed. J. C. Hilson, M. M. B. Jones, and J. R. Watson (Leicester: Leicester University Press, 1978), pp. 153 – 64.

88. Cibber, *Apology*, 1 : 79 – 80. See Joseph Roach, *The Player's Passion: Stud-ies in the Science of Acting* (Newark: University of Delaware Press; London: As-sociated University Presses, 1985).

89. Cibber, *Apology*, 1 : 82 – 83.

90. Garber devotes a whole section of *Vested Interests* to the androgynous potential expressed in the habits of religious orders.

91. Probably Elkanah Settle's *The Female Prelate: Being the History of the Life and Death of Pope Joan* (London, 1680).

92. Charlotte Charke, *A Narrative of the Life of Mrs. Charlotte Charke*, ed. Leonard R. N. Ashley (Gainesville, Fla.: Scholars' Facsimiles and Reprints, 1969), p. 170.

93. Fidelis Morgan, *The Well-Known Troublemaker: A Life of Charlotte Charke* (London: Faber and Faber, 1988), pp. 128 – 29.

94. Straub, *Sexual Suspects*, p. 131.

95. Morgan, *The Well-Known Troublemaker*, p. 204. Rudolf M. Dekker and Lotte C. van de Pol, *The Tradition of Female Transvestism in Early Modern Eu-rope*, foreword by Peter Burke (New York: St. Martin's Press, 1989), p. 99. See also Erin Mackie, "Desperate Measures: The Narratives of the Life of Mrs. Charlotte Charke," *ELH* 58 (1991), 841 – 65.

96. Senelick, "Mollies or Men of Mode?" p. 36.

97. Madeleine Bingham, *Masks and Façades: Sir John Vanbrugh, The Man in His Setting* (London: George Allen and Unwin, 1974), p. 55. Zimansky, in his edition of the play, also sees a neutralization in effect here: "Coupler's homosexual gestures must have lost some effect with Fashion played by a woman" (*The Relapse*, p. 8).

98. A characteristic for which the actor who played Coupler was known; see Cibber, *Apology*, 2 : 361.

99. Garber, *Vested Interests*, p. 389.

100. [Tom Brown], *The Stage-Beaux Toss'd in a Blanket or, Hypocrisie Alamode; expos'd in a True Picture of Jerry —— , a Pretending Scourge to the English Stage: a comedy* (London: J. Nutt, 1704), "Epistle Dedicatory" (to Mr. Rich), aiv (all italics in quotations in original).

101. John Gardiner, *The Speech of John Gardiner, esquire, delivered in the House of Representatives on Thursday, the 26th of January, 1792, on the subject of the Report of the Committee, appointed to Consider the Expediency of Repealing the Law against Theatrical Exhibitions within the Commonwealth* (Boston: for the Author, 1792), pp. 16, 18, 69–70, "To the Public," ix (italics in original).

ACT TWO. THEY LIE

1. Jean Baptiste Morvan, abbé de Bellegarde, *Reflections upon ridicule: or, What it is that makes a man ridiculous; and the means to avoid it. Wherein are represented the different manners and characters of persons of the present age; Of unpoliteness. Indiscretion. Affectation. Foolish vanity. The bad taste. Imposture. The morose humour. Impertinence. Of prejudice. Interest. Sufficiency. Absurdities. Caprice. False delicacy. Decorum*, 2 vols., here quoted from the 4th ed. (London: for D. Midwinter et al., 1727), 1 : 107, 109, 111. A fifth edition (Dublin: R. Reilly, 1738) intriguingly attributes the anonymous translation to Jeremiah Collier, A.M. Is the translator Jeremy himself?

2. [Richard Head], *Proteus redivivus: or The Art of Wheedling, or Insinuation* (London: by W. D., 1675), title page, pp. 5, 87 (all italics in quotations in original). Bellegarde's English translator uses the word, too: "Wheedling and Decoying are stains to Civil Society, and the signs of a weak Soul" (2 : 178).

SCENE ONE. ROUSSEAU AND THE CULT OF SINCERITY

3. Jean-Jacques Rousseau, *Politics and the Arts: Letter to M. D'Alembert on the Theatre*, trans., with notes and an introduction, by Allan Bloom, Agora Editions, gen. ed., Allan Bloom (Glencoe, Ill.: Free Press, 1960), p. xxv.

4. Ibid., pp. 60–63. Jean-Jacques Rousseau, *Lettre à D'Alembert*, in *Oeuvres complètes V: Ecrits sur la musique, la langue et le théâtre*, Bibliothèque de la Pléiade, ed. Bernard Gagnebin, Marcel Raymond, et al. (Paris: Gallimard, 1995), p. 55: "peut-être unique sur la terre"; "L'hiver surtout, tems où la hauteur des neiges leur ôte une communication facile, chacun renfermé bien chaudement, avec sa nombreuse famille, dans sa jolie et propre maison de bois, qu'il a bâtie lui-même, s'occupe de mille travaux amusans, qui chassent l'ennui de son azile,

et ajoutent à son bien-être" (p. 56); "Supposons encore qu'ils prennent du goût pour ce même Spectacle; et cherchons ce qui doit résulter de son établissement"; "relâchement de travail" (p. 57); "[a]ugmentation de dépense"; "[d]iminution de débit"; "[é]tablissement d'impôts"; "[i]ntroduction du luxe" (p. 58).

5. James F. Hamilton, *Rousseau's Theory of Literature: The Poetics of Art and Nature* (York, S.C.: French Literature Publications Co., 1979), pp. xiii, 22; quotation from preface to *Narcisse* on p. 52: "Elles détruisent la vertu, mais elles en laissent le simulacre public qui est toujours une belle chose. Elles introduisent à sa place la politesse et les bienséances, et à la crainte de paroître méchant elles substituent celle de paroître ridicule" (my translation).

6. John Hope Mason, "The *Lettre à D'Alembert* and Its Place in Rousseau's Thought," in *Rousseau and the Eighteenth Century: Essays in Memory of R. A. Leigh*, ed. Marian Hobson, J. T. A. Leigh, and Robert Wokler (Oxford: Voltaire Foundation at the Taylor Institution, 1992), pp. 255, 261, 258.

7. Rousseau, *Politics and the Arts*, pp. 25, 113, 115. "En donnant des pleurs à ces fictions, nous avons satisfait à tous les droits de l'humanité, sans avoir plus rien à mettre du nôtre; au lieu que les infortunés en personne exigeroient de nous des soins, des soulagemens, des consolations, des travaux qui pourroient nous associer à leurs peines, qui coûteroient du moins à notre indolence, et dont nous sommes bien aises d'être exemptés" (*Lettre*, p. 23); "le pauvre au delà de ses forces" (p. 104); "les spectacles modernes, où l'on n'assiste qu'à prix d'argent, tendent partout à favoriser et augmenter l'inégalité des fortunes" (p. 105).

8. David Marshall, *The Surprising Effects of Sympathy: Marivaux, Diderot, Rousseau, and Mary Shelley* (Chicago: University of Chicago Press, 1988), pp. 137–38.

9. Patrick Coleman, *Rousseau's Political Imagination: Rule and Representation in the "Lettre à D'Alembert"* (Geneva: Droz, 1984), p. 102.

10. Rousseau, *Politics and the Arts*, p. 47. "L'amour est le régne des femmes. Ce sont elles qui nécessairement y donnent la loi; parce que, selon l'ordre de la Nature, la resistance leur appartient et que les hommes ne peuvent vaincre cette résistance qu'aux dépens de leur liberté. Un effet naturel de ces sortes de piéces est donc d'étendre l'empire du *Sexe*, de rendre des femmes et des jeunes filles les precepteurs du public, et de leur donner sur les spectateurs le même pouvoir qu'elles ont sur leurs amans. Pensez-vous, Monsieur, que cet ordre soit sans inconvenient, et qu'en augmentant avec tant de soin l'ascendant des femmes, les hommes en seront mieux gouvernés?" (*Lettre*, pp. 43–44; italics in original).

11. Henri Peyre, *Literature and Sincerity* (1963; rpt. Westport, Conn.: Greenwood Press, 1978), p. 49.

12. Jean-Jacques Rousseau, *Oeuvres complètes*, 33 vols. (Lyon, 1796): "Rien n'est si dissemblable à moi que moi-même: c'est pourquoi il seroit inutile de tenter de me définir autrement que par cette variété singulière: elle est telle dans mon esprit qu'elle influe de temps à autre jusques sur mes sentimens. Quelquefois je suis un dur et féroce misanthrope; en d'autres momens, j'entre en extase

au milieu des charmes de la société et dans les délices de l'amour. Tantôt je suis austere et dévot, et pour le bien de mon âme je fais tous mes efforts pour rendre durables ces saintes dispositions: mais je deviens bientôt un franc libertin, et comme je m'occupe alors beaucoup plus de mes sens que de ma raison, je m'abstiens constamment d'écrire dans ces momens-là: c'est sur quoi il est bon que mes lecteurs soient suffisamment prévenus, de peur qu'ils ne s'attendent à trouver dans mes feuilles des choses que certainement ils n'y verront jamais. En un mot, un Protée, un Caméléon, une femme sont des êtres moins changeans que moi" (13:334–35; my translation). Ruth W. Grant, *Hypocrisy and Integrity: Machiavelli, Rousseau, and the Ethics of Politics* (Chicago: University of Chicago Press, 1997), pp. 58–59.

13. Elizabeth Wingrove, "Sexual Performance as Political Performance in the *Lettre à M. D'Alembert sur les spectacles,*" *Political Theory* 23 (1995), 592; quoting *Emile*, p. 595. Wingrove's argument has since appeared in her book *Rousseau's Republican Romance* (Princeton: Princeton University Press, 2000).

14. Nina Auerbach, *Private Theatricals*, pp. 4, 8, 83; Matthew Arnold, "The Study of Poetry," in *The Complete Prose Works of Matthew Arnold, Volume 9: English Literature and Irish Politics*, ed. R. H. Super, 11 vols. (Ann Arbor: University of Michigan Press, 1973), p. 184.

15. See Jean Starobinski, *Jean-Jacques Rousseau: La transparence et l'obstacle*, 2nd ed. (Paris: Gallimard, 1971), for a study of Rousseau in terms of a quest for transparency. Grant offers her critique of Starobinski in *Hypocrisy and Integrity*, pp. 58–59, 91. Willy Loman reference on p. 15.

16. Thomas M. Kavanagh, *Writing the Truth: Authority and Desire in Rousseau* (Berkeley: University of California Press, 1987), pp. 37, 41.

17. *The Misanthrope* quoted from Molière, *The Misanthrope and Other Plays*, trans. Donald M. Frame, Signet Classics (New York: NAL, 1968); "Morbleu! C'est une chose indigne, lâche, infâme, / De s'abaisser ainsi jusqu'à trahir son âme" (*Le Tartuffe, Dom Juan, Le misanthrope*, ed. Couton, 1.1.25–26).

18. Rousseau, *Lettre*: "homme droit, sincére, estimable, un véritable homme de bien" (p. 34); "Ce Philinte est le Sage de la piéce; un de ces honnêtes gens du grand monde, dont les maximes ressemblent beaucoup à celles des fripons; de ces gens si doux, si modérés, qui trouvent toujours que tout va bien, parce qu'ils ont intérêt que rien n'aille mieux; qui sont toujours contens de tout le monde, parce qu'ils ne se soucient de personne; qui, autour d'une bonne table, soutiennent qu'il n'est pas vrai que le peuple ait faim; qui, le gousset bien garni, trouvent fort mauvais qu'on déclame en faveur des pauvres; qui, de leur maison bien fermée, verroient voler, piller, égorger, massacrer tout le genre humain sans se plaindre: attendu que Dieu les a doüés d'une douceur très méritoire à supporter les malheurs d'autrui" (p. 36; my translation).

19. Philippe-François-Nazaire Fabre de L'Eglantine, *Le Philinte de Molière*, in *Répertoire général du théâtre français (second ordre)*, 67 vols. (Paris: Menard et Raymond, 1813), 51:299–300. "Je vous déclare net, qu'à votre ame endurcie, / Nul goût, nul sentiment, et rien ne m'associe. / Je vous rejette; au loin,

parmi ces êtres froids / Qui du beau nom d'homme ont perdu les droits. . . . *l'hon-neur, la bienfaisance, l'equité, la candeur, l'amour et l'amitié*, n'existèrent jamais dans un coeur sans *PITIÉ*." "Philinte (confondu): j'ai tort"; "un ami si parfait" (my translation; italics in original).

SCENE TWO. PLAYING JOSEPH SURFACE

20. Charles Lamb, *Lamb as Critic*, ed. Roy Park (Lincoln and London: University of Nebraska Press, 1980), pp. 60, 65 (all italics in quotations in original).

21. Michael Cordner, "Introduction" to Richard Brinsley Sheridan, *School for Scandal and Other Plays*, Oxford World's Classics (Oxford and New York: Oxford University Press, 1998), p. xxxv. All references to this edition are cited in the text.

22. James Morwood, "Sheridan, Molière, and the Idea of the School in *The School for Scandal*," in *Sheridan Studies*, ed. James Morwood and David Crane (Cambridge: Cambridge University Press, 1995), p. 75.

23. Colley Cibber, *The Careless Husband*, in *British Dramatists from Dryden to Sheridan*, ed. George H. Nettleton and Arthur E. Case (Boston: Houghton Mifflin, 1939); all italics in quotations in original. This edition reproduces the 1731 frontispiece, p. 402. Paul E. Parnell, "The Sentimental Mask," *PMLA* 78 (1963), 530.

24. Ann Jessie Van Sant, *Eighteenth-Century Sensibility and the Novel: The Senses in Social Context*, Cambridge Studies in Eighteenth-Century Literature and Thought (Cambridge: Cambridge University Press, 1993), pp. 5, 1.

25. Butler is quoted in James P. Spiegel, *Hypocrisy: Moral Fraud and Other Vices* (Grand Rapids: Baker Books, 1999), p. 22.

26. Jean-Paul Sartre, *Being and Nothingness*, trans. Hazel E. Barnes (New York: Washington Square Press, 1956), p. 89. See Spiegel's discussion in his third chapter, "Taking Oneself In" (*Hypocrisy*, 44–67).

27. There is a brief biography of Frances Abington, née Barton, in Christopher Lennox-Boyd, Guy Shaw, and Sarah Halliwell, *Theatre: The Age of Garrick, English Mezzotints from the Collection of the Hon. Christopher Lennox-Boyd* (London: Published in conjunction with an exhibition at the Courtauldt Institute Galleries, Christopher Lennox-Boyd, 1994), 104–5. John Taylor quoted on p. 105.

28. Judith Shklar, *Ordinary Vices* (Cambridge, Mass.: Harvard University Press, 1984); Arthur M. Melzer, "Rousseau and the Modern Cult of Sincerity," in *The Legacy of Rousseau*, ed. Clifford Orwin and Nathan Tarcov (Chicago: University of Chicago Press, 1997), pp. 276, 282, 292, 291.

SCENE THREE. IBSEN'S SMALL STAGE OF FOOLS

29. Gina Ekdal in Henrik Ibsen, *The Complete Major Prose Plays*, trans. and intro. by Rolf Fjelde (New York: New American Library, 1978), p. 431; all quotations from Ibsen from this edition are cited in the text; all italics in original.

30. See Joan Templeton, *Ibsen's Women* (Cambridge: Cambridge University

Press, 1997), where Hedda's career in criticism as an "Unreal Character in a Realistic Play" is considered: "Ibsen's protagonist remains an enigma and his drama a work about nothing but its strange self" (p. 205).

31. Brian Johnston, *The Ibsen Cycle: The Design of the Plays from "The Pillars of Society" to "When We Dead Awaken,"* rev. ed. (University Park: Pennsylvania State University Press, 1992), p. 148.

32. Shklar, *Ordinary Vices*, pp. 57–58.

33. M. C. Bradbrook, *Ibsen the Norwegian* (London: Oxford University Press, 1966), p. 120; Raymond Williams, *Drama from Ibsen to Brecht* (New York: Oxford University Press, 1969), p. 63.

34. Jens Arup, "On *Hedda Gabler*," *Orbis Litterarum* 12 (1957), 13, 37.

35. *Hedda Gabler*, trans. Jens Arup, in *The Oxford Ibsen*, ed. James Walter McFarlane, vol. 7 (London: Oxford University Press, 1966), p. 255. "I alt dette — løjerlige — Jørgen" is what Hedda says in the original: *Ibsens samlede verker*, 21 vols. (Oslo: Gyldendal Norsk Forlag, 1928–57), 11 : 380. The word *løjerlige* denotes ridiculous incongruities in general rather than specifically theatrical ones. In the authorized German version of Ibsen's *Sämtliche Werke*, 5 vols. (Berlin: Fischer Verlag, 1913) Hedda's line reads "In all dem — komischen, Jorgen" (8 : 321). Fjelde suggests a later modern theatrical context in his translation: "Of all these — absurdities — George" (p. 767).

36. *Hedda Gabler*, in *The Oxford Ibsen*, vol. 7, pp. 484, 487.

37. Thomas Whitaker, *Fields of Play in Modern Drama* (Princeton: Princeton University Press, 1977), p. 54.

38. Johnston, *The Ibsen Cycle*, p. 149 (italics in original). "Frantically dissatisfied with civilized life but unwilling to realize the ecstatic deliverance from it that lies at hand, Hedda is a crippled Maenad," says Theoharis Theoharis in *Ibsen's Drama: Right Action and Tragic Joy* (New York: St. Martin's Press, 1996). Nonetheless, in her suicide she achieves a "Bacchic end" (p. 272). Templeton, too, sees the death as liberating: "In doing what 'people don't do,' deviant Hedda dies acclaiming her difference, the pistol shot her final 'Non Serviam'" (*Ibsen's Women*, p. 232). "With Lovborg's sordid end, classical tragedy topples; with Hedda's suicide, she transcends the historical moment," argues Nina da Vinci Nichols in *Ariadne's Lives* (Madison: Fairleigh Dickinson University Press, 1995), p. 125.

39. John Northam, *Ibsen: A Critical Study* (Cambridge: Cambridge University Press, 1973), p. 184.

40. Hermann Weigand, *The Modern Ibsen* (New York, 1925, 1953; rpt. Freeport, N.Y.: Books for Libraries Press, 1970), p. 262.

41. Ronald Gray, *Ibsen: A Dissenting View* (Cambridge: Cambridge University Press, 1977), p. 143.

42. Gay Gibson Cima, *Performing Women: Female Characters, Male Playwrights, and the Modern Stage* (Ithaca, N.Y.: Cornell University Press, 1993), pp. 53, 48; Robins quoted on p. 49.

43. Templeton uses the phrase "Hedda's perverse phallicism" (*Ibsen's Women*, p. 209).

44. G. Wilson Knight, *Ibsen* (Edinburgh: Oliver and Boyd, 1962), p. 65.

45. Templeton, *Ibsen's Women*, p. 217.

46. Michel de Montaigne, "Of the Inconstancie of Our Actions," in *The Essayes of Michel Lord of Montaigne*, trans. John Florio, World's Classics, 3 vols. (London: Henry Frowde, Oxford University Press, 1906), 2:10.

47. Michael Goldman, *Ibsen: The Dramaturgy of Fear* (New York: Columbia University Press, 1999), p. 35.

48. Marshall, *The Surprising Effects of Sympathy*.

49. Goldman, *Ibsen*, p. 62.

SCENE FOUR. PRINCELY HYPOCRITE

50. Niccolò Machiavelli, *The Prince*, new ed., trans. George Bull (Harmondsworth: Penguin Books, 1999), p. 57.

51. The dolphin was considered amphibious because it was a fish that breathed air. The OED entry *dolphin* also mentions the dorado or dolphin-fish, "celebrated for its beautiful colors, which, when it is taken out of water, or is dying, undergo rapid changes of hue" (*OED*, s.v. Dolphin, 2).

52. Hegel quoted in Hayden White, *The Content of the Form: Narrative Discourse and Historical Representation* (Baltimore: Johns Hopkins University Press, 1990), pp. 12, 30.

53. Anne Righter [Barton], *Shakespeare and the Idea of the Play* (London: Chatto and Windus, 1962); James Calderwood, *Metadrama in Shakespeare's Henriad: "Richard II" to "Henry V"* (Berkeley and Los Angeles: University of California Press, 1979).

54. Thomas Heywood, *Apologie for Actors* (London: 1612; rpt. New York: Garland, 1974), C3v; I. G., *A Refutation of the Apologie for Actors* (London: 1615; rpt. New York: Garland, 1973), p. 17 (italics in original).

55. Susan C. Jarratt, *Rereading the Sophists: Classical Rhetoric Refigured* (Carbondale: Southern Illinois University Press, 1991).

56. Thomas F. Van Laan, *Role-Playing in Shakespeare* (Toronto: University of Toronto Press, 1978), p. 150.

57. Calderwood, *Metadrama in Shakespeare's Henriad*, p. 88.

58. Richard Levin, *The Multiple Plot in English Renaissance Drama* (Chicago: University of Chicago Press, 1971), pp. 143, 146.

59. E. M. W. Tillyard, *Shakespeare's History Plays* (New York: Macmillan, 1947); Joseph A. Porter, *The Drama of Speech Acts: Shakespeare's Lancastrian Tetralogy* (Berkeley and Los Angeles: University of California Press, 1979), p. 115.

60. Robert B. Pierce, *Shakespeare's History Plays: The Family and the State* (Columbus: Ohio State University Press, 1971), p. 174.

61. John Wilders, *The Lost Garden: A View of Shakespeare's English and Roman History Plays* (London: Macmillan, 1978), p. 90.

62. John W. Blanpied, *Time and the Artist in Shakespeare's Histories* (Newark: University of Delaware Press, 1983), p. 163.

63. Alvin B. Kernan, *The Playwright as Magician* (New Haven: Yale University Press, 1979), p. 116.

64. John D. Cox, *Shakespeare and the Dramaturgy of Power* (Princeton:

Princeton University Press, 1989), pp. 120, 127.

65. Frank Whigham, *Ambition and Privilege: The Social Tropes of Elizabethan Courtesy Theory* (Berkeley and Los Angeles: University of California Press, 1984), p. 130.

66. David Scott Kastan, "Proud Majesty Made a Subject: Shakespeare and the Spectacle of Rule," *Shakespeare Quarterly* 37 (1986), 474. This article is revised and expanded in Kastan's book *Shakespeare after Theory* (New York: Routledge, 1999).

67. Paul Yachnin, "The Powerless Theater," *English Literary Renaissance* 21 (1991), 51.

68. Herbert Blau, *The Audience*, Parallax: Re-visions of Culture and Society, series eds. Stephen G. Nichols, Gerald Price, and Wendy Steiner (Baltimore: Johns Hopkins University Press, 1990), pp. 48-49.

69. Jean E. Howard and Phyllis Rackin, *Engendering a Nation: A Feminist Account of Shakespeare's English Histories* (London: Routledge, 1997), p. 191.

70. Robert Ornstein, *A Kingdom for a Stage: The Achievement of Shakespeare's History Plays* (Cambridge, Mass.: Harvard University Press, 1972), p. 138.

71. Jean-Christophe Agnew, *Worlds Apart: The Market and the Theatre in Anglo-American Thought, 1550-1750* (Cambridge: Cambridge University Press, 1986), p. 148.

72. Norman Rabkin, "Rabbits, Ducks, and *Henry V*," *Shakespeare Quarterly* 28 (1977), 279-96.

73. Stephen Greenblatt, "Invisible Bullets: Renaissance Authority and Its Subversion," in *Shakespearean Negotiations* (Berkeley and Los Angeles: University of California Press, 1988), p. 56.

74. Michael Manheim, "The English History Play on Screen," in *Shakespeare and the Moving Image*, ed. Anthony Davies and Stanley Wells (Cambridge: Cambridge University Press, 1994), pp. 125, 129-30, 128 (italics in original), 125.

75. Quoted by Michael Billington, "A 'New Olivier' Is Taking on *Henry V* on the Screen," *New York Times*, January 8, 1989, sec. 2, p. 18.

76. Ace G. Pilkington, in *Screening Shakespeare from "Richard II" to "Henry V"* (Newark: University of Delaware Press, 1991), points out the parallel between Scroop and Falstaff and excuses the omission of the Scroop scene as a kind of substitution: Olivier offers the "little play" of Falstaff's death instead: "Olivier has simply substituted one incident (the more theatrically resonant one) for the other" (p. 117).

77. Michael Goldman, *Shakespeare and the Energies of Drama* (Princeton: Princeton University Press, 1972), p. 70.

78. Montaigne, *Essayes*, 3:153.

79. See Lance Wilcox, "Katherine of France as Victim and Bride," *Shakespeare Studies* 17 (1985), 61-76.

80. Olivier as Ronald Reagan to Branagh's Bill Clinton?

81. Donald K. Hedrick, "War Is Mud: Branagh's Dirty Harry V and the

Types of Political Ambiguity," in *Shakespeare, The Movie*, ed. Lynda E. Boose and Richard Burt (London and New York: Routledge, 1997), pp. 52, 53.

82. Manheim, "English History Play," pp. 130–31.

83. Susanne Fabricius, "The Face of Honour: On Kenneth Branagh's Screen Adaptation of *Henry V*," in *Screen Shakespeare*, ed. Michael Skovmand, Dolphin, no. 24 (Aarhus: Aarhus University Press, 1994), p. 96.

84. Pilkington, *Screening Shakespeare*, p. 192.

ACT THREE. THEY DRINK

1. Prynne, *Histriomastix*, pp. 511, 512.

2. Thomas Adams, "The White Devil, or, the Hypocrite Uncased, in a Sermon preached at St. Paul's Cross, March 7, 1612," in *The Works of Thomas Adams*, Nichol's Series of Standard Divines: Puritan Period, 3 vols. (Edinburgh: James Nichol, 1862), 2:230.

3. Rousseau, *Lettre à M. D'Alembert*, in *Oeuvres complètes* V (1995), p. 69: "je vois en général que l'état de Comédien est un état de licence et de mauvais moeurs; que les hommes y sont livrés au désordre; que les femmes y ménent une vie scandaleuse; que les uns et les autres, avares et prodigues tout à la fois, toujours accablés de dettes et toujours versant de l'argent à pleines mains, sont aussi peu retenus sur leurs dissipations, que peu scrupuleux sur les moyens d'y pourvoir" (my translation).

4. Stephen Gosson, *The School of Abuse*, in *Shakespeare Society of London: Publications, Vol. 15 (#14; #2)* (Nendeln, Liechtenstein: Kraus Reprint Ltd., 1966), pp. 25, 35.

5. [Head], *Proteus redivivus: or The Art of Wheedling, or Insinuation*, p. 122 (italics in original).

6. Joseph Lenz, "Base Trade: Theater as Prostitution," *ELH* 60 (1993), 845, 841. In this article Lenz closely follows Steven Mullaney, *The Place of the Stage: License, Play, and Power in Renaissance England* (Chicago: University of Chicago Press, 1988); Mullaney emphasizes the geographical proximity of brothels, theaters, lazar-houses, and taverns in the Liberties. See also Jean E. Howard, *The Stage and Social Struggle in Early Modern England* (London: Routledge, 1994): antitheatricalists "obviously regarded the whole playhouse — pit, galleries, and stage — as an arena of visual display encouraging transgressive" behavior (p. 34).

7. Quoted by Lenz, "Base Trade," p. 839.

8. John Alcock, *Observations on the Defects of the Poor Laws* (London: for R. Baldwin, Jun., 1752), pp. 8, 11, 29, 45, 47–48.

9. Herbert Blau, *To All Appearances: Ideology and Performance* (New York and London: Routledge, 1992), p. 16.

SCENE ONE. THE TAVERN

10. William Vaughan, *The Golden Fleece*, 3 vols. (London: for Francis Williams, 1626), 2:75 [Kk2r] (all italics in quotations in original).

11. Thomas Nashe, *The Unfortunate Traveller and Other Works*, ed. J. B. Steane (Harmondsworth: Penguin Books, 1972), pp. 107–8.

12. Burton quoted from Barish, *The Antitheatrical Prejudice*, p. 102.

13. Anya Taylor, *Bacchus in Romantic England: Writers and Drink, 1780–1830*, Romanticism in Perspective: Texts, Cultures, Histories, gen. eds. Marilyn Gaull and Stephen Prickett (London: Macmillan; New York: St. Martin's Press, 1999), p. 9.

14. Buckner B. Trawick, *Shakespeare and Alcohol* (Amsterdam: Rodopi, 1978), points out that the scene of Cassio's drunken quarrel "helps to reveal several of Othello's traits" and foreshadows the tragedy (p. 22).

15. Graham Bradshaw, in *Misrepresentations: Shakespeare and the Materialists* (Ithaca: Cornell University Press, 1993), devotes an entire chapter to "The New Historicist as Iago," 223–57; like a new historicist, Iago is committed to "a materialistically reductive account of human motives," Bradshaw declares (p. 226). Temperance speakers in the nineteenth century, too, were drawn to the representation of the sudden and violent effects of drink in *Othello*.

16. A. C. Bradley, *Shakespearean Tragedy* (1904; rpt. New York: Meridian Books, 1955), p. 187: "[H]e is an artist. His action is a plot, the intricate plot of a drama, and in the conception and execution of it he experiences the tension and the joy of artistic creation." Bradley himself cites William Hazlitt and Algernon Charles Swinburne as precursors to this observation. Bernard Spivack, *Shakespeare and the Allegory of Evil* (New York: Columbia University Press, 1958), pays much attention to the stage traditions to which Iago belongs as a stage villain (pp. 2–59). "As a johannes factotum of the theater himself — actor, director, playwright, prompter — Iago is the antithesis of realism," says James Calderwood, *The Properties of "Othello"* (Amherst: University of Massachusetts Press, 1989), p. 116.

17. Ben Jonson, *Everyman in His Humour*, prologue, line 18, quoted from *English Drama, 1580–1642*, ed. C. F. Tucker Brooke and Nathan Burton Paradise (Lexington, Mass.: D. C. Heath and Co., 1933), p. 437.

18. James Calderwood, *If It Were Done: "Macbeth" and Tragic Action* (Amherst: University of Massachusetts Press, 1986), pp. 69, 65, 70.

19. C. L. Barber and Richard P. Wheeler, *The Whole Journey: Shakespeare's Power of Development* (Berkeley and Los Angeles: University of California Press, 1986), pp. 54, 56. Emile Legouis went further in his 1926 Annual Shakespeare Lecture, asking whether the "whole evolution of the Shakespearian drama might not be plausibly accounted for from the Bacchic point of view." "Nothing would indeed be easier," he answers himself. From an "optimistic period" in which "all is jovial, frolicsome, jocose," Shakespeare in the tragedy declines into "days of surfeit and penance," followed by a recovery period in which the poet, "just as if he was obeying the prescription of a wise and friendly physician, gives as much of his time as he can to his native Stratford" (*The Bacchic Element in Shakespeare's Plays*, Annual Shakespeare Lecture, June 23, 1926, Proceedings of the British Academy [Oxford: Oxford University Press, 1926], pp. 16–17, 18).

20. *The Complete Works of Shakespeare*, ed. Bevington, p. 1074*n*.

21. Donald Foster, "A Romance of Electronic Scholarship: With the True and Lamentable Tragedies of *Hamlet, Prince of Denmark*, Part 1: The Words," *Early Modern Literary Studies* 3, special issue 1 (1998), 5.11 (URL: http://purl .oclc.org/emls/03-3/fostshak.html).

22. But consider *OED*'s first meaning for the adjective *stale*: stale ale is ale that has stood long enough to leave its dregs behind; it is clear (*OED*, Stale, a. 1).

23. Peter Clark, *The English Alehouse: A Social History 1200–1830* (London: Longman, 1983), pp. 145, 153. George Evans Light, in "Drunken Politics: Alcohol, Alehouses, and Theater in England, 1555–1700" (diss., Stanford, 1994), offers a broad survey of the association of alehouses with theaters in the period. The performance at Warrington is fully reported in *Records of Early English Drama: Lancashire*, ed. David George (Toronto: University of Toronto Press, 1991), p. 96.

24. King James VI and I, *Political Writings*, ed. Johann P. Sommerville, Cambridge Texts in the History of Political Thought (Cambridge: Cambridge University Press, 1994), p. 224.

25. *The Drunkard's Character: or, A True Drunkard with such sins etc.*, by "R. Iunius" (London: for George Latham, 1638), pp. 14–15 (italics in original).

26. For example, see the instances of church ales requiring intervention of the authorities in the Lancashire records: "Most of the other people who appeared in court because of ales seem to have been prosecuted for holding them on the sabbath or for disorders that broke out at their ales rather than for holding an ale as such," reports David George (*Records of Early English Drama*, p. li).

27. Sarah Augusta Dickson, *Panacea or Precious Bane: Tobacco in Sixteenth Century Literature* (New York: New York Public Library, 1954), p. 167; the quotation refers readers to Edna St. Vincent Millay's *Letters*, ed. Allan Ross Macdougall (New York: Harper, 1952), p. 244.

28. Fretchwill quoted in Harris Gray Hudson, *A Study of Social Regulations in England under James I and Charles I: Drink and Tobacco* (Chicago: University of Chicago Libraries, 1933), p. 22; Riche quoted in Clark, *The English Alehouse*, p. 134.

29. Vaughan, *The Golden Fleece*, p. 79 [Kk(4)].

30. George Louis Beer, *The Origin of the British Colonial System* (New York: Macmillan, 1908), p. 80; he quotes Charles I on p. 149.

31. Quoted in Hudson, *A Study of Social Regulations*, p. 25.

32. Jacques Bonneau, *Les législations françaises sur les tabacs sous l'ancien régime* (Paris: Librairie de la Société du Recueil J-B. Sircy, 1910), p. 12: "ne prohiba pas le tabac; il fit mieux: il l'imposa."

33. Leah S. Marcus, *The Politics of Mirth: Jonson, Herrick, Milton, Marvell, and the Defense of Old Holiday Pastimes* (Chicago: University of Chicago Press, 1986). As Marcus notes, James I, too, participated in the self-contradictions of

the tobacco trade: he inveighed against the evil weed in a *Counter-blast to To-bacco* (1604) and declared the tobacco trade a royal monopoly in 1612 (p. 55).

34. See Act One, note 18 above.

SCENE TWO. LIBERTY HALL

35. Oliver Goldsmith, "A Reverie at the Boar's-head-tavern in Eastcheap," in *Collected Works of Oliver Goldsmith*, ed. Arthur Friedman, 5 vols. (Oxford: Clarendon Press, 1966), 3:98, 99.

36. "I would 'twere bedtime, Hal, and all well," *1 Henry IV* (5.1.125). *She Stoops to Conquer* quoted from *Collected Works of Oliver Goldsmith*, vol. 5, by page number: 5:116. Subsequent citations in the text are in this form; all italics in original.

37. Bernard Harris, "Goldsmith in the Theatre," in *The Art of Oliver Goldsmith*, ed. Andrew Swarbrick (London: Vision Press; New York: Barnes and Noble, 1984), pp. 163, 162, 164.

38. Frank Donoghue, "'He Never Gives us Nothing That's *Low*': Goldsmith's Plays and the Reviewers," *ELH* 55 (1988), 665.

39. The phrase is from Marlies K. Danziger, *Oliver Goldsmith and Richard Brinsley Sheridan*, World Dramatists (New York: Ungar, 1978), p. 57. See T. G. A. Nelson, "Stooping to Conquer in Goldsmith, Haywood, and Wycherley," *Essays in Criticism* 46 (1996), 324–25 and note 8.

40. See Nelson, "Stooping to Conquer," for a Freudian analysis. For a feminist analysis, see Christopher K. Brooks, "Goldsmith's Feminist Drama: *She Stoops to Conquer*, Silence, and Language," *Papers on Language and Literature* 28 (1992), 38–51, and "Marriage in Goldsmith: The Single Woman, Feminine Space, and 'Virtue,'" in *Joinings and Disjoinings: The Significance of Marital Status in Literature*, ed. JoAnna Stephens Mink and Janet Doubler Ward (Bowling Green, Ohio: Bowling Green State University Popular Press, 1991), pp. 19–35.

41. C. L. Barber, *Shakespeare's Festive Comedy: A Study of Dramatic Form and Its Relation to Social Custom* (Princeton: Princeton University Press, 1959), pp. 6, 7.

42. Northrop Frye, *A Natural Perspective: The Development of Shakespearean Comedy and Romance* (New York: Columbia University Press, 1963), p. 73.

43. As William J. Burling suggests in "Entrapment in Eighteenth-Century Drama from Congreve to Goldsmith," in *Reader Entrapment in Eighteenth-Century Literature*, ed. Carl R. Kropf, Georgia State Literary Studies, no. 8 (New York: AMS Press, 1992), p. 196: "Precisely the mirror opposite of her namesake Kate in *The Taming of the Shrew*, Kate Hardcastle, we are led to believe, *becomes* a shrew . . . and we have the unmistakable irony of the epilogue that traces the transition in Kate's character after she and Charles marry: she becomes a loud, impudent coquette who indulges in every vanity of London highlife."

44. Jane Collier, *An Essay on the Art of Ingeniously Tormenting with proper rules for the use of that pleasant art, humbly addressed in the first part, to the master, husband, &c, in the second part to the wife, friend, &c, with some general instruc-*

tions for plaguing all your acquaintance (London: printed for A. Millar, in the Strand, 1753), p. 146 (all italics in quotations in original).

45. *Tormentors*, of course, are also features of the theater: "In C18 theatre, they were sliding extensions of the proscenium wing," says Martin Harrison in *The Language of Theatre* (New York: Routledge, 1998). "Whilst I can find no corroboration of this," Harrison continues, "I should hazard a guess that the term comes from the tormenting effect on those in the audience who might have liked to see what was going on in the wing-space more than the proceedings on stage, since the verb has no other recorded sense" (p. 285). *Teasers* get their name "from the pun on the sense of the tease as a small torment" (p. 271).

SCENE THREE. HARRY HOPE'S SALOON

46. George Henry Nettleton, *English Drama of the Restoration and Eighteenth Century* (1932; rpt. New York: Cooper Square Publishers, 1968), p. 286.

47. Raymond Williams, *The Long Revolution* (London: Chatto and Windus, 1961), p. 260.

48. Louis Sheaffer, *O'Neill: Son and Playwright* (Boston: Little, Brown, 1968), pp. 418–19.

49. Quoted by Sheaffer, *Son and Playwright*, p. 481; attributed to John Lahr on the back cover of *File on O'Neill*, ed. Stephen Black (London: Methuen, 1991).

50. Quoted with approval by Sheaffer, *O'Neill: Son and Artist* (Boston: Little, Brown [1973]; rpt. New York: AMS Press, 1988), pp. 245–46.

51. Quoted in Richard F. Moorton, "Introduction," in *Eugene O'Neill's Century: Centennial Views on America's Foremost Tragic Dramatist*, Contributions in Drama and Theatre Studies, no. 36 (Westport, Conn.: Greenwood Press, 1991), p. xxii.

52. Henri Peyre, *Literature and Sincerity* (1963; rpt. Westport, Conn.: Greenwood Press, 1978), pp. 336, 334.

53. Egil Törnqvist, *A Drama of Souls: Studies in O'Neill's Super-Naturalistic Technique* (New Haven: Yale University Press, 1969), p. 149.

54. See, for example, Michael Manheim, "The Transcendence of Melodrama in O'Neill's *The Iceman Cometh*," in *Critical Essays on Eugene O'Neill*, ed. James J. Martine, Critical Essays on American Literature (Boston: Hall, 1984), pp. 145–58; Michael Manheim, "The Transcendence of Melodrama in *Long Day's Journey into Night*," in *Perspectives on O'Neill: New Essays*, ed. Shaymal Bagchee, English Literary Studies Monograph Series, no. 43 (Victoria: University of Victoria Press, 1988), pp. 33–42.

55. John Gassner, "Introduction," in *O'Neill: A Collection of Critical Essays*, ed. John Gassner (Englewood Cliffs, N.J.: Prentice-Hall, 1964), p. 4.

56. Joel Pfister, *Staging Depth: Eugene O'Neill and the Politics of Psychological Discourse* (Chapel Hill: University of North Carolina Press, 1995): the phrase refers to "the hothouse configuration of affectionate mothers, competitive fathers, and needy sons later christened by psychoanalysts the oedipal family" (pp. 28, 25).

57. Moorton, *Eugene O'Neill's Century*, p. xviii; Macgowan quoted in Sheaffer, *Son and Playwright*, p. 481.

58. Thomas Postlewait, "From Melodrama to Realism: The Suspect History of American Drama," in *Melodrama: The Cultural Emergence of a Genre*, ed. Michael Hays and Anastasia Nikolopoulou (New York: St. Martin's, 1996), pp. 39-60.

59. Arthur Gelb and Barbara Gelb, *O'Neill* (New York: Harper and Row, 1962, 1973), p. 870.

60. Postlewait, "From Melodrama to Realism," p. 46.

61. Virgil Geddes, *The Melodramadness of Eugene O'Neill* (Brookfield, Conn., 1934; rpt. Norwood, Pa.: Norwood Editions, 1977), pp. 8-9. Geddes's main claim to fame was that his first New York production featured the young Bette Davis in her first New York appearance. Geddes's play, *The Earth Between*, a tragedy set on a farm and rich with hints of incest, appeared on a double bill with O'Neill's grim 1916 one-act *Before Breakfast* with the Provincetown Players in 1929.

62. Eugene O'Neill, *Long Day's Journey into Night* (New Haven: Yale University Press, 1955), p. 151 (all italics in quotations in original).

63. Moorton, *Eugene O'Neill's Century*, pp. xviii-xix. Steiner seems fond of using the word *morass* when he refers to O'Neill: for example, see his comments on *Mourning Becomes Electra* in *The Death of Tragedy* (London: Faber and Faber, 1961): "O'Neill commits inner vandalism by sheer inadequacy of style. In the morass of his language the high griefs of the house of Atreus dwindle to a case of adultery and murder in some provincial rathole" (p. 327).

64. Harold Bloom, "Introduction," in *Eugene O'Neill: Modern Critical Views* (New York: Chelsea House, 1987), pp. 5, 12.

65. Eric Bentley, "The Life and Hates of Eugene O'Neill," in *Thinking about the Playwright: Comments from Four Decades* (Evanston: Northwestern University Press, 1987), p. 32.

66. Eugene O'Neill, *Selected Letters*, ed. Travis Bogard and Jackson R. Breyer (New Haven: Yale University Press, 1988), p. 339. In this same letter, O'Neill again affirms his desire to "wind up writing plays to be published with 'No Productions Allowed' in red letters on the first page. . . ."

67. Robert Benchley, *Benchley at the Theatre: Dramatic Criticism, 1920-40*, ed. Charles Gethcell (Ipswich, Mass.: Ipswich Press, 1985), p. 97.

68. John Henry Raleigh, *The Plays of Eugene O'Neill*, with a preface by Harry T. Moore (Carbondale and Edwardsville: Southern Illinois University Press, 1965), p. 184.

69. Kurt Eisen, *The Inner Strength of Opposites: O'Neill's Novelistic Drama and the Melodramatic Imagination* (Athens: University of Georgia Press, 1994), pp. 26, 30.

70. William Henry Smith, *The Drunkard, or, The Fallen Saved: A Moral Domestic Drama* (1872; rept. Boston: Literature House, Gregg Press, 1972), p. 26.

71. Jeffrey D. Mason, *Melodrama and the Myth of America*, Drama and Per-

formance Studies, gen. ed. Timothy Wiles (Bloomington: University of Indiana Press, 1993), p. 76 (italics in original).

72. For discussion of the narrative structures of AA narratives, see Edmund B. O'Reilly, *Sobering Tales: Narratives of Alcohol and Recovery* (Amherst: University of Massachusetts Press, 1997), and "'Bill's Story': Form and Meaning in A. A. Recovery Narratives," in *The Serpent in the Cup: Temperance in American Literature*," ed. David S. Reynolds and Debra J. Rosenthal (Amherst: University of Massachusetts Press, 1997), pp. 180-204; in the same collection, see also "'Alcoholism' and the Modern Temper," by John W. Crowley, pp. 165-79.

73. McCarthy quoted in Steven F. Bloom, "Drinking and Drunkenness in *The Iceman Cometh*: A Response to Mary McCarthy," *Eugene O'Neill Newsletter* 9 (1985), 3 (italics in original). The issue incorporates a special "focus section" on drinking and addiction.

74. August Strindberg, *Preface* to *Miss Julie*, in *Five Plays*, trans. and with intro. by Harry G. Carlson, Signet Classic (New York: NAL, 1984), p. 53.

75. Strindberg's *Preface*, of course, does not describe his actual dramatic practice: even in *Miss Julie*, both Jean and Julie revert to type; and the later Strindberg abounds in caricatures and exaggerated stereotypical figures.

76. Fernand Braudel, *Capitalism and Material Life, 1400-1800*, trans. Miriam Kochan (New York: Harper and Row, 1973), p. 158. Quoted by Taylor, *Bacchus in Romantic England*, p. 12.

77. Thomas Brennan, *Public Drinking and Popular Culture in Eighteenth-Century Paris* (Princeton: Princeton University Press, 1988), pp. 203-4. Brennan concurs with "an English visitor" that spirits did not wreak the kind of havoc in Paris that gin did in eighteenth-century London: "this vice is almost unknown in France," wrote a visitor in 1776 (p. 204). Brennan's book makes it clear that the persistent linkage of acting with drinking that can be found in English pamphlets and plays and in American contexts does not occur in France. In French literature actors are no more likely than anyone else to frequent bars or commit homicides.

78. Eugene O'Neill, *The Iceman Cometh* (New York: Random House, 1946), act 3, p. 206. Subsequent references are in the text; all italics in quotations in original.

79. "Bill's Story," quoted by O'Reilly, "Bill's Story," p. 189. I am not contending that Hickey, in 1912 when the play is set, has read "Bill's Story," first published in 1939; nor am I contending that O'Neill, working on the play in the 1940s, had done so. As O'Reilly points out, the dynamics of the AA narrative were already anticipated in the stories told by earlier temperance movements like the Washingtonians.

80. O'Reilly, "Bill's Story," p. 194.

81. For Thomas B. Gilmore, Hickey's presentation is a "parody or travesty of genuine adherence to AA principles and procedures" (*Equivocal Spirits: Alcoholism and Drinking in Twentieth-Century American Literature* [Chapel Hill, N.C.: University of North Carolina Press, 1987], p. 49).

82. Michael Manheim, *Eugene O'Neill's New Language of Kinship* (Syracuse, N.Y.: Syracuse University Press, 1982), p. 155.

83. "Natural history of the human heart" from *Son of a Servant*; "perceive myself as an object," from *Black Banners*; both Strindberg novels quoted and trans. by Michael Robinson, *Strindberg and Autobiography* (Norwich: Norvik Press, 1986), p. 3.

84. Gunnar Brandell, *Freud och hans tid* (Stockholm, 1970), p. 16; quoted and trans. by Robinson, *Strindberg and Autobiography*, p. 21.

85. Pfister, *Staging Depth*, p. 99; Moorton, *Eugene O'Neill's Century*, p. xxii.

86. Sheaffer, *Son and Playwright*, p. 351: "O'Neill was an emotional hemophiliac; his wounds, his grievances, would never heal. This was a primary source of the anguished feeling and pounding power in his plays, as well as part of the lifelong price he had to pay for his talent." Sheaffer repeats the phrase "emotional hemophiliac" in *Son and Artist* (p. ix) and continues, "he always wrote from his guts. . . ."

87. Steven F. Bloom has argued that the repetitive behavior of the Tyrones is a realistic depiction of a substance-addicted family: "this is the life of an alcoholic, and, for O'Neill, this is the life of modern man" ("Empty Bottles, Empty Dreams: O'Neill's Use of Drinking and Alcoholism in *Long Day's Journey into Night*," in *Critical Essays on O'Neill*, ed. Thomas Martine [Boston: G. K. Hall, 1984], p. 177).

88. Bennett Simon, *Tragic Drama and the Family: Psychoanalytic Studies from Aeschylus to Beckett* (New Haven: Yale University Press, 1988), p. 181 (italics in original).

89. Walter A. Davis, *Get the Guests: Psychoanalysis, Modern American Drama, and the Audience*, Wisconsin Project on American Writers, gen. ed. Frank Lentricchia (Madison: University of Wisconsin Press, 1994), p. 207.

SCENE FOUR. CONTESTED SITES

90. Glenn D. Wilson, *Psychology for Performing Artists: Butterflies and Bouquets* (London and Bristol, Pa.: Jessica Kingsley Publishers, 1994), pp. 171–72.

91. Meredith Anne Skura, *Shakespeare the Actor and the Purposes of Playing* (Chicago: University of Chicago Press, 1993), p. 4.

92. Jane Lilienfeld, "Introduction," in *The Languages of Addiction*, ed. Jane Lilienfeld and Jeffrey Oxford (New York: St. Martin's Press, 1999), p. 22.

93. Stephen Aaron, *Stage Fright: Its Role in Acting* (Chicago: University of Chicago Press, 1986), pp. 131, 130, 131.

94. Gregg Franzwa, "Aristotle and the Languages of Addiction," in *The Languages of Addiction*, ed. Lilienfeld and Oxford, p. 23.

95. *The Gamester*, in *The Plays of Susanna Centlivre: Volume 1*, ed. Richard C. Frushell, Eighteenth-Century Drama, gen. ed. Paula Backscheider (New York: Garland, 1982), act 3, p. 36 (all italics in quotations in original).

96. *A Modest Defence of Gaming*, in *Fugitive Pieces on Various Subjects*, ed. Robert Dodsley, 3 vols. (London: for R. and J. Dodsley, 1761), 1:181.

97. Skura, *Shakespeare the Actor*, p. 40.

98. Alcock, *Observations on the Defects of the Poor Laws*, p. 48 (italics in original).

99. Edward Moore, *The Foundling: A Comedy and The Gamester: A Tragedy*, ed. Anthony Amberg (Newark: University of Delaware Press; London: Associated University Presses, 1996); all italics in quotations in original.

100. Mason, *Melodrama and the Myth of America*, p. 77.

101. Shearer West, *The Image of the Actor: Verbal and Visual Representation in the Age of Garrick and Kemble* (New York: St. Martin's, 1991), p. 25. See also Mendel Kohansky, *The Disreputable Profession: The Actor in Society*, Contributions in American Studies, no. 72 (Westport, Conn.: Greenwood Press, 1984), p. 92: "Garrick spent a great deal of time, effort, and money in cultivating his public image."

102. Joseph Roach, *The Player's Passion: Studies in the Science of Acting* (Newark: University of Delaware Press; London: Associated University Presses, 1985), p. 56.

103. Jean Duvignaud, *L'Acteur: Esquisse d'une sociologie du comédien* (Paris: Gallimard, 1965), p. 93: "Le 'naturel' qui envahit le siècle correspond à la baisse d'influence des cours royales et à l'acroissance d'importance des publics urbains." "Déraciné de son terreau 'bourgeois,' devenu le transmetteur des modèles de culture, nomade ou fixé dans une troupe, créateur d'une image de la personne humaine sans laquel il n'y aurait point de théâtre, vassal d'un prince ou serviteur du public, le comédien reste en marge de la société monarchique, qui, pourtant, trouve dans le théâtre son expression la plus haute" (p. 104); "On accepte du comédien célèbre ce que l'on admettait au prince – qu'il consomme plus q'un autre, qu'il dépense et gaspille, qu'il se livre à un 'potlatch' où il exalte son existence, tout comme le souverain d'autrefois pour conquérir de prestige et acquérir une importance qui maintienne son crédit auprès du public" (pp. 132–33).

104. Quoted by Amberg, "Introduction" to *The Gamester*, p. 102 (italics in original).

105. Burns, *Theatricality*, pp. 146–47 (italics in original).

106. West, *The Image of the Actor*, p. 15.

107. Quoted by Stephen D. Cox, *"The Stranger within Thee": Concepts of the Self in Late Eighteenth-Century Literature* (Pittsburgh: University of Pittsburgh Press, 1980), p. 39.

108. Quoted by Van Sant, *Eighteenth-Century Sensibility and the Novel*, p. 11.

109. William B. Worthen, *The Idea of the Actor: Drama and the Ethics of Performance* (Princeton: Princeton University Press, 1984), p. 96.

110. Blau, *The Audience*, pp. 280, 314 (italics in original).

111. Aaron, *Stage Fright*, pp. 39, 40. "It is a commonplace among directors,"

concurs Skura, "that actors are like children, but this means more than being spoiled" (*Shakespeare the Actor*, p. 18).

112. Goldman, *The Actor's Freedom*, pp. 7, 37.

113. Reading and eating are related through the phenomenon of "introjection," according to David Cole, in *Acting as Reading: The Place of the Reading Process in the Actor's Work*, Theater: Theory/Text/Performance, series ed. Enoch Brater (Ann Arbor: University of Michigan Press, 1992): actors exist in "an eat-or-be-eaten relationship with a text" (p. 83). Cole sketches out connections between acting, reading, and drinking in a lively discussion of *The Tempest*: "For introjection, to eat is to be eaten; for reading, to absorb is to be absorbed; for Stephano, to drink is to be drunk" (p. 66).

114. Worthen, *The Idea of the Actor*, pp. 152, 154.

115. Euripides, *The Bacchae*, trans. William Arrowsmith, in *The Complete Greek Tragedies, Euripides V*, ed. David Greene and Richmond Lattimore (Chicago: University of Chicago Press, 1959), line 863, p. 193. E. R. Dodds, *The Greeks and the Irrational* (Berkeley: University of California Press, 1968), p. 76 (italics in original).

116. Aaron, *Stage Fright*, p. 131, is among many commentators who invoked John Keats's famous phrase to describe what actors do.

EPILOGUE

1. Roberto Calasso, *The Marriage of Cadmus and Harmony*, trans. Tim Parks (New York: Vintage Books, 1994), pp. 38−39.

2. W. J. T. Mitchell, *Picture Theory: Essays on Verbal and Visual Representation* (Chicago: University of Chicago Press, 1994), p. 420.

3. Burns, *Theatricality*, p. 146.

4. Michel Foucault, *The Order of Things: An Archaeology of the Human Sciences* (New York: Vintage Books, 1973), p. 16.

5. Susan Wells, *The Dialectics of Representation* (Baltimore: Johns Hopkins University Press, 1985), p. 60.

6. Christopher Prendergast, *The Triangle of Representation* (New York: Columbia University Press, 2000), pp. 2, 4, 2.

7. Friedrich Nietzsche, *Die Geburt der Tragödie aus dem Geiste der Musik (Griechentum und Pessimismus)* (Munich: Wilhelm Goldmann Verlag, 1967), p. 160: "im Wandeln unter hohen ionischen Säulengängen, aufwärtsblickend zu dem Horizont, der durch reine und edle Linien abgeschnitten ist, neben sich Widerspiegelungen seiner verklärten Gestalt in leuchtendem Marmor, rings um sich feierlich schreitende oder zart bewegte Menschen, mimt harmonisch tönenden Lauten und rhythmischer Gebärdensprache — würde er nicht, bei diesem forwährenden Einströmen der Schönheit, zu Apollo die Hand erhebend ausrufen müssen: 'Seliges Volk der Hellenen! Wie gross muss unter euch Dionysus sein, wenn de delische Gott solche Zauber für nötig hält, um euren dithyrambischen Wahnsinn zu heilen!' — Einem so Gestimmten dürfte aber

ein greiser Athener, mit dem erhabene Auge des Äschylus zu ihm aufblickend, entgegen: 'Sage aber auch dies, du wunderlicher Fremdling: Wieviel musste dies Volk leiden, um so schön werden zu können! Jetzt aber folge mir zur Tragödie un *opfere* mit mir *im Tempel beider Gottheiten!*'" (my translation; italics in original).

Index

STUDIES IN

THEATRE HISTORY & CULTURE

Shakespeare on the American Yiddish Stage
  By Joel Berkowitz

The Show and the Gaze of Theatre: A European Perspective
  By Erika Fischer-Lichte

Textual and Theatrical Shakespeare: Questions of Evidence
  Edited by Edward Pechter

The Theatrical Event: Dynamics of Performance and Perception
  By Willmar Sauter

The Trick of Singularity: *Twelfth Night* and the Performance Editions
  By Laurie E. Osborne

Wandering Stars: Russian Emigré Theatre, 1905–1940
  Edited by Laurence Senelick